WEBBOTS, SPIDERS, AND SCREEN SCRAPERS

D1534531

WEBBOTS, SPIDERS, AND SCREEN SCRAPERS

A Guide to Developing Internet Agents with PHP/CURL

by Michael Schrenk

NO STARCH PRESS

San Francisco

WEBBOTS, SPIDERS, AND SCREEN SCRAPERS. Copyright © 2007 by Michael Schrenk.

 Printed on recycled paper in the United States of America

11 10 09 08 07   1 2 3 4 5 6 7 8 9

ISBN-10: 1-59327-120-4
ISBN-13: 978-1-59327-120-6

Publisher: William Pollock
Production Editor: Christina Samuell
Cover and Interior Design: Octopod Studios
Developmental Editors: Tyler Ortman and William Pollock
Technical Reviewer: Peter MacIntyre
Copyeditor: Megan Dunchak
Compositors: Megan Dunchak, Riley Hoffman, and Christina Samuell
Proofreader: Stephanie Provines
Indexer: Nancy Guenther

For information on book distributors or translations, please contact No Starch Press, Inc. directly:

No Starch Press, Inc.
555 De Haro Street, Suite 250, San Francisco, CA 94107
phone: 415.863.9900; fax: 415.863.9950; info@nostarch.com; www.nostarch.com

Library of Congress Cataloging-in-Publication Data

Schrenk, Michael.
  Webbots, spiders, and screen scrapers : a guide to developing internet agents with PHP/CURL / Michael Schrenk.
       p. cm.
  Includes index.
  ISBN-13: 978-1-59327-120-6
  ISBN-10: 1-59327-120-4
  1. Web search engines. 2. Internet programming. 3. Internet searching. 4. Intelligent agents (Computer software) I. Title.
  TK5105.884.S37 2007
  025.04--dc22
                                           2006026680

In loving memory

Charlotte Schrenk
1897–1982

ACKNOWLEDGMENTS

I needed support and inspiration from family, friends, and colleagues to write this book. Unfortunately, I did not always acknowledge their contributions when they offered them. Here is a delayed thanks to all of those who helped me.

Thanks to Donna, my wife, who convinced me that I could actually do this, and to my kids, Ava and Gordon, who have always supported my crazy schemes, even though they know it means fewer coffees and chess matches together.

Andy King encouraged me to find a publisher for this project, and Daniel Stenberg, founder of the cURL project, helped me organize my thoughts when this book was barely an outline.

No Starch Press exhibited saint-like patience while I split my time between *writing* webbots and *writing about* webbots. Special thanks to Bill, who trusted the concept, Tyler, who edited most of the manuscript, and Christina, who kept me on task. Peter MacIntyre was instrumental in checking for technical errors, and Megan's copyediting improved the book throughout.

Anamika Mishra assisted with the book's website and consistently covered for me when I was busy writing or too tired to code.

Laurie Curtis helped me explore what it might be like to *finish* a book.

Finally, a tip of the hat goes to Mark, Randy, Megan, Karen, Terri, Susan, Dennis, Dan, and Matt, who were thoughtful enough to ask about my book's progress before inquiring about the status of *their* projects.

BRIEF CONTENTS

PART III: ADVANCED TECHNICAL CONSIDERATIONS

PART IV: LARGER CONSIDERATIONS

CONTENTS IN DETAIL

3
DOWNLOADING WEB PAGES   21

4
PARSING TECHNIQUES   35

19
PROCUREMENT WEBBOTS AND SNIPERS 187

20
WEBBOTS AND CRYPTOGRAPHY 195

21
AUTHENTICATION 199

22
ADVANCED COOKIE MANAGEMENT 211

23
SCHEDULING WEBBOTS AND SPIDERS   217

PART IV
LARGER CONSIDERATIONS

24
DESIGNING STEALTHY WEBBOTS AND SPIDERS   227

25
WRITING FAULT-TOLERANT WEBBOTS   235

INTRODUCTION

My introduction to the World Wide Web was also the beginning of my relationship with the browser. The first browser I used was Mosaic, pioneered by Eric Bina and Marc Andreessen. Andreessen later co-founded Netscape.

Shortly after I discovered the World Wide Web, I began to associate the wonders of the Internet with the simplicity of the browser. By just clicking a hyperlink, I could enjoy the art treasures of the Louvre; if I followed another link, I could peruse a fan site for *The Brady Bunch*.[1] The browser was more than a software application that facilitated use of the World Wide Web: It *was* the World Wide Web. It was the new television. And just as television tamed distant video signals with simple channel and volume knobs, browsers demystified the complexities of the Internet with hyperlinks, bookmarks, and back buttons.

---

[1] I stumbled across a fan site for *The Brady Bunch* during my first World Wide Web experience.

Old-School Client-Server Technology

My big moment of discovery came when I learned that I didn't need a browser to view web pages. I realized that Telnet, a program used since the early '80s to communicate with networked computers, could also download web pages, as shown in Figure 1.

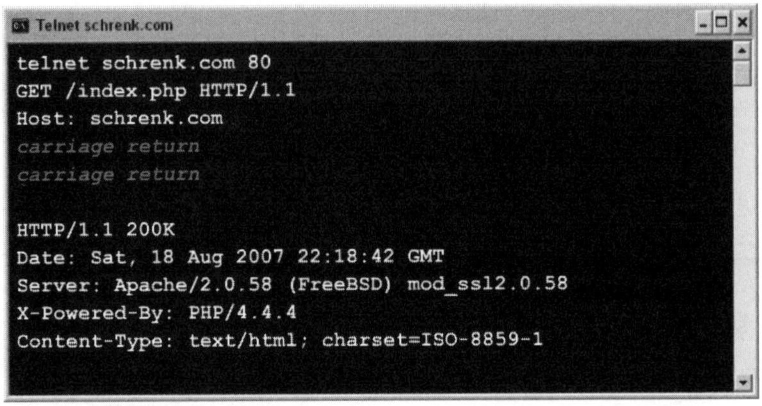

```
Telnet schrenk.com                                          _ □ ×

telnet schrenk.com 80
GET /index.php HTTP/1.1
Host: schrenk.com
carriage return
carriage return


HTTP/1.1 200K
Date: Sat, 18 Aug 2007 22:18:42 GMT
Server: Apache/2.0.58 (FreeBSD) mod_ssl2.0.58
X-Powered-By: PHP/4.4.4
Content-Type: text/html; charset=ISO-8859-1
```

Figure 1: Viewing a web page with Telnet

Suddenly, the World Wide Web was something I could understand without a browser. It was a familiar *client-server architecture* where simple clients worked on tasks found on remote servers. The difference here was that the clients were browsers and the servers dished up web pages.

The only revolutionary thing was that, unlike previous client-server client applications, browsers were easy for anyone to use and soon gained mass acceptance. The Internet's audience shifted from physicists and computer programmers to the public. Unfortunately, the general public didn't understand client-server technology, so the dependency on browsers spread further. They didn't understand that there were other ways to use the World Wide Web.

As a programmer, I realized that if I could use Telnet to download web pages, I could also write programs to do the same. I could write my own browser if I desired, or I could write automated agents (webbots, spiders, and screen scrapers) to solve problems that browsers couldn't.

The Problem with Browsers

The basic problem with browsers is that they're manual tools. Your browser only downloads and renders websites: You still need to decide if the web page is relevant, if you've already seen the information it contains, or if you need to follow a link to another web page. What's worse, your browser can't think for itself. It can't notify you when something important happens online, and it certainly won't anticipate your actions, automatically complete forms, make purchases, or download files for you. To do these things, you'll need the automation and intelligence only available with a *webbot,* or a web robot.

What to Expect from This Book

This book identifies the limitations of typical web browsers and explores how you can use webbots to capitalize on these limitations. You'll learn how to design and write webbots through sample scripts and example projects. Moreover, you'll find answers to larger design questions like these:

- Where do ideas for webbot projects come from?
- How can I have fun with webbots and stay out of trouble?
- Is it possible to write stealthy webbots that run without detection?
- What is the trick to writing robust, fault-tolerant webbots that won't break as Internet content changes?

Learn from My Mistakes

I've written webbots, spiders, and screen scrapers for nearly 10 years, and in the process I've made most of the mistakes someone can make. Because webbots are capable of making unconventional demands on websites, system administrators can confuse webbots' requests with attempts to hack into their systems. Thankfully, none of my mistakes has ever led to a courtroom, but they have resulted in intimidating phone calls, scary emails, and very awkward moments. Happily, I can say that I've learned from these situations, and it's been a very long time since I've been across the desk from an angry system administrator. You can spare yourself a lot of grief by reading my stories and learning from my mistakes.

Master Webbot Techniques

You will learn about the technology needed to write a wide assortment of webbots. Some technical skills you'll master include these:

- Programmatically downloading websites
- Decoding encrypted websites
- Unlocking authenticated web pages
- Managing cookies
- Parsing data
- Writing spiders
- Managing the large amounts of data that webbots generate

Leverage Existing Scripts

This book uses several code libraries that make it easy for you to write webbots, spiders, and screen scrapers. The functions and declarations in these libraries provide the basis for most of the example scripts used in this book. You'll save time by using these libraries because they do the underlying work, leaving the upper-level planning and development to you. All of these libraries are available for download at this book's website.

About the Website

This book's website (http://www.schrenk.com/nostarch/webbots) is an additional resource for you to use. To the extent that it's possible, all the example projects in this book use web pages on the companion site as *targets*, or resources for your webbots to download and take action on. These targets provided a consistent (unchanging) environment for you to hone your webbot writing skills. A controlled learning environment is important because, regardless of our best efforts, webbots can fail when their target websites change. Knowing that your targets are unchanging makes the task of debugging a little easier.

The companion website also has links to other sites of interest, white papers, book updates, and an area where you can communicate with other webbot developers (see Figure 2). From the website, you will also be able to access all of the example code libraries used in this book.

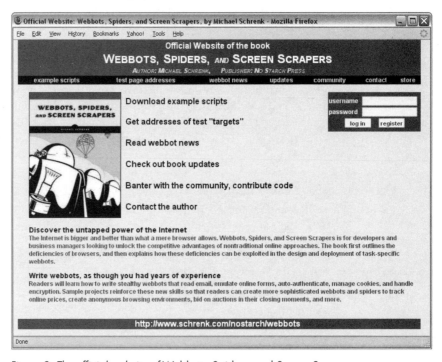

Figure 2: The official website of Webbots, Spiders, and Screen Scrapers

About the Code

Most of the scripts in this book are straight PHP. However, sometimes PHP and HTML are intermixed in the same script—and in many cases, on the same line. In those situations, a bold typeface differentiates PHP scripts from HTML, as shown in Listing 1.

You may use any of the scripts in this book for your own personal use, as long as you agree not to redistribute them. If you use any script in this book, you also consent to bear full responsibility for its use and execution and agree not to sell or create derivative products, under any circumstances. However, if you do improve any of these scripts or develop entirely new (related) scripts, you are encouraged to share them with the webbot community via the book's website.

```html
<h1>Coding Conventions for Embedded PHP</h1>
<table border="0" cellpadding="1" cellspacing="0">
<tr>
<th>Name</th>
    <th>Address</th>
  </tr>
  <? for ($x=0; $x<sizeof($person_array); $x++)
     {    ?>
     <tr>
        <td><? echo person_array[$x]['NAME']?></td>
           <td><? echo person_array[$x]['ADDRESS']?></td>
     </tr>
<?    }    ?>
</table>
```

Listing 1: Bold typeface differentiates PHP from HTML script

The other thing you should know about the example scripts is that they are teaching aids. The scripts may not reflect the most efficient programming method, because their primary goal is readability.

NOTE   *The code libraries used by this book are governed by the W3C Software Notice and License (http://www.w3.org/Consortium/Legal/2002/copyright-software-20021231) and are available for download from the book's website. The website is also where the software is maintained. If you make meaningful contributions to this code, please go to the website to see how your improvements may be part of the next distribution. The software examples depicted in this book are protected by this book's copyright.*

Requirements

Knowing HTML and the basics of how the Internet works will be necessary for using this book. If you are a beginning programmer with even nominal computer network experience, you'll be fine. It is important to recognize, however, that this book will not teach you how to program or how TCP/IP, the protocol of the Internet, works.

Hardware

You don't need elaborate hardware to start writing webbots. If you have a secondhand 33 MHz Pentium computer, you have the minimum requirement to play with all the examples in this book. Any of the following hardware is appropriate for using the examples and information in this book:

- A personal computer that uses a Windows 95, Windows XP, or Windows Vista operating system
- Any reasonably modern Linux-, Unix-, or FreeBSD-based computer
- A Macintosh running OS X (or later)

It will also prove useful to have ample storage. This is particularly true if your plan is to write *spiders*, self-directed webbots, which can consume all available resources (especially hard drives) if they are allowed to download too many files.

Software

In an effort to be as relevant as possible, the software examples in this book use PHP,[2] cURL,[3] and MySQL.[4] All of these software technologies are available as free downloads from their respective websites. In addition to being free, these software packages are wonderfully portable and function well on a variety of computers and operating systems.

NOTE *If you're going to follow the script examples in this book, you will need a basic knowledge of PHP. This book assumes you know how to program.*

Internet Access

A connection to the Internet is very handy, but not entirely necessary. If you lack a network connection, you can create your own local *intranet* (one or more webservers on a private network) by loading Apache[5] onto your computer, and if that's not possible, you can design programs that use local files as targets. However, neither of these options is as fun as writing webbots that use a live Internet connection. In addition, if you lack an Internet connection, you will not have access to the online resources, which add a lot of value to your learning experience.

A Disclaimer (This Is Important)

As with anything you develop, you must take responsibility for your own actions. From a technology standpoint, there is little to distinguish a beneficial webbot from one that does destructive things. The main difference is the intent of the developer (and how well you debug your scripts). Therefore, it's up to you to do constructive things with the information in this book and not violate copyright law, disrupt networks, or do anything else that would be troublesome or illegal. And if you do, don't call me.

Please reference Chapter 28 for insight into how to write webbots ethically. Chapter 28 will help you do this, but it won't provide legal advice. If you have questions, talk to a lawyer before you experiment.

---

[2] See http://www.php.net.

[3] See http://curl.haxx.se.

[4] See http://www.mysql.com.

[5] See http://www.apache.org.

PART I

FUNDAMENTAL CONCEPTS AND TECHNIQUES

While most web development books explain how to create websites, this book teaches developers how to combine, adapt, and automate existing websites to fit their specific needs. Part I introduces the concept of web automation and explores elementary techniques to harness the resources of the Web.

Chapter 1: What's in It for You?
This chapter explores why it is fun to write webbots and why webbot development is a rewarding career with expanding possibilities.

Chapter 2: Ideas for Webbot Projects
We've been led to believe that the only way to use a website is with a browser. If, however, you examine what you *want* to do, as opposed to what a browser *allows* you to do, you'll look at your favorite web resources in a whole new way. This chapter discusses existing as well as potential webbots.

Chapter 3: Downloading Web Pages
This chapter introduces PHP/CURL, the free library that makes it easy to download web pages—even when the targeted web pages use advanced techniques like forwarding, encryption, authentication, and cookies.

Chapter 4: Parsing Techniques

Downloaded web pages aren't of any use until your webbot can separate the data you need from the data you don't need.

Chapter 5: Automating Form Submission

To truly automate web agents, your application needs the ability to automatically upload data to online forms.

Chapter 6: Managing Large Amounts of Data

Spiders in particular can generate huge amounts of data. That's why it's important for you to know how to effectively store and reduce the size of web pages, text, and images.

You may already have experience from other areas of computer science that you can apply to these activities. However, even if these concepts are familiar to you, developing webbots may force you to view these skills in a different context, so the following chapters are still worth reading. If you don't already have experience in these areas, the next six chapters will provide the basics for designing and developing webbots. You'll use this groundwork in the other projects and advanced considerations discussed later.

1

WHAT'S IN IT FOR YOU?

Whether you're a software developer looking for new skills or a business leader looking for a competitive advantage, this chapter is where you will discover how webbots create opportunities.

Uncovering the Internet's True Potential

Webbots present a virtually untapped resource for software developers and business leaders. This is because the public has yet to realize that most of the Internet's potential lies outside the capability of the existing browser/website paradigm. For example, in today's world, people are satisfied with pointing a browser at a website and using whatever information or services they find there. With webbots, the focus of the Internet will shift from what's available on individual websites toward what people actually want to accomplish. To this end, webbots will use as many online resources as required to satisfy their individual needs.

To be successful with webbots, you need to stop thinking like other Internet users. Namely, you need to stop thinking about the Internet in terms of a browser viewing one website at a time. This will be difficult, because we've all become dependent on browsers. While you can do a wide variety of things with a browser, you also pay a price for that versatility—browsers need to be sufficiently generic to be useful in a wide variety of circumstances. As a result, browsers can do general things well, but they lack the ability to do specific things exceptionally well.[1] Webbots, on the other hand, can be programmed for specific tasks and can perform those tasks with perfection. Additionally, webbots have the ability to automate anything you do online or notify you when something needs to be done.

What's in It for Developers?

Your ability to write a webbot can distinguish you from a pack of lesser developers. Web developers—who've gone from designing the new economy of the late 1990s to falling victim to it during the dot-com crash of 2001—know that today's job market is very competitive. Even today's most talented developers can have trouble finding meaningful work. Knowing how to write webbots will expand your ability as a developer and make you more valuable to your employer or potential employers.

A webbot writer differentiates his or her skill set from that of someone whose knowledge of Internet technology extends only to creating websites. By designing webbots, you demonstrate that you have a thorough understanding of network technology and a variety of network protocols, as well as the ability to use existing technology in new and creative ways.

Webbot Developers Are in Demand

There are many growth opportunities for webbot developers. You can demonstrate this for yourself by looking at your website's file access logs and recording all the non-browsers that have visited your website. If you compare current server logs to those from a year ago, you should notice a healthy increase in traffic from nontraditional web clients or webbots. Someone has to write these automated agents, and as the demand for webbots increases, so does the demand for webbot developers.

Hard statistics on the growth of webbot use are hard to come by, since many webbots defy detection and masquerade as traditional web browsers. In fact, the value that webbots bring to businesses forces most webbot projects underground. I can't talk about most of the webbots I've developed because they create competitive advantages for clients, and they'd rather keep those techniques secret. Regardless of the actual numbers, it's a fact that webbots and spiders comprise a large amount of today's Internet traffic and that many developers are required to both maintain existing webbots and develop new ones.

---

[1] For example, they can't act on your behalf, filter content for relevance, or perform tasks automatically.

Webbots Are Fun to Write

In addition to solving serious business problems, webbots are also fun to write. This should be welcome news to seasoned developers who no longer experience the thrill of solving a problem or using a technology for the first time. Without a little fun, it's easy for developers to get bored and conclude that software is simply a sequence of instructions that do the same thing every time a program runs. While predictability makes software dependable, it also makes it tiresome to write. This is especially true for computer programmers who specialize in a specific industry and lack diversity in tasks. At some point in their careers, nearly all of the programmers I know have become very tired of what they do, in spite of the fact that they still like to write computer programs.

Webbots, however, are almost like games, in that they can pleasantly surprise their developers with their unpredictability. This is because webbots operate on data that changes frequently, and they respond slightly differently every time they run. As a result, webbots become impulsive and lifelike. Unlike other software, webbots feel organic! Once you write a webbot that does something wonderfully unexpected, you'll have a hard time describing the experience to those writing traditional software applications.

Webbots Facilitate "Constructive Hacking"

By its strict definition, *hacking* is the process of creatively using technology for a purpose other than the one originally intended. By using web pages, news groups, email, or other online technology in unintended ways, you join the ranks of innovators that combine and alter existing technology to create totally new and useful tools. You'll also broaden the possibilities for using the Internet.

Unfortunately, hacking also has a dark side, popularized by stories of people breaking into systems, stealing private data, and rendering online services unusable. While some people do write destructive webbots, I don't condone that type of behavior here. In fact, Chapter 28 is dedicated to this very subject.

What's in It for Business Leaders?

Few businesses gain a competitive advantage simply by *using* the Internet. Today, businesses need a unique online strategy to gain a competitive advantage. Unfortunately, most businesses limit their online strategy to a website—which, barring some visual design differences, essentially functions like all the other websites within the industry.

Customize the Internet for Your Business

Most of the webbot projects I've developed are for business leaders who've become frustrated with the Internet as it is. They want added automation and decision-making capability on the websites they use to run their businesses. Essentially, they want webbots that customize other people's websites (and the data those sites contain) for the specific way they do business. Progressive businesses use webbots to improve their online experience, optimizing how they buy things, how they gather facts, how they're notified when things change, and how to enforce business rules when making online purchases.

Businesses that use webbots aren't limited to envisioning the Internet as a set of websites that are accessed by browsers. Instead, they see the Internet as a stockpile of varied resources that they can customize (using webbots) to serve their specific needs.

There has always been a lag between when people figure out how to do something manually and when they figure out how to automate the process. Just as chainsaws replaced axes and as sewing machines superseded needles and thimbles, it is only natural to assume that new (automated) methods for interacting with the Internet will follow the methods we use today. The companies that develop these processes will be the first to enjoy the competitive advantage created by their vision.

Capitalize on the Public's Inexperience with Webbots

Most people have very little experience using the Internet with anything other than a browser, and even if people have used other Internet clients like email or news readers, they have never thought about how their online experience could be improved through automation. For most, it just hasn't been an issue.

For businesspeople, blind allegiance to browsers is a double-edged sword. In one respect, it's good that people aren't familiar with the benefits that webbots provide—this provides opportunities for you to develop webbot projects that offer competitive advantages. On the other hand, if your supervisors are used to the Internet as seen through a browser alone, you may have a hard time selling your webbot projects to management.

Accomplish a Lot with a Small Investment

Webbots can achieve amazing results without elaborate setups. I've used obsolete computers with slow, dial-up connections to run webbots that create completely new revenue channels for businesses. Webbots can even be designed to work with existing office equipment like phones, fax machines, and printers.

Final Thoughts

One of the nice things about webbots is that you can create a large effect without making something difficult for customers to use. In fact, customers don't even need to know that a webbot is involved. For example, your webbots can deliver services through traditional-looking websites. While you know that you're doing something radically innovative, the end users don't realize what's going on behind the scenes—and they don't really need to know about the hordes of hidden webbots and spiders combing the Internet for the data and services they need. All they know is that they are getting an improved Internet experience. And in the end, that's all that matters.

2

IDEAS FOR WEBBOT PROJECTS

It's often more difficult to find applications for new technology than it is to learn the technology itself. Therefore, this chapter focuses on encouraging you to generate ideas for things that you can do with webbots. We'll explore how webbots capitalize on browser limitations, and we'll see a few examples of what people are currently doing with webbots. We'll wrap up by throwing out some wild ideas that might help you expand your expectations of what can be done online.

Inspiration from Browser Limitations

A useful method for generating ideas for webbot projects is to study what *cannot* be done by simply pointing a browser at a typical website. You know that browsers, used in traditional ways, cannot automate your Internet experience. For example, they have these limitations:

- Browsers cannot aggregate and filter information for relevance
- Browsers cannot interpret what they find online
- Browsers cannot act on your behalf

However, a browser may leverage the power of a webbot to do many things that it could not do alone. Let's look at some real-life examples of how browser limitations were leveraged into actual webbot projects.

Webbots That Aggregate and Filter Information for Relevance

TrackRates.com (http://www.trackrates.com, shown in Figure 2-1) is a website that deploys an army of webbots to aggregate and filter hotel room prices from travel websites. By identifying room prices for specific hotels for specific dates, it determines the actual market value for rooms up to three months into the future. This information helps hotel managers intelligently price rooms by specifically knowing what the competition is charging for similar rooms. TrackRates.com also reveals market trends by performing statistical analysis on room prices, and it tries to determine periods of high demand by indicating dates on which hotels have booked all of their rooms.

Figure 2-1: TrackRates.com

I wrote TrackRates.com to help hotel managers analyze local markets and provide facts for setting room prices. Without the TrackRates.com webbot, hotel managers either need to guess what their rooms are worth, rely on less current information about their local hotel market, or go through the arduous task of manually collecting this data.

Webbots That Interpret What They Find Online

WebSiteOptimization.com (http://www.websiteoptimization.com) uses a webbot to help web developers create websites that use resources effectively. This webbot accepts a web page's URL (as shown in Figure 2-2) and analyzes how each graphic, CSS, and JavaScript file is used by the web page. In the interest of full disclosure, I should mention that I wrote the back end for this web page analyzer.

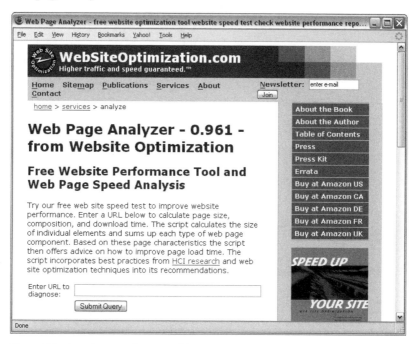

Figure 2-2: A website-analyzing webbot

The WebSiteOptimization.com webbot analyzes the data it collects and offers suggestions for optimizing website performance. Without this tool, developers would have to manually parse through their HTML code to determine which files are required by web pages, how much bandwidth they are using, and how the organization of the web page affects its performance.

Webbots That Act on Your Behalf

Pokerbots, webbots that play online poker, are a response to the recent growth in online gambling sites, particularly gaming sites with live poker rooms. While the action in these pokers sites is live, not all the players are. Some online poker players are webbots, like Poker Robot, shown in Figure 2-3.

Webbots designed to play online poker not only know the rules of Texas hold 'em but use predetermined business rules to expertly read how others play. They use this information to hold, fold, or bet appropriately. Reportedly, these automated players can very effectively pick the pockets of new and inexperienced poker players. Some *collusion webbots* even allow one virtual player to play multiple hands at the same table, while making it look like a separate person is playing each hand. Imagine playing against a group of people who not only know each other's cards, but hold, fold, and bet against you as a team!

Obviously, such webbots that play expert poker (and cheat) provide a tremendous advantage. Nobody knows exactly how prevalent pokerbots are, but they have created a market for anti-pokerbot software like Poker BodyGuard, distributed by StopPokerCheaters.com.

Figure 2-3: An example pokerbot

A Few Crazy Ideas to Get You Started

One of the goals of this book is to encourage you to write new and experimental webbots of your own design. A way to jumpstart this process is to brainstorm and generate some ideas for potential projects. I've taken this opportunity to list a few ideas to get you started. These ideas are not here necessarily because they have commercial value. Instead, they should act as inspiration for your own webbots and what you want to accomplish online.

When designing a webbot, remember that the more specifically you can define the task, the more useful your webbot will be. What can you do with a webbot? Let's look at a few scenarios.

Help Out a Busy Executive

Suppose you're a busy executive type and you like to start your day reading your online industry publication. Time is limited, however, and you only let yourself read industry news until you've finished your first cup of coffee. Therefore, you don't want to be bothered with stories that you've read before or that you know are not relevant to your business. You ask your developer to create a specialized webbot that consolidates articles from your favorite industry news sources and only displays links to stories that it has not shown you before.

The webbot could ignore articles that contain certain key phrases you previously entered in an *exclusion list*[1] and highlight articles that contain references to you or your competitors. With such an application, you could quickly scan what's happening in your industry and only spend time reading relevant articles. You might even have more time to enjoy your coffee.

Save Money by Automating Tasks

It's possible to design a webbot that automatically buys inventory for a store, given a predetermined set of buying criteria. For example, assume you own a store that sells used travel gear. Some of your sources for inventory are online auction websites.[2] Say you are interested in bidding on under-priced Tumi suitcases during the closing minute of their auctions. If you don't use a webbot of some sort, you will have to use a web browser to check each auction site periodically.

Without a webbot, it can be expensive to use the Internet in a business setting, because repetitive tasks (like procuring inventory) are time consuming without automation. Additionally, the more mundane the task, the greater the opportunity for human error. Checking online auctions for products to resell could easily consume one or two hours a day—up to 25 percent of a 40-hour work week. At that rate, someone with an annual salary of $80,000 would cost a company $20,000 a year to procure inventory (without a webbot). That cost does not include the cost of opportunities lost while the employee manually surfs auction sites. In scenarios like this, it's easy to see how product acquisition with a webbot saves a lot of money—even for a small business with small requirements. Additionally, a webbot may uncover bargains missed by someone manually searching the auction site.

Protect Intellectual Property

You can write a webbot to protect your online intellectual property. For example, suppose you spent many hours writing a JavaScript program. It has commercial value, and you license the script for others to use for a fee. You've been selling the program for a few months and have learned that some people

---

[1] An *exclusion list* is a list of keywords or phrases that are ignored by a webbot.

[2] Some online auctions actually provide tools to help you write webbots that manage auctions. If you're interested in automating online auctions, check out eBay's Developers Program (http://developer.ebay.com).

are downloading and using your program without paying for it. You write a webbot to find websites that are using your JavaScript program without your permission. This webbot searches the Internet and makes a list of URLs that reference your JavaScript file. In a separate step, the webbot does a *whois* lookup on the domain to determine the owner from the domain registrar.[3] If the domain is not one of your registered users, the webbot compiles contact information from the domain registrar so you can contact the parties who are using unlicensed copies of your code.

Monitor Opportunities

You can also write webbots that alert you when particular opportunities arise. For example, let's say that you have an interest in acquiring a Jack Russell Terrier.[4] Instead of devoting part of each day to searching for your new dog, you decide to write a webbot to search for you and notify you when it finds a dog meeting your requirements. Your webbot performs a daily search of the websites of local animal shelters and dog rescue organizations. It parses the contents of the sites, looking for your dog. When the webbot finds a Jack Russell Terrier, it sends you an email notification describing the dog and its location. The webbot also records this specific dog in its database, so it doesn't send additional notifications for the same dog in the future. This is a fairly common webbot task, which could be modified to automatically discover job listings, sports scores, or any other timely information.

Verify Access Rights on a Website

Webbots may prevent the potentially nightmarish situation that exists for any web developer who mistakenly gives one user access to another user's data. To avoid this situation, you could commission a webbot to verify that all users receive the correct access to your site. This webbot logs in to the site with every viable username and password. While acting on each user's behalf, the webbot accesses every available page and compares those pages to a list of appropriate pages for each user. If the webbot finds a user is inadvertently able to access something he or she shouldn't, that account is temporarily suspended until the problem is fixed. Every morning before you arrive at your office, the webbot emails a report of any irregularities it found the night before.

Create an Online Clipping Service

Suppose you're very vain, and you'd like a webbot to send an email to your mother every time a major news service mentions your name. However, since you're not vain enough to check all the main news websites on a regular basis, you write a webbot that accomplishes the task for you. This webbot accesses a collection of websites, including CNN, Forbes, and Fortune.

---

[3] *whois* is a service that returns information about the owner of a website. You can do the equivalent of a whois from a shell script or from an online service.

[4] I actually met my dog online.

You design your webbot to look only for articles that mention your name, and you employ an exclusion list to ignore all articles that contain words or phrases like *shakedown, corruption,* or *money laundering.* When the webbot finds an appropriate article, it automatically sends your mother an email with a link to the article. Your webbot also blind copies you on all emails it sends so you know what she's talking about when she calls.

Plot Unauthorized Wi-Fi Networks

You could write a webbot that aids in maintaining network security on a large corporate campus. For example, suppose that you recently discovered that you have a problem with employees attaching unauthorized wireless access points to your network. Since these unauthorized access points occur inside your firewalls and proxies, you recognize that these unauthorized Wi-Fi networks pose a security risk that you need to control. Therefore, in addition to a new security policy, you decide to create a webbot that automatically finds and records the location of all wireless networks on your corporate campus.

You notice that your mail room uses a small metal cart to deliver mail. Because this cart reaches every corner of the corporate campus on a daily basis, you seek and obtain permission to attach a small laptop computer with a webbot and Global Positioning System (GPS) card to the cart. As your webbot hitches a ride through the campus, it looks for open wireless network connections. When it finds a wireless network, it uses the open network to send its GPS location to a special website. This website logs the GPS coordinates, IP address, and date of uplink in a database. If you did your homework correctly, in a few days your webbot should create a map of all open Wi-Fi networks, authorized and unauthorized, in your entire corporate campus.

Track Web Technologies

You could write webbots that use *web page headers,* the information that servers send to browsers so they may correctly render websites, to maintain a list of web technologies used by major corporations. Headers typically indicate the type of webserver (and often the operating system) that websites use, as shown in Figure 2-4.

Figure 2-4: A web page header showing server technology

Your webbot starts by accessing the headers of each website from a list that you keep in a database. It then parses web technology information from the header. Finally, the webbot stores that information in a database that is used by a graphing program to plot how server technology choices change over time.

Allow Incompatible Systems to Communicate

In addition to creating human-readable output, you could design a webbot that only talks to other computers. For example, let's say that you want to synchronize two databases, one on a local private network and one that's behind a public website. In this case, *synchronization* (ensuring that both databases contain the same information) is difficult because the systems use different technologies with incompatible synchronization techniques. Given the circumstances, you could write a webbot that runs on your private network and, for example, analyzes the public database through a password-protected web service every morning. The webbot uses the Internet as a common protocol between these databases, analyzes data on both systems, and exchanges the appropriate data to synchronize the two databases.

Final Thoughts

Studying browser limitations is one way to uncover ideas for new webbot designs. You've seen some real-world examples of webbots in use and read some descriptions of conceptual webbot designs. But, enough with theory—let's head to the lab!

The next four chapters describe the basics of webbot development: downloading pages, parsing data, emulating form submission, and managing large amounts of data. Once you master these concepts, you can move on to actual webbot projects.

3

DOWNLOADING WEB PAGES

The most important thing a webbot does is move web pages from the Internet to your computer. Once the web page is on your computer, your webbot can parse and manipulate it.

This chapter will show you how to write simple PHP scripts that download web pages. More importantly, you'll learn PHP's limitations and how to overcome them with *PHP/CURL*, a special binding of the cURL library that facilitates many advanced network features. cURL is used widely by many computer languages as a means to access network files with a number of protocols and options.

NOTE *While web pages are the most common targets for webbots and spiders, the Web is not the only source of information for your webbots. Later chapters will explore methods for extracting data from newsgroups, email, and FTP servers, as well.*

Prior to discovering PHP, I wrote webbots in a variety of languages, including Visual Basic, Java, and Tcl/Tk. But due to its simple syntax, in-depth string parsing capabilities, networking functions, and portability, PHP proved ideal for webbot development. However, PHP is primarily a server language, and its chief purpose is to help webservers interpret incoming requests and send the appropriate web pages in response. Since webbots don't serve pages (they request them), this book supplements PHP built-in functions with PHP/CURL and a variety of libraries, developed specifically to help you learn to write webbots and spiders.

Think About Files, Not Web Pages

To most people, the Web appears as a collection of web pages. But in reality, the Web is collection of files that form those web pages. These files may exist on servers anywhere in the world, and they only create web pages when they are viewed together. Because browsers simplify the process of downloading and rendering the individual files that make up web pages, you need to know the nuts and bolts of how web pages are put together before you write your first webbot.

When your browser requests a file, as shown in Figure 3-1, the webserver that fields the request sends your browser a *default* or *index file*, which maps the location of all the files that the web page needs and tells how to render the text and images that comprise that web page.

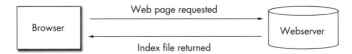

Figure 3-1: When a browser requests a web page, it first receives an index file.

As a rule, this index file also contains references to the other files required to render the complete web page,[1] as shown in Figure 3-2. These may include images, JavaScript, style sheets, or complex media files like Flash, QuickTime, or Windows Media files. The browser downloads each file separately, as it is referenced by the index file.

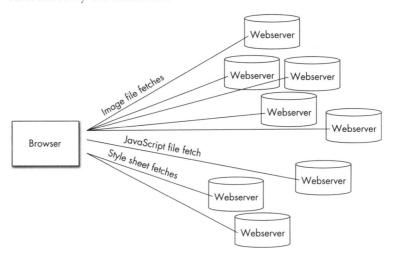

Figure 3-2: Downloading files, as they are referenced by the index file

---

[1] Some very simple websites consist of only one file.

For example, if you request a web page with references to eight items your single web page actually executes nine separate file downloads (one for the web page and one for each file referenced by the web page). Usually, each file resides on the same server, but they could just as easily exist on separate domains, as shown in Figure 3-2.

Downloading Files with PHP's Built-in Functions

Before you can appreciate PHP/CURL, you'll need to familiarize yourself with PHP's built-in functions for downloading files from the Internet.

Downloading Files with fopen() and fgets()

PHP includes two simple built-in functions for downloading files from a network—fopen() and fgets(). The fopen() function does two things. First, it creates a *network socket*, which represents the link between your webbot and the network resource you want to retrieve. Second, it implements the HTTP *protocol*, which defines how data is transferred. With those tasks completed, fgets() leverages the networking ability of your computer's operating system to pull the file from the Internet.

Creating Your First Webbot Script

Let's use PHP's built-in functions to create your first webbot, which downloads a "Hello, world!" web page from this book's companion website. The short script is shown in Listing 3-1.

```
# Define the file you want to download
$target      = "http://www.schrenk.com/nostarch/webbots/hello_world.html";
$file_handle = fopen($target, "r");

# Fetch the file
while (!feof($file_handle))
    echo fgets($file_handle, 4096);
fclose($file_handle);
```

Listing 3-1: Downloading a file from the Web with fopen() and fgets()

As shown in Listing 3-1, fopen() establishes a network connection to the *target*, or file you want to download. It references this connection with a *file handle*, or network link called $file_handle. The script then uses fopen() to fetch and echo the file in 4,096-byte chunks until it has downloaded and displayed the entire file. Finally, the script executes an fclose() to tell PHP that it's finished with the network handle.

Before we can execute the example in Listing 3-1, we need to examine the two ways to execute a webbot: You can run a webbot either in a browser or in a command shell.[2]

---

[2] See Chapter 23 for more information on executing webbots as scheduled events.

Executing Webbots in Command Shells

If you have a choice, it is usually better to execute webbots from a shell or command line. Webbots generally don't care about web page formatting, so they will display exactly what is returned from a webserver. Browsers, in contrast, will interpret HTML tags as instructions for rendering the web page. For example, Figure 3-3 shows what Listing 3-1 looks like when executed in a shell.

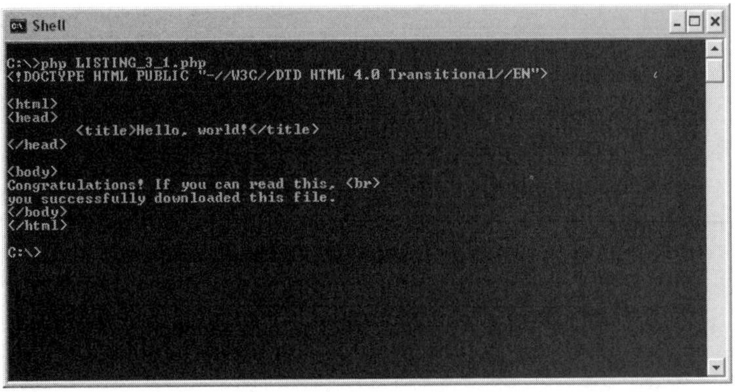

Figure 3-3: Running a webbot script in a shell

Executing Webbots in Browsers

To run a webbot script in a browser, simply load the script on a webserver and execute it by loading its URL into the browser's location bar as you would any other web page. Contrast Figure 3-3 with Figure 3-4, where the same script is run within a browser. The HTML tags are gone, as well as all of the structure of the returned file; the only things displayed are two lines of text. Running a webbot in a browser only shows a partial picture and often hides important information that a webbot needs.

NOTE   *To display HTML tags within a browser, surround the output with <xmp> and </xmp> tags.*

Figure 3-4: Browser "rendering" the output of a webbot

Browser buffering is another complication you might run into if you try to execute a webbot in a browser. Buffering is useful when you're viewing web pages because it allows a browser to wait until it has collected enough of a web page before it starts *rendering* or displaying the web page. However, browser buffering is troublesome for webbots because they frequently run for extended periods of time—much longer than it would take to download a typical web page. During prolonged webbot execution, status messages written by the webbot may not be displayed by the browser while it is buffering the display.

I have one webbot that runs continuously; in fact, it once ran for seven months before stopping during a power outage. This webbot could never run effectively in a browser because browsers are designed to render web pages with files of finite length. Browsers assume short download periods and may buffer an entire web page before displaying anything—therefore, never displaying the output of your webbot.

NOTE   *Browsers can still be very useful for creating interfaces that set up or control the actions of a webbot. They can also be useful for displaying the results of a webbot's work.*

Downloading Files with file()

An alternative to fopen() and fgets() is the function file(), which downloads formatted files and places them into an array. This function differs from fopen() in two important ways: One way is that, unlike fopen(), it does not require you to create a file handle, because it creates all the network preparations for you. The other difference is that it returns the downloaded file as an array, with each line of the downloaded file in a separate array element. The script in Listing 3-2 downloads the same web page used in Listing 3-1, but it uses the file() command.

```
<?
// Download the target file
$target = "http://www.schrenk.com/nostarch/webbots/hello_world.html";
$downloaded_page_array = file($target);

// Echo contents of file
for($xx=0; $xx<count($downloaded_page_array); $xx++)
    echo $downloaded_page_array[$xx];
?>
```

Listing 3-2: Downloading files with file()

The file() function is particularly useful for downloading *comma-separated value (CSV) files*, in which each line of text represents a row of data with columnar formatting (as in an Excel spreadsheet). Loading files line-by-line into an array, however, is not particularly useful when downloading HTML files because the data in a web page is not defined by rows or columns; in a CSV file, however, rows and columns have specific meaning.

Introducing PHP/CURL

While PHP is capable when it comes to simple file downloads, most real-life applications require additional functionality to handle advanced issues such as form submission, authentication, redirection, and so on. These functions are difficult to facilitate with PHP's built-in functions alone. Therefore, most of this book's examples use PHP/CURL to download files.

The open source cURL project is the product of Swedish developer Daniel Stenberg and a team of developers. The cURL library is available for use with nearly any computer language you can think of. When cURL is used with PHP, it's known as PHP/CURL.

The name *cURL* is either a blend of the words *client* and *URL* or an acronym for the words *client URL Request Library*—you decide. cURL does everything that PHP's built-in networking functions do and a lot more. Appendix A expands on cURL's features, but here's a quick overview of the things PHP/CURL can do for you, a webbot developer.

Multiple Transfer Protocols

Unlike the built-in PHP network functions, cURL supports multiple transfer protocols, including FTP, FTPS, HTTP, HTTPS, Gopher, Telnet, and LDAP. Of these protocols, the most important is probably HTTPS, which allows webbots to download from encrypted websites that employ the Secure Sockets Layer (SSL) protocol.

Form Submission

cURL provides easy ways for a webbot to emulate browser form submission to a server. cURL supports all of the standard *methods*, or form submission protocols, as you'll learn in Chapter 5.

Basic Authentication

cURL allows webbots to enter password-protected websites that use basic authentication. You've encountered authentication if you've seen this familiar gray box, shown in Figure 3-5, asking for your username and password. PHP/CURL makes it easy to write webbots that enter and use password-protected websites.

Figure 3-5: A basic authentication prompt

Cookies

Without cURL, it is difficult for webbots to read and write *cookies*, those small bits of data that websites use to create session variables that track your movement. Websites also use cookies to manage shopping carts and authenticate users. cURL makes it easy for your webbot to interpret the cookies that webservers send it; it also simplifies the process of showing webservers all the cookies your webbot has written. Chapters 21 and 22 have much more to say on the subject of webbots and cookies.

Redirection

Redirection occurs when a web browser looks for a file in one place, but the server tells it that the file has moved and that it should download it from another location. For example, the website www.company.com may use redirection to force browsers to go to www.company.com/spring_sale when a seasonal promotion is in place. Browsers handle redirections automatically, and cURL allows webbots to have the same functionality.

Agent Name Spoofing

Every time a webserver receives a file request, it stores the requesting agent's name in a log file called an *access log file*. This log file stores the time of access, the IP address of the requester, and the *agent name*, which identifies the type of program that requested the file. Generally, agent names identify the browser that the web surfer was using to view the website.

Some agent names that a server log file may record are shown in Listing 3-3. The first four names are browsers; the last is the Google spider.

```
Mozilla/5.0 (Windows; U; Windows NT 5.1; rv:1.7.6) Gecko/20050225 Firefox/1.0.1
Mozilla/4.0 (compatible; MSIE 5.0; Windows 2000) Opera 6.03 [en]
Mozilla/5.0 (compatible; Konqueror/3.1-rc3; i686 Linux; 20020515)
Mozilla/4.0 (compatible; MSIE 7.0b; Windows NT 5.1)
Googlebot/2.1 (+http://www.google.com/bot.html)
```

Listing 3-3: Agent names as seen in a file access log

A webbot using cURL can assume any appropriate (or inappropriate) agent name. For example, sometimes it is advantageous to identify your webbots, as Google does. Other times, it is better to make your webbot look like a browser. If you write webbots that use the LIB_http library (described later), your webbot's agent name will be *Test Webbot*. If you download a file from a webserver with PHP's fopen() or file() functions, your agent name will be the version of PHP installed on your computer.

Referer Management

cURL allows webbot developers to change the *referer*, which is the reference that servers use to detect which link the web surfer clicked. Sometimes webservers use the referer to verify that file requests are coming from the correct place. For example, a website might enforce a rule that prevents downloading of images unless the referring web page is also on the same webserver. This prohibits people from *bandwidth stealing*, or writing web pages using images on someone else's server. cURL allows a webbot to set the referer to an arbitrary value.

Socket Management

cURL also gives webbots the ability to recognize when a webserver isn't going to respond to a file request. This ability is vital because, without it, your webbot might hang (forever) waiting for a server response that will never happen. With cURL, you can specify how long a webbot will wait for a response from a server before it gives up and moves on.

Installing PHP/CURL

Since PHP/CURL is tightly integrated with PHP, installation should be unnecessary, or at worst, easy. You probably already have PHP/CURL on your computer; you just need to enable it in php.ini, the PHP configuration file. If you're using Linux, FreeBSD, OS X, or another Unix-based operating system, you may have to recompile your copy of Apache/PHP to enjoy the benefits of PHP/CURL. Installing PHP/CURL is similar to installing any other PHP library. If you need help, you should reference the PHP website (http://www.php.net) for the instructions for your particular operating system and PHP version.

LIB_http

Since PHP/CURL is very flexible and has many configurations, it is often handy to use it within a *wrapper function*, which simplifies the complexities of a code library into something easier to understand. For your convenience, this book uses a library called LIB_http, which provides wrapper functions to the PHP/CURL features you'll use most. The remainder of this chapter describes the basic functions of the LIB_http library.

LIB_http is a collection of PHP/CURL routines that simplify downloading files. It contains defaults and abstractions that facilitate downloading files, managing cookies, and completing online forms. The name of the library refers to the HTTP protocol used by the library. Some of the reasons for using this library will not be evident until we cover its more advanced features. Even simple file downloads, however, are made easier and more robust with LIB_http because of PHP/CURL. The most recent version of LIB_http is available at this book's website.

Familiarizing Yourself with the Default Values

To simplify its use, LIB_http sets a series of default conditions for you, as described below:

- Your webbot's agent name is *Test Webbot.*
- Your webbot will time out if a file transfer doesn't complete within 25 seconds.
- Your webbot will store cookies in the file c:\cookie.txt.
- Your webbot will automatically follow a maximum of four redirections, as directed by servers in HTTP headers.
- Your webbot will, if asked, tell the remote server that you do not have a local authentication certificate. (This is only important if you access a website employing SSL encryption, which is used to protect confidential information on e-commerce websites.)

These defaults are set at the beginning of the file. Feel free to change any of these settings to meet your specific needs.

Using LIB_http

The LIB_http library provides a set of wrapper functions that simplify complicated PHP/CURL interfaces. Each of these interfaces calls a common routine, http(), which performs the specified task, using the values passed to it by the wrapper interfaces. All functions in LIB_http share a similar format: A target and referring URL are passed, and an array is returned, containing the contents of the requested file, transfer status, and error conditions.

While LIB_http has many functions, we'll restrict our discussion to simply fetching files from the Internet using HTTP. The remaining features are described as needed throughout the book.

http_get()

The function http_get() downloads files with the GET method; it has many advantages over PHP's built-in functions for downloading files from the Internet. Not only is the interface simple, but this function offers all the previously described advantages of using PHP/CURL. The script in Listing 3-4 shows how files are downloaded with http_get().

```
# Usage: http_get()
array http_get (string target_url, string referring_url)
```

Listing 3-4: Using http_get()

These are the inputs for the script in Listing 3-4:

> *target_url* is the fully formed URL of the desired file
>
> *referring_url* is the fully formed URL of the referer

These are the outputs for the script in Listing 3-4:

> *$array['FILE']* contains the contents of the requested file
>
> *$array['STATUS']* contains status information regarding the file transfer
>
> *$array['ERROR']* contains a textual description of any errors

http_get_withheader()

When a web agent requests a file from the Web, the server returns the file contents, as discussed in the previous section, along with the *HTTP header*, which describes various properties related to a web page. Browsers and webbots rely on the HTTP header to determine what to do with the contents of the downloaded file.

The data that is included in the HTTP header varies from application to application, but it may define cookies, the size of the downloaded file, redirections, encryption details, or authentication directives. Since the information in the HTTP header is critical to properly using a network file, LIB_http configures cURL to automatically handle the more common header directives. Listing 3-5 shows how this function is used.

```
# Usage: http_get_withheader()
array http_get_withheader (string target_url, string referring_url)
```

Listing 3-5: Using http_get()

These are the inputs for the script in Listing 3-5:

> *target_url* is the fully formed URL of the desired file
>
> *referring_url* is the fully formed URL of the referer

These are the outputs for the script in Listing 3-5:

> *$array['FILE']* contains the contents of the requested file, including the HTTP header
>
> *$array['STATUS']* contains status information about the file transfer
>
> *$array['ERROR']* contains a textual description of any errors

The example in Listing 3-6 uses the http_get_withheader() function to download a file and display the contents of the returned array.

```
# Include http library
include("LIB_http.php");
```

```
# Define the target and referer web pages
$target = "http://www.schrenk.com/publications.php";
$ref    = "http://www.schrenk.com";

# Request the header
$return_array = http_get_withheader($target, $ref);

# Display the header
echo "FILE CONTENTS \n";
var_dump($return_array['FILE']);

echo "ERRORS \n";
var_dump($return_array['ERROR']);

echo "STATUS \n";
var_dump($return_array['STATUS']);
```

Listing 3-6: Using http_get_withheader()

The script in Listing 3-6 downloads the page and displays the requested page, any errors, and a variety of status information related to the fetch and download.

Listing 3-7 shows what is produced when the script in Listing 3-6 is executed, with the array that includes the page header, error conditions, and status. Notice that the contents of the returned file are limited to only the HTTP header, because we requested only the header and not the entire page. Also, notice that the first line in a HTTP header is the *HTTP code*, which indicates the status of the request. An HTTP code of 200 tells us that the request was successful. The HTTP code also appears in the status array element.[3]

```
FILE CONTENTS
string(215) "HTTP/1.1 200 OK
Date: Sat, 08 Oct 2008 16:38:51 GMT
Server: Apache/2.0.53 (FreeBSD) mod_ssl/2.0.53 OpenSSL/0.9.7g PHP/4.4.0
X-Powered-By: PHP/4.4.0
Content-Type: text/html; charset=ISO-8859-1

"
ERRORS
string(0) ""

STATUS
array(20) {
  ["url"]=>
  string(39) "http://www.schrenk.com/publications.php"
  ["content_type"]=>
  string(29) "text/html; charset=ISO-8859-1"
  ["http_code"]=>
  int(200)
```

---

[3] A complete list of HTTP codes can be found in Appendix B.

```
["header_size"]=>
int(215)
["request_size"]=>
int(200)
["filetime"]=>
int(-1)
["ssl_verify_result"]=>
int(0)
["redirect_count"]=>
int(0)
["total_time"]=>
float(0.683)
["namelookup_time"]=>
float(0.005)
["connect_time"]=>
float(0.101)
["pretransfer_time"]=>
float(0.101)
["size_upload"]=>
float(0)
["size_download"]=>
float(0)
["speed_download"]=>
float(0)
["speed_upload"]=>
float(0)
["download_content_length"]=>
float(0)
["upload_content_length"]=>
float(0)
["starttransfer_time"]=>
float(0.683)
["redirect_time"]=>
float(0)
}
```

Listing 3-7: File contents, errors, and the download status array returned by LIB_http

The information returned in $array['STATUS'] is extraordinarily useful for learning how the fetch was conducted. Included in this array are values for download speed, access times, and file sizes—all valuable when writing diagnostic webbots that monitor the performance of a website.

Learning More About HTTP Headers

When a Content-Type line appears in an HTTP header, it defines the *MIME*, or the media type of file sent from the server. The MIME type tells the web agent what to do with the file. For example, the Content-Type in the previous example was *text/html*, which indicates that the file is a web page. Knowing if the file they just downloaded was an image or an HTML file helps browsers know if they should display the file as text or render an image. For example, the HTTP header information for a JPEG image is shown in Listing 3-8.

```
HTTP/1.1 200 OK
Date: Mon, 23 Mar 2009 00:06:13 GMT
Server: Apache/1.3.12 (Unix) mod_throttle/3.1.2 tomcat/1.0 PHP/4.0.3pl1
Last-Modified: Wed, 23 Jul 2008 18:03:29 GMT
ETag: "74db-9063-3d3eebf1"
Accept-Ranges: bytes
Content-Length: 36963
Content-Type: image/jpeg
```

Listing 3-8: An HTTP header for an image file request

Examining LIB_http's Source Code

Most webbots in this book will use the library LIB_http to download pages from the Internet. If you plan to explore any of the webbot examples that appear later in this book, you should obtain a copy of this library; the latest version is available for download at this book's website. We'll explore some of the defaults and functions of LIB_http here.

LIB_http Defaults

At the very beginning of the library is a set of defaults, as shown in Listing 3-9.

```
define("WEBBOT_NAME", "Test Webbot");      # How your webbot will appear in server logs
define("CURL_TIMEOUT", 25);                # Time (seconds) to wait for network response
define("COOKIE_FILE", "c:\cookie.txt");    # Location of cookie file
```

Listing 3-9: LIB_http defaults

LIB_http Functions

The functions shown in Listing 3-10 are available within LIB_http. All of these functions return the array defined earlier, containing downloaded files, error messages, and the status of the file transfer.

```
http_get($target, $ref)                                # Simple get request (w/o header)
http_get_withheader($target, $ref)                     # Simple get request (w/ header)
http_get_form($target, $ref, $data_array)              # Form (method ="GET", w/o header)
http_get_form_withheader($target, $ref, $data_array)   # Form (method ="GET", w/ header)
http_post_form($target, $ref, $data_array)             # Form (method ="POST", w/o header)
http_post_withheader($target, $ref, $data_array)       # Form (method ="POST", w/ header)
http_header($target, $ref)                             # Only returns header
```

Listing 3-10: LIB_http functions

Final Thoughts

Some of these functions use an additional input parameter, $data_array, when form data is passed from the webbot to the webserver. These functions are listed below:

- http_get_form()
- http_get_form_withheader()
- http_post_form()
- http_post_form_withheader()

If you don't understand what all these functions do now, don't worry. Their use will become familiar to you as you go through the examples that appear later in this book. Now might be a good time to thumb through Appendix A, which details the features of cURL that webbot developers are most apt to need.

4

PARSING TECHNIQUES

Parsing is the process of segregating what's desired or useful from what is not. In the case of webbots, parsing involves detecting and separating image names and addresses, key phrases, hyper-references, and other information of interest to your webbot. For example, if you are writing a spider that follows links on web pages, you will have to separate these links from the rest of the HTML. Similarly, if you write a webbot to download all the images from a web page, you will have to write parsing routines that identify all the references to image files.

Parsing Poorly Written HTML

One of the problems you'll encounter when parsing web pages is poorly written HTML. A large amount of HTML is machine generated and shows little regard for human readability, and hand-written HTML often disregards standards by ignoring closing tags or misusing quotes around values. Browsers may correctly render web pages that have substandard HTML, but poorly written HTML interferes with your webbot's ability to parse web pages.

Fortunately, a software library known as HTMLTidy[1] will clean up poorly written web pages. PHP includes HTMLTidy in its standard distributions, so you should have no problem getting it running on your computer. Installing HTMLTidy (also known as just *Tidy*) should be similar to installing cURL. Complete installation instructions are available at the PHP website.[2]

The parse functions (described next) rely on Tidy to put unparsed source code into a known state, with known delimiters and known closing tags of known case.

NOTE   *If you do not have HTMLTidy installed on your computer, the parsing described in this book may not work correctly.*

Standard Parse Routines

I have simplified parsing by identifying a few useful functions and placing them into a library called LIB_parse. These functions (or a combination of them) provide everything needed for 99 percent of your parsing tasks. Whether or not you use the functions in LIB_parse, I highly suggest that you standardize your parsing routines. Standardized parse functions make your scripts easier to read and faster to write—and perhaps just as importantly, when you limit your parsing options to a few simple solutions, you're forced to consider simpler approaches to parsing problems. The latest version of LIB_parse is available from this book's website.

Using LIB_parse

The parsing library used in this book, LIB_parse, provides easy-to-read parsing functions that should meet most parsing tasks your webbots will encounter. Primarily, LIB_parse contains wrapper functions that provide simple interfaces to otherwise complicated routines. To use the examples in this book, you should download the latest version of this library from the book's website.

One of the things you may notice about LIB_parse is the lack of regular expressions. Although regular expressions are the mainstay for parsing text, you won't find many of them here. Regular expressions can be difficult to read and understand, especially for beginners. The built-in PHP string manipulation functions are easier to understand and usually more efficient than regular expressions.

The following is a description of the functions in LIB_parse and the parsing problems they solve. These functions are also described completely within the comments of LIB_parse.

---

[1] See http://tidy.sourceforge.net.

[2] See http://www.php.net.

Splitting a String at a Delimiter: split_string()

The simplest parsing function returns a string that contains everything before or after a delimiter term. This simple function can also be used to return the text between two terms. The function provided for that task is split_string(), shown in Listing 4-1.

```
/*
string split_string (string unparsed, string delimiter, BEFORE/AFTER, INCL/EXCL)
Where
    unparsed is the string to parse
    delimiter defines boundary between substring you want and substring you don't want
    BEFORE indicates that you want what is before the delimiter
    AFTER indicates that you want what is after the delimiter
    INCL indicates that you want to include the delimiter in the parsed text
    EXCL indicates that you don't want to include the delimiter in the parsed text
*/
```

Listing 4-1: Using split_string()

Simply pass split_string() the string you want to split, the delimiter where you want the split to occur, whether you want the portion of the string that is before or after the delimiter, and whether or not you want the delimiter to be included in the returned string. Examples using split_string() are shown in Listing 4-2.

```
include("LIB_parse.php");
$string = "The quick brown fox";

# Parse what's before the delimiter, including the delimiter
$parsed_text = split_string($string, "quick", BEFORE, INCL);
// $parsed_text = "The quick"

# Parse what's after the delimiter, but don't include the delimiter
$parsed_text = split_string($string, "quick", AFTER, EXCL);
// $parsed_text = "brown fox"
```

Listing 4-2: Examples of split_string() usage

Parsing Text Between Delimiters: return_between()

Sometimes it is useful to parse text between two delimiters. For example, to parse a web page's title, you'd want to parse the text between the <title> and </title> tags. Your webbots can use the return_between() function in LIB_parse to do this.

The return_between() function uses a start delimiter and an end delimiter to define a particular part of a string your webbot needs to parse, as shown in Listing 4-3.

```
/*
string return_between (string unparsed, string start, string end, INCL/EXCL)
Where
    unparsed is the string to parse
    start identifies the starting delimiter
    end identifies the ending delimiter
    INCL indicates that you want to include the delimiters in the parsed text
    EXCL indicates that you don't want to include delimiters in the parsed text
*/
```

Listing 4-3: Using return_between()

The script in Listing 4-4 uses return_between() to parse the HTML title of a web page.

```
# Include libraries
include("LIB_parse.php");
include("LIB_http.php");

# Download a web page
$web_page = http_get($target="http://www.nostarch.com", $referer="");

# Parse the title of the web page, inclusive of the title tags
$title_incl = return_between($web_page['FILE'], "<title>", "</title>", INCL);

# Parse the title of the web page, exclusive of the title tags
$title_excl = return_between($web_page['FILE'], "<title>", "</title>", EXCL);

# Display the parsed text
echo "title_incl = ".$title_incl;
echo "\n";
echo "title_excl = ".$title_excl;
```

Listing 4-4: Using return_between() to find the title of a web page

When Listing 4-4 is run in a shell, the results should look like Figure 4-1.

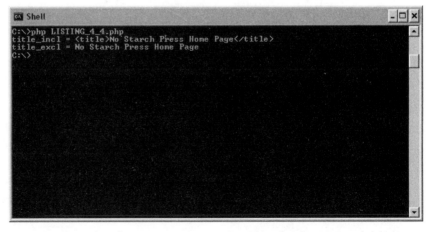

Figure 4-1: Examples of using return_between(), with and without returned delimiters

Parsing a Data Set into an Array: parse_array()

Sometimes the things your webbot needs to parse, like links, appear more than once in a web page. In these cases, a single parsed result isn't as useful as an array of results. Such a parsed array could contain all the links, meta tags, or references to images in a web page. The parse_array() function does essentially the same thing as the return_between() function, but it returns an array of all items that match the parse description or all occurrences of data between two delimiting strings. This function, for example, makes it extremely easy to extract all the links and images from a web page.

The parse_array() function , shown in Listing 4-5, is most useful when your webbots need to parse the content of reoccurring tags. For example, returning an array of everything between every occurrence of <img and > returns information about all the images in a web page. Alternately, returning an array of everything between <script and </script> will parse all inline JavaScript. Notice that in each of these cases, the opening tag is not completely defined. This is because <img and <script are sufficient to describe the tag, and additional parameters (that we don't need to define in the parse) may be present in the downloaded page.

This simple parse is also useful for parsing tables, meta tags, formatted text, video, or any other parts of web pages defined between reoccurring HTML tags.

```
/*
array return_array (string unparsed, string beg, string end)
Where
    unparsed is the string to parse
    beg is a reoccurring beginning delimiter
    end is a reoccurring ending delimiter
    array contains every occurrence of what's found between beginning and end.
*/
```

Listing 4-5: Using parse_array()

The script in Listing 4-6 uses the parse_array() function to parse and display all the meta tags on the FBI website. Meta tags are primarily used to define a web page's content to a search engine.

The following code, which uses parse_array() to gather the meta tags from a web page, could be incorporated with the project in Chapter 11 to determine how adjustments in your meta tags affect your ranking in search engines. To parse all the meta tags, the function must be told to return all instances that occur between <meta and >. Again, notice that the script only uses enough of each delimiter to uniquely identify where a meta tag starts and ends. Remember that the definitions you apply for start and stop variables must apply for each data set you want to parse.

```
include("LIB_parse.php");    # Include parse library
include("LIB_http.php");     # Include cURL library

$web_page = http_get($target="http://www.fbi.gov", $referer="");
$meta_tag_array = parse_array($web_page['FILE'], "<meta", ">");

for($xx=0; $xx<count($meta_tag_array); $xx++)
    echo $meta_tag_array[$xx]."\n";
```

Listing 4-6: Using parse_array() to parse all the meta tags from http://www.fbi.gov

When the script in Listing 4-6 runs, the result should look like Figure 4-2.

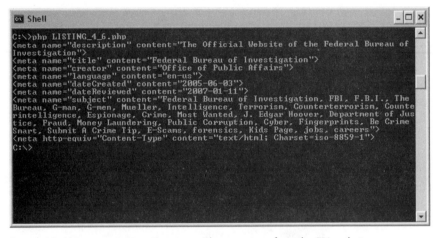

Figure 4-2: Using parse_array() to parse the meta tags from the FBI website

Parsing Attribute Values: get_attribute()

Once your webbot has parsed tags from a web page, it is often important to parse attribute values from those tags. For example, if you're writing a spider that harvests links from web pages, you will need to parse all the link tags, but you will also need to parse the specific href attribute of the link tag. For these reasons, LIB_parse includes the get_attribute() function.

The get_attribute() function provides an interface that allows webbot developers to parse specific attribute values from HTML tags. Its usage is shown in Listing 4-7.

```
/*
string get_attribute( string tag, string attribute)
Where
    tag is the HTML tag that contains the attribute you want to parse
    attribute is the name of the specific attribute in the HTML tag
*/
```

Listing 4-7: Using get_attribute()

This parse is particularly useful when you need to get a specific attribute from a previously parsed array of tags. For example, Listing 4-8 shows how to parse all the images from http://www.schrenk.com, using get_attribute() to get the src attribute from an array of <img> tags.

```
include("LIB_parse.php");     # include parse library
include("LIB_http.php");      # include curl library

// Download the web page
$web_page = http_get($target="http://www.schrenk.com", $referer="");

// Parse the image tags
$meta_tag_array = parse_array($web_page['FILE'], "<img", ">");

// Echo the image source attribute from each image tag
for($xx=0; $xx<count($meta_tag_array); $xx++)
    {
    $name = get_attribute($meta_tag_array[$xx],  $attribute="src");
    echo $name ."\n";
    }
```

Listing 4-8: Parsing the src attributes from image tags

Figure 4-3 shows the output of Listing 4-8.

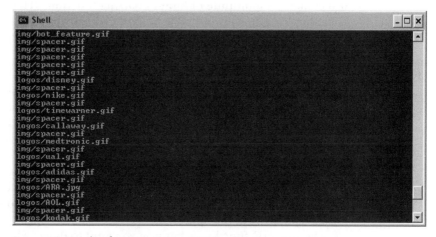

Figure 4-3: Results of running Listing 4-8, showing parsed image names

Removing Unwanted Text: remove()

Up to this point, parsing meant extracting desired text from a larger string. Sometimes, however, parsing means manipulating text. For example, since webbots usually lack JavaScript interpreters, it's often best to delete JavaScript from downloaded files. In other cases, your webbots may need to remove all images or email addresses from a web page. For these reasons, LIB_parse includes the remove() function. The remove() function is an easy-to-use interface for removing unwanted text from a web page. Its usage is shown in Listing 4-9.

```
/*
string remove( string web page, string open_tag, string close_tag)
Where
    web_page  is the contents of the web page you want to affect
    open_tag defines the beginning of the text that you want to remove
    close_tag defines the end of the text you want to remove
*/
```

Listing 4-9: Using remove()

By adjusting the input parameters, the remove() function can remove a variety of text from web pages, as shown in Listing 4-10.

```
$uncommented_page    = remove($web_page, "<!--", "-->");
$links_removed       = remove($web_page, "<a", "</a>");
$images_removed      = remove($web_page, "<img", " >");
$javascript_removed  = remove($web_page, "<script", "</script>");
```

Listing 4-10: Using remove()

Useful PHP Functions

In addition to the previously described parsing functions in LIB_parse, PHP also contains a multitude of built-in parsing functions. The following is a brief sample of the most valuable built-in PHP parsing functions, along with examples of how they are used.

Detecting Whether a String Is Within Another String

You can use the stristr() function to tell your webbot whether or not a string contains another string. The PHP community commonly uses the term *haystack* to refer to the entire unparsed text and the term *needle* to refer to the substring within the larger string. The function stristr() looks for an occurrence of *needle* in *haystack*. If found, stristr() returns a substring of *haystack* from the occurrence of *needle* to the end of the larger string. In normal use, you're not always concerned about the actual returned text. Generally, the fact that something was returned is used as an indication that you found the existence of *needle* in the *haystack*.

The stristr() function is handy if you want to detect whether or not a specific word is mentioned in a web page. For example, if you want to know if a web page mentions dogs, you can execute the script shown in Listing 4-11.

```
if(stristr($web_page, "dogs"))
    echo "This is a web page that mentions dogs.";
else
    echo "This web page does not mention dogs";
```

Listing 4-11: Using stristr() to see if a string contains another string

In this example, we're not specifically interested in what the stristr() function returns, but whether is returns anything at all. If something is returned, we know that the web page contained the word *dogs*.

The stristr() function is not case sensitive. If you need a case-sensitive version of stristr(), use strstr().

Replacing a Portion of a String with Another String

The PHP built-in function str_replace() puts a new string in place of all occurrences of a substring within a string, as shown in Listing 4-12.

```
$org_string = "I wish I had a Cat.";
$result_string = str_replace("Cat", "Dog", $org_string);
# $result_string contains "I wish I had a Dog."
```

Listing 4-12: Using str_replace() to replace all occurrences of Cat with Dog

The str_repalce() function is also useful when a webbot needs to remove a character or set of characters from a string. You do this by instructing str_replace() to replace text with a null string, as shown in Listing 4-13.

```
$result = str_replace("$","","$100.00");     // Remove the dollar sign
# $result contains 100.00
```

Listing 4-13: Using str_replace() to remove leading dollar signs

Parsing Unformatted Text

The script in Listing 4-14 uses a variety of built-in functions, along with a few functions from LIB_http and LIB_parse, to create a string that contains unformatted text from a website. The result is the contents of the web page without any HTML formatting.

```
include("LIB_parse.php");     # Include parse library
include("LIB_http.php");      # Include cURL library

// Download the page
$web_page = http_get($target="http://www.cnn.com", $referer="");

// Remove all JavaScript
$noformat = remove($web_page['FILE'], "<script", "</script>");
// Strip out all HTML formatting
$unformatted = strip_tags($only_text);

// Remove unwanted white space
$noformat = str_replace("\t", "", $noformat);      // Remove tabs
$noformat = str_replace(" ", "", $noformat); // Remove non-breaking spaces
$noformat = str_replace("\n", "", $noformat);      // Remove line feeds
echo $noformat;
```

Listing 4-14: Parsing the content from the HTML used on http://www.cnn.com

Measuring the Similarity of Strings

Sometimes it is convenient to calculate the similarity of two strings without necessarily parsing them. PHP's similar_text() function returns a value that represents the percentage of similarity between two strings. The syntax for using similar_text() is shown in Listing 4-15.

```
$similarity_percentage = similar_text($string1, $string2);
```

Listing 4-15: Example of using PHP's similar_text() function

You may use similar_text() to determine if a new version of a web page is significantly different than a cached version.

Final Thoughts

As demonstrated, a wide variety of parsing tasks can be performed with the standardized parsing routines in LIB_parse, along with a few of PHP's built-in functions. Here are a few more suggestions that may help you in your parsing projects.

NOTE *You'll get plenty of parsing experience as you explore the projects in this book. The projects also introduce a few advanced parsing techniques. In Chapter 7, we'll cover advanced methods for parsing data in tables. In Chapter 11, you'll learn about the insertion parse, which makes it easier to parse and debug difficult-to-parse web pages.*

Don't Trust a Poorly Coded Web Page

While the scripts in LIB_parse attempt to handle most situations, there is no guarantee that you will be able to parse poorly coded or nonsensical web pages. Even the use of Tidy will not always provide proper results. For example, code like this:

```
<img src="width='523'" alt >
```

may drive your parsing routines crazy. If you're having trouble debugging a parsing routine, check to see if the page has errors. If you don't check for errors, you may waste many hours trying to parse unparseable web pages.

Parse in Small Steps

When you are writing a script that depends on several levels of parsing, avoid the temptation to write your parsing script in one pass. Since succeeding sections of your code will depend on earlier parses, write and debug your scripts one parse at a time.

Don't Render Parsed Text While Debugging

If you are viewing the results of your parse in a browser, remember that the browser will attempt to render your output as a web page. If the results of your parse contain tags, display your parses within <xmp> and </xmp> tags. These tags will tell the browser not to render the results of your parse as HTML. Failure to analyze the unformatted results of your parse may cause you to miss things that are inside tags.[3]

Use Regular Expressions Sparingly

The use of regular expressions is a parsing language in itself, and most modern programming languages support aspects of regular expressions. In the right hands, regular expressions are also useful for parsing and substituting text; however, they are famous for their sharp learning curve and cryptic syntax. I avoid regular expressions whenever possible.

The regular expression engine used by PHP is not as efficient as engines used in other languages, and it is certainly less efficient than PHP's built-in functions for parsing HTML. For those reasons, my preference is to limit regular expression use to instances in which there are few alternatives; in those cases, I use wrapper functions to take advantage of the functionality of regular expressions while shielding the developer from their complexities.

---

[3] Chapter 3 describes additional methods for viewing text downloaded from websites.

5

AUTOMATING FORM
SUBMISSION

You learned how to download files from the Internet in Chapter 3. In this chapter, you'll learn how to fill out forms and upload information to websites. When your webbots have the ability to exchange information with target websites, as opposed to just asking for information, they become capable of acting on your behalf. Interactive webbots can do these kinds of things:

- Transfer funds between your online bank accounts when an account balance drops below a predetermined limit
- Buy items in online auctions when an item and its price meet preset criteria
- Autonomously upload files to a photo sharing website
- Advise a distributor to refill a vending machine when product inventory is low

Webbots send data to webservers by mimicking what people do as they fill out standard HTML forms on websites. This process is called *form emulation*. Form emulation is not an easy task, since there are many ways to submit form information. In addition, it's important to submit forms *exactly* as the webserver expects them to be filled out, or else the server will generate errors in its log files. People using browsers don't have to worry about the format of the data they submit in a form. Webbot designers, however, must reverse engineer the form interface to learn about the data format the server is expecting. When the form interface is properly debugged, the form data from a webbot appears exactly as if it were submitted by a person using a browser.

If done poorly, form emulation can get webbot designers into trouble. This is especially true if you are creating an application that delivers a competitive advantage for a client and you want to conceal the fact that you are using a webbot. A number of things could happen if your webbot gets into trouble, ranging from leaking (to your competitors) that you're gaining an advantage through the use of a webbot to having your website privileges revoked by the owner of the target website.

The first rule of form emulation is staying legal: Represent yourself truthfully, and don't violate a website's user agreement. The second rule is to send form data to the server exactly as the server expects to receive it. If your emulated form data deviates from the format that is expected, you may generate suspicious-looking errors in the server's log. In either case, the server's administrator will easily figure out that you are using a webbot. Even though your webbot is legitimate, the server log files your webbot creates may not resemble browser activity. They may indicate to the website's administrator that you are a hacker and lead to a blocked IP address or termination of your account. It is best to be both stealthy and legal. For these reasons, you may want to read Chapters 24 and 28 before you venture out on your own.

Reverse Engineering Form Interfaces

Webbot developers need to look at online forms differently than people using the same forms in a browser. Typically, when people use browsers to fill out online forms, performing some task like paying a bill or checking an account balance, they see various fields that need to be selected or otherwise completed.

Webbot designers, in contrast, need to view HTML forms as interfaces or specifications that tell a webbot how a server expects to see form data after it is submitted. A webbot designer needs to have the same perspective on forms as the server that receives the form. For example, a person filling out the form in Figure 5-1 would complete a variety of form elements—text boxes, text areas, select lists, radio controls, checkboxes, or hidden elements—that are identified by text labels.

Figure 5-1: A simple form with various form elements

While a human associates the text labels shown in Figure 5-1 with the form elements, a webbot designer knows that the text labels and types of form elements are immaterial. All the form needs to do is send the correct name/data pairs that represent these data fields to the correct server page, with the expected protocol. This isn't nearly as complicated as it sounds, but before we can go further, it's important that you understand the various parts of HTML forms.

Form Handlers, Data Fields, Methods, and Event Triggers

Web-based forms have four main parts, as shown in Figure 5-2:

- A form handler
- One or more data fields
- A method
- One or more event triggers

I'll examine each of these parts in detail and then show how a webbot emulates a form.

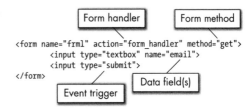

Figure 5-2: Parts of a form

Form Handlers

The action attribute in the <form> tag defines the web page that interprets the data entered into the form. We'll refer to this page as the *form handler*. If there is no defined action, the form handler is the same as the page that contains the form. The examples in Table 5-1 compare the location of form handlers in a variety of conditions.

Table 5-1: Variations in Form-Handler Descriptions

action Attribute	Meaning

`<form`
`  name="myForm"`
`  action="search.php"`
`>`
	The script called *search.php* will accept and interpret the form data. This script shares the same server and directory as the page that served the form.

`<form`
`  name="myForm"`
`  action="../cgi/search.php"`
`>`
	A script called *search.php* handles this form and is in the cgi directory, which is parallel to the current directory.

`<form`
`   name="myForm"`
`   action="/search.php"`
`>`
	The script called *search.php*, in the home directory of the server that served the page, handles this form.

`<form`
`   name="myForm"`
`   action="www.schrenk.com/search.php"`
`>`
	The contents of this form are sent to the specified page at http://www.schrenk.com.

(continued)

Table 5-1: Variations in Form-Handler Descriptions (continued)

action Attribute	Meaning
`<form name="myForm">`	There isn't an action (or form handler) specified in the `<form>` tag. In these cases, the same page that delivered the form is also the page that interprets the completed form.

Servers have no use for the form's name, which is the variable that identifies the form. This variable is only used by JavaScript, which associates the form name with its form elements. Since servers don't use the form's name, webbots (and their designers) have no use for it either.

Data Fields

Form input tags define data fields and the name, value, and user interface used to input the value. The user interface (or widget) can be a text box, text area, select list, radio control, checkbox, or hidden element. Remember that while there are many types of interfaces, they are completely meaningless to the webbot that emulates the form and the server that handles the form. From a webbot's perspective, there is no difference between data entered via a text box or a select list. The input tag's name and its value are the only things that matter.

Every data field must have a name.[1] These names become *form data variables*, or containers for their data values. In Listing 5-1, a variable called session_id is set to 0001, and the value for search is whatever was in the text box labeled *Search* when the user clicked the submit button. Again, from a webbot designer's perspective, it doesn't matter what type of data elements define the data fields (hidden, select, radio, text box, etc.). It is important that the data has the correct name and that the value is within a range expected by the form handler.

```
<form method="GET">
    <input type="hidden" name="session_id" value="0001">
    <input type="text"   name="search" value="">
    <input type="submit">
</form>
```

Listing 5-1: Data fields in a HTML form

Methods

The form's *method* describes the protocol used to send the form data to the form handler. The most common methods for form data transfers are GET and POST.

---

[1] The HTML value of any form element is only its stating or default value. The user may change the final element with JavaScript or by editing the form before it is sent to the form handler.

The GET Method

You are already familiar with the GET method, because it is identical to the protocol you used to request web pages in previous chapters. With the GET protocol, the URL of a web page is combined with data from form elements. The address of the page and the data are separated by a ? character, and individual data variables are separated by & characters, as shown in Listing 5-2. The portion of the URL that follows the ? character is known as a *query string*.

```
URL http://www.schrenk.com/search.php?term=hello&sort=up
```

Listing 5-2: Data values passed in a URL (GET method)

Since GET form variables may be combined with the URL, the web page that accepts the form will not be able to tell the difference between the form submitted in Listing 5-3 and the form emulation techniques shown in Listings 5-4 and 5-5. In either case, the variables term and sort will be submitted to the web page http://www.schrenk.com/search with the GET protocol.[2]

```
<form name="frm1" action="http://www.schrenk.com/search.php">
   <input type="text" name="term" value="hello">
   <input type="text" name="sort" value="up">
   <input type="submit">
</form>
```

Listing 5-3: A GET method performed by a form submission

Alternatively, you could use LIB_http to emulate the form, as in Listing 5-4.

```
include("LIB_http.php");

$action = "http://www.schrenk.com/search.php";    // Address of form handler
$method="GET";                                     // GET method
$ref = "";                                         // Referer variable
$data_array['term'] = "hello";                     // Define term
$data_array['sort'] = "up";                        // Define sort
$response = http($target=$action, $ref, $method, $data_array, EXCL_HEAD);
```

Listing 5-4: Using LIB_http to emulate the form in Listing 5-3 with data passed in an array

Conversely, since the GET method places form information in the URL's query string, you could also emulate the form with a script like Listing 5-5.

```
include("LIB_http.php");

$action = "http://www.schrenk.com/search.php?term=hello&sort=up";
$method=""GET";
$ref = "" ;
$response = http($target=$action, $ref, $method, $data_array="", EXCL_HEAD);
```

Listing 5-5: Emulating the form in Listing 5-3 by combining the URL with the form data

---

[2] In forms where no form method is defined, like the form shown in Listing 5-3, the default form method is GET.

The reason we might choose Listing 5-4 over Listing 5-5 is that the code is cleaner when form data is treated as array elements, especially when many form values are passed to the form handler. Passing form variables to the form's handler with an array is also more *symmetrical*, meaning that the procedure is nearly identical to the one required to pass values to a form handler expecting the POST method.

The POST Method

While the GET method tacks on form data at the end of the URL, the POST method sends data in a separate file. The POST method has these advantages over the GET method:

- POST methods can send more data to servers than GET methods can. The maximum length of a GET method is typically around 250 characters. POST methods, in contrast, can easily upload several megabytes of information during a single form upload.

- Since URL fetch requests are sent in HTTP headers, and since headers are never encrypted, sensitive data should always be transferred with POST methods. POST methods don't transfer form data in headers, and thus, they may be encrypted. Obviously, this is only important for web pages using encryption.

- GET method requests are always visible on the location bar of the browser. POST requests only show the actual URL in the location bar.

Regardless of the advantages of POST over GET, you must match your method to the method of form you are emulating. Keep in mind that methods may also be combined in the same form. For example, forms with POST methods may also use form handlers that contains query strings.

To submit a form using the POST method with LIB_http, simply specify the POST protocol, as shown in Listing 5-6.

```
include("LIB_http.php");

$action = "http://www.schrenk.com/search.php";      // Address of form handler
$method="POST ";                                     // POST method
$ref = "";                                           // Referer variable
$data_array['term'] = "hello";                       // Define term
$data_array['sort'] = "up";                          // Define sort
$response = http($target=$action, $ref, $method, $data_array, EXCL_HEAD);
```

Listing 5-6: Using LIB_http to emulate a form with the POST method

Regardless of the number of data elements, the process is the same. Some form handlers, however, access the form elements as an array, so it's always a good idea to match the order of the data elements that is defined in the HTML form.

Event Triggers

A submit button typically acts as the event trigger, which causes the form data to be sent to the form handler using the defined form method. While the submit button is the most common event trigger, it is not the only way to submit a form. It is very common for web developers to employ JavaScript to verify the contents of the form before it is submitted to the server. In fact, any JavaScript event like onClick or onMouseOut can submit a form, as can any other type of human-generated JavaScript event. Sometimes, JavaScript may also change the value of a form variable before the form is submitted. The use of JavaScript as an event trigger causes many difficulties for webbot designers, but these issues are remedied by the use of special tools, as you'll soon see.

Unpredictable Forms

You may not be able to tell exactly what the form requires by looking at the source HTML. There are three primary reasons for this: the use of JavaScript, the readability of machine generated HTML, and the presence of cookies.

JavaScript Can Change a Form Just Before Submission

Forms often use JavaScript to manipulate data before sending it to the form handler. These manipulations are usually the result of checking the validity of data entered into the form data field. Since these manipulations happen dynamically, it is nearly impossible to predict what will happen unless you actually run the JavaScript and see what it does—or unless you have a JavaScript parser in your head.

Form HTML Is Often Unreadable by Humans

You cannot expect to look at the source HTML for a web page and determine, with any precision, what the form does. Regardless of the fact that all browsers have a *View Source* option, it is important to remember that HTML is rendered by machines and does not have to be readable by people—and it frequently isn't. It is also important to remember that much of the HTML served on web pages is dynamically generated by scripts. For these reasons, you should never expect HTML pages to be easy to read, and you should never count on being able to accurately analyze a form by looking at a script.

Cookies Aren't Included in the Form, but Can Affect Operation

While cookies are not evident in a form, they can often play an important role, since they may contain session variables or other important data that isn't readily visible but is required to process a form. You'll learn more about webbots that use cookies in Chapters 21 and 22.

Analyzing a Form

Since it is so hard to accurately analyze an HTML form by hand, and since the importance of submitting a form correctly is critical, you may prefer to use a tool to analyze the format of forms. This book's website has a form handler that provides this service. The form analyzer works by substituting the form's original form handler with the URL of the form analyzer. When the analyzer receives form data, it creates a web page that describes the method, data variables, and cookies sent by the form *exactly* as they are seen by the original form handler, even if the web page uses JavaScript.

To use the emulator, you must first create a copy of the web page that contains the form you want to analyze, and place that copy on your hard drive. Then you must replace the form handler on the web page with a form handler that will analyze the form structure. For example, if the form you want to analyze has a <form> tag like the one in Listing 5-7, you must substitute the original form handler with the address of my form analyzer, as shown in Listing 5-8.

```
<form
    method="POST"
    action="https://panel.schrenk.com/keywords/search/"
>
```

Listing 5-7: Original form handler

```
<form
    method="POST"
    action="http://www.schrenk.com/nostarch/webbots/form_analyzer.php"
>
```

Listing 5-8: Substituting the original form handler with a handler that analyzes the form

To analyze the form, save your changes to your hard drive and load the modified web page into a browser. Once you fill out the form (by hand) and submit it, the form analyzer will provide an analysis similar to the one in Figure 5-3.

This simple diagnosis isn't perfect—use it at your own risk. However, it does allow a webbot developer to verify the form method, agent name, and GET and POST variables as they are presented to the actual form handler. For example, in this particular exercise, it is evident that the form handler expects a POST method with the variables sessionid, email, message, status, gender, and vol.

Forms with a session ID point out the importance of downloading and analyzing the form before emulating it. In this typical case, the session ID is assigned by the server and cannot be predicted. The webbot can accurately use session IDs only by first downloading and parsing the web page containing the form.

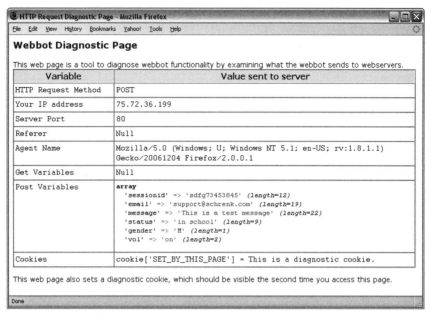

Figure 5-3: Using a form analyzer

If you were to write a script that emulates the form submitted and analyzed in Figure 5-3, it would look something like Listing 5-9.

```
include("LIB_http.php");

# Initiate addresses
$action="http://www.schrenk.com/nostarch/webbots/form_analyzer.php";
$ref = "" ;

# Set submission method
$method="POST";

# Set form data and values
$data_array['sessionid'] = "sdfg73453845";
$data_array['email'] = "sales@schrenk.com";
$data_array['message'] = "This is a test message";
$data_array['status'] = "in school";
$data_array['gender'] = "M";
$data_array['vol'] = "on";

$response = http($target=$action, $ref, $method, $data_array, EXCL_HEAD);
```

Listing 5-9: Using LIB_http to emulate the form analysis in Figure 5-3

After you write a form-emulation script, it's a good idea to use the analyzer to verify that the form method and variables match the original form you are attempting to emulate. If you're feeling ambitious, you could improve on this simple form analyzer by designing one that accepts both the submitted and emulated forms and compares them for you.

The script in Listing 5-10 is similar to the one running at http://www
.schrenk.com/nostarch/webbots/form_analyzer.php. This script is for
reference only. You can download the latest copy from this book's website.
Note that the PHP sections of this script appear in bold.

```php
<?
setcookie("SET BY THIS PAGE", "This is a diagnostic cookie.");
?>
<head>
    <title>HTTP Request Diagnostic Page</title>
    <style type="text/css">
        p { color: black; font-weight: bold; font-size: 110%; font-family: arial}
          .title { color: black; font-weight: bold; font-size: 110%; font-family: arial}
          .text {font-weight: normal; font-size: 90%;}
        TD { color: black; font-size: 100%; font-family: courier; vertical-align: top;}
          .column_title { color: black; font-size: 100%; background-color: eeeeee;
                          font-weight: bold; font-family: arial}
    </style>
</head>

<p class="title">Webbot Diagnostic Page</p>
<p class="text">This web page is a tool to diagnose webbot functionality by examining what the
webbot sends to webservers.
<table border="1" cellspacing="0" cellpadding="3" width="800">
    <tr class="column_title">
        <th width="25%">Variable</th>
        <th width="75%">Value sent to server</th>
    </tr>
    <tr>
        <td>HTTP Request Method</td><td><?echo $_SERVER["REQUEST_METHOD"];?></td>
    </tr>
    <tr>
        <td>Your IP Address</td><td><?echo $_SERVER["REMOTE_ADDR"];?></td>
    </tr>
    <tr>
        <td>Server Port</td><td><?echo $_SERVER["SERVER_PORT"];?></td>
    </tr>
    <tr>
        <td>Referer</td>
        <td><?
            if(isset($_SERVER['HTTP_REFERER']))
                echo $_SERVER['HTTP_REFERER'];
            else
                echo "Null<br>";
            ?>
        </td>
    </tr>
    <tr>
        <td>Agent Name</td>
        <td><?
            if(isset($_SERVER['HTTP_USER_AGENT']))
                echo $_SERVER['HTTP_USER_AGENT'];
            else
                echo "Null<br>";
            ?>
        </td>
    </tr>
```

```
<tr>
    <td>Get Variables</td>
    <td><?
        if(count($_GET)>0)
            var_dump($_GET);
        else
            echo "Null";
        ?>
    </td>
</tr>
<tr>
    <td>Post Variables</td>
    <td><?
        if(count($_POST)>0)
            var_dump($_POST);
        else
            echo "Null";
        ?>
    </td>
</tr>
<tr>
    <td>Cookies</td>
    <td><?
        if(count($_COOKIE)>0)
            var_dump($_COOKIE);
        else
            echo "Null";
        ?>
    </td>
</tr>
</table>
<p class="text">This web page also sets a diagnostic cookie, which should be
visible the second time you access this page.
```

Listing 5-10: A simple form analyzer

Final Thoughts

Years of experience have taught me a few tricks for emulating forms. While it's not hard to write a webbot that submits a form, it is often difficult to do it right the first time. Moreover, as you read earlier, there are many reasons to submit a form correctly the first time. I highly suggest reading Chapters 24, 25, and 28 before creating webbots that emulate forms. These chapters provide additional insight into potential problems and perils that you're likely to encounter when writing webbots that submit data to webservers.

Don't Blow Your Cover

If you're using a webbot to create a competitive advantage for a client, you don't want that fact to be widely known—especially to the people that run the targeted site.

There are two ways a webbot can blow its cover while submitting a form:

- It emulates the form but not the browser.
- It generates an error either because it poorly analyzed the form or poorly executed the emulation. Either error may create a condition that isn't possible when the form is submitted by a browser, creating a questionable entry in a server activity log.

NOTE   *This topic is covered in more detail in Chapter 24.*

Correctly Emulate Browsers

Emulating a browser is easy, but you should verify that you're doing it correctly. Your webbot can look like any browser you desire if you properly declare the name of your web agent. If you're using the LIB_http library, the constant WEBBOT_NAME defines how your webbot identifies itself, and furthermore, how servers log your web agent's name in their log files. In some cases, webservers verify that you are using a particular web browser (most commonly Internet Explorer) before allowing you to submit a form.

If you plan to emulate a browser as well as the form, you should verify that the name of your webbot is set to something that looks like a browser (as shown in Listing 5-11). Obviously, if you don't change the default value for your webbot's name in the LIB_http library, you'll tell everyone who looks at the server logs that you're using a test webbot.

```
# Define how your webbot will appear in server logs
define("WEBBOT_NAME", "Internet Explorer");
```

Listing 5-11: Setting the name of your webbot to Internet Explorer in LIB_http

Strange user agent names will often be noticed by webmasters, since they routinely analyze logs to see which browsers people use to access their sites to ensure that they don't run into browser compatibility problems.

Avoid Form Errors

Even more serious than using the wrong agent name is submitting a form that couldn't possibly be sent from the form the webserver provides on its website. These mistakes are logged in the server's error log and are subject to careful scrutiny. Situations that could cause server errors include the following:

- Using the wrong form protocol
- Submitting the form to the wrong action (form handler)
- Submitting form variables in the wrong order
- Ignoring an expected variable that the form handler needs
- Adding an extra variable that the form handler doesn't expect
- Emulating a form that is no longer available on the website

Using the wrong method can have several undesirable outcomes. If your webbot sends too much data with a GET method when the form specifies a POST method, you risk the danger of losing some of your data. (Most webservers restrict the length of a GET method.[3]) Another danger of using the wrong form method is that many form handlers expect variables to be members of either a $_GET or $_POST array, which is a keyed name/value array similar to the $data_array used in LIB_http. If you're sending the form a POST variable called 'name', and the server is expecting $_GET['name'], your webbot will generate an entry in the server's error log because it didn't send the variable the server was looking for.

Also, remember that protocols aren't limited to the form method. If the form handler expects an SSL-encrypted https protocol, and you deliver the emulated form to an unencrypted http address, the form handler won't understand you because you'll be sending data to the wrong server port. In addition, you're potentially sending sensitive data over an unencrypted connection.

The final thing to verify is that you are sending your emulated form to a web page that exists on the target server. Sometimes mistakes like this are the result of sloppy programming, but this can also occur when a webmaster updates the site (and form handler). For this reason, a proactive webbot designer verifies that the form handler hasn't changed since the webbot was written.

---

[3] Servers routinely restrict the length of a GET request to help protect the server from extremely long requests, which are commonly used by hackers attempting to compromise servers with buffer overflow exploits.

6

MANAGING LARGE
AMOUNTS OF DATA

You will soon find that your webbots are capable of collecting massive amounts of data. The amount of data a simple automated webbot or spider can collect, even if it runs only once a day for several months, is colossal. Since none of us have unlimited storage, managing the quality and volume of the data our programs collect and store becomes very important. In this chapter, I will describe methods to organize the data that your webbots collect and then investigate ways to reduce the size of what you save.

Organizing Data

Organizing the resources that your webbots download requires planning. Whether you employ a well-defined file structure or a relational database, the result should meet the needs of the particular problem your application attempts to solve. For example, if the data is primarily text, is accessed by many people, or is in need of sort or search capability, then you may prefer to store information in a relational database, which addresses these needs.

If, on the other hand, you are storing many images, PDFs, or Word documents, you may favor storing files in a structured filesystem. You may even create a hybrid system where a database references media files stored in structured directories.

Naming Conventions

While there is no "correct" way to organize data, there are many bad ways to store the data webbots generate. Most mistakes arise from assigning non-descriptive or confusing names to the data your webbots collect. For this reason, your designs must incorporate naming conventions that uniquely identify files, directories, and database properties. Define names for things early, during your planning stages, as opposed to naming things as you go along. Always name in a way that allows your data structure to grow. For example, a real estate webbot that refers to properties as *houses* may be difficult to maintain if your application later expands to include raw land, offices, or businesses. Updating names for your data can become tedious, since your code and documentation will reference those names many times.

Your naming convention can enforce any rules you like, but you should consider the following guidelines:

- You need to enforce any naming standards with an iron fist, or they will cease to be standards.

- It's often better to assign names based on the type of thing an object is, rather than what is actually is. For example, in the previous real estate example, it may have been better to name the database table that describes houses *properties*, so when the scope of the project expands,[1] it can handle a variety of real estate. With this method, if your project grows, you could add another column to the table to describe the type of property. It is always easier to expand data tables than to rename columns.

- Consider who (or what) will be using your data organization. For example, a directory called *Saturday_January_23* might be easy for a person to read, but a directory called *0123* might be a better choice if a computer accesses its contents. Sequential numbers are easier for computer programs to interpret.

- Define the format of your names. People will often use compound words and separate the word with underscores for readability, as in *name_first*. Other times, people separate compound words with case, as in *nameFirst*; this is commonly referred to as *CamelCase*. These format definitions should include things like case, language, and parts of speech. For example, if you decide to separate terms with underscores, you shouldn't use Camel-Case to name other terms later. It's very common for developers to use different standards to help identify differences between functions, data variables, and objects.

---

[1] Projects *always* expand in scope.

- If you give members of a certain group labels that are all the same part of speech, don't occasionally throw in a label with another grammatical form. For example, if you have a group of directories named with nouns, don't name another directory in the same group with a verb—and if you do, chances are it probably doesn't belong in that group of things in the first place.

- If you are naming files in a directory, you may want to give the files names that will later facilitate easy grouping or sorting. For example, if you are using a filename that defines a date, filenames with the format *year_month_day* will make more sense when sorted than filenames with the format *month_day_year*. This is because year, month, and day is a sequential progression from largest to smallest and will accurately reflect order when sorted.

Storing Data in Structured Files

To successfully store files in a structured series of directories, you need to find out what the files have in common. In most cases, the problem you're trying to solve and the means for retrieving the data will dictate the common factors among your files. Figuratively, you need to look for the lowest common denominator for all your files. Figure 6-1 shows a file structure for storing data retrieved by a webbot that runs once a day. Its common theme is time.

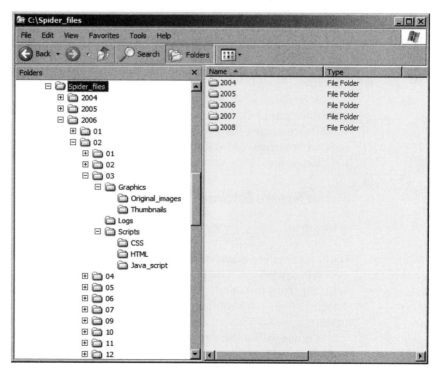

Figure 6-1: Example of a structured filesystem primarily based on dates

With the structure defined in Figure 6-1, you could easily locate thumbnail images created by the webbot on February 3, 2006 because the folders comply with the following specification:

```
drive:\project\year\month\day\category\subcategory\files
```

Therefore, the path would look like this:

```
c:\Spider_files\2006\02\03\Graphics\Thumbnails\
```

People may easily decipher this structure, and so will programs, which need to determine the correct file path programmatically. Figure 6-2 shows another file structure, primarily based on geography.

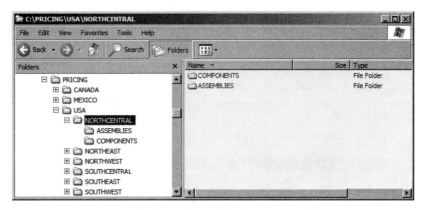

Figure 6-2: A geographically themed example of a structured filesystem

Ensure that all files have a unique path and that either a person or a computer can easily make sense of these paths.

File structures, like the ones shown in the previous figures, are commonly created by webbots. You'll see how to write webbots that create file structures in Chapter 8.

Storing Text in a Database

While many applications call for file structures similar to the ones shown in Figures 6-1 or 6-2, the majority of projects you're likely to encounter will require that data is stored in a database. A database has many advantages over a file structure. The primary advantage is the ability to query or make requests from the database with a query language called *Structured Query Language* or *SQL* (pronounced *SEE-quill*). SQL allows programs to sort, extract, update, combine, insert, and manipulate data in nearly any imaginable way.

It is not within the scope of this book to teach SQL, but this book does include the LIB_mysql library, which simplifies using SQL with the open source database called *MySQL*[2] (pronounced *my-esk-kew-el*).

---

[2] More information about MySQL is available at http://www.mysql.com and http://www.php.net.

LIB_mysql

LIB_mysql consists of a few server configurations and three functions, which should handle most of your database needs. These functions act as *abstractions* or simplifications of the actual interface to the program. Abstractions are important because they allow access to a wide variety of database functions with a common interface and error-reporting method. They also allow you to use a database other than MySQL by creating a similar library for a new database. For example, if you choose to use another database someday, you could write abstractions with the same function names used in LIB_mysql. In this way, you can make the code in this book work with Oracle, SQL Server, or any other database without modifying any scripts.

The source code for LIB_mysql is available from this book's website. There are other fine database abstractions available from projects like PEAR and PECL; however, the examples in this book use LIB_mysql.

Listing 6-1 shows the configuration area of LIB_mysql. You should configure this area for your specific MySQL installation before you use it.

```
MySQL Constants (scope = global)

define("MYSQL_ADDRESS", "localhost"); // Define IP address of your MySQL Server
define("MYSQL_USERNAME", "");          // Define your MySQL username
define("MYSQL_PASSWORD", "");          // Define your MySQL password
define("DATABASE", "");                // Define your default database
```

Listing 6-1: LIB_mysql server configurations

As shown in Listing 6-1, the configuration section provides an opportunity to define where your MySQL server resides and the credentials needed to access it. The configuration section also defines a constant, "DATABASE", which you may use to define the default database for your project.

There are three functions in LIB_mysql that facilitate the following:

- Inserting data into the database
- Updating data already in the database
- Executing a raw SQL query

Each function uses a similar interface, and each provides error reporting if you request an erroneous query.

The insert() Function

The insert() function in LIB_mysql simplifies the process of inserting a new entry into a database by passing the new data in a keyed array. For example, if you have a table like the one in Figure 6-3, you can insert another row of data with the script in Listing 6-2, making it look like the table in Figure 6-4.

ID	NAME	CITY	STATE	ZIP
1	Kelly Garrett	Culver City	CA	90232
2	Sabrina Duncan	Anaheim	CA	92812

Figure 6-3: Example table people before the insert()

```
$data_array['NAME']  = "Jill Monroe";
$data_array['CITY']  = "Irvine";
$data_array['STATE'] = "CA";
$data_array['ZIP']   = "55410";
insert(DATABASE, $table="people", $data_array);
```

Listing 6-2: Example of using insert()

ID	NAME	CITY	STATE	ZIP
1	Kelly Garrett	Culver City	CA	90232
2	Sabrina Duncan	Anaheim	CA	92812
3	Jill Monroe	Irvine	CA	55410

Figure 6-4: Example table people after executing the insert() in Listing 6-2

The update() Function

Alternately, you can use update() to update the record you just inserted with the script in Listing 6-3, which changes the ZIP code for the record.

```
$data_array['NAME']  = "Jill Monroe";
$data_array['CITY']  = "Irvine";
$data_array['STATE'] = "CA";
$data_array['ZIP']   = "92604";
update(DATABASE, $table="people", $data_array, $key_column="ID", $id="3");
```

Listing 6-3: Example script for updating data in a table

Running the script in Listing 6-3 changes values in the table, as shown in Figure 6-5.

ID	NAME	CITY	STATE	ZIP
1	Kelly Garrett	Culver City	CA	90232
2	Sabrina Duncan	Anaheim	CA	92812
3	Jill Monroe	Irvine	CA	92604

Figure 6-5: Example table people after updating ZIP codes with the script in Listing 6-3

The exe_sql() Function

For database functions other than inserting or updating records, LIB_mysql provides the exe_sql() function, which executes a SQL query against the database. This function is particularly useful for extracting data with complex queries or for deleting records, altering tables, or anything else you can do with SQL. Table 6-1 shows various uses for this function.

Table 6-1: Example Usage Scenarios for the `LIB_mysql_exe_sql()` Function

Instruction	Result
`$array = exe_sql(DATABASE, "select * from people");`	`$array[1]['ID']="1";`
	`$array[1]['NAME']="Kelly Garrett";`
	`$array[1]['CITY']="Culver City";`
	`$array[1]['STATE']="CA";`
	`$array[1]['ZIP']="90232";`
	`$array[2]['ID']="2";`
	`$array[2]['NAME']="Sabrina Duncan";`
	`$array[2]['CITY']="Anaheim";`
	`$array[2]['STATE']="CA";`
	`$array[2]['ZIP']="92812";`
	`$array[3]['ID']="3";`
	`$array[3]['NAME']="Jill Monroe";`
	`$array[3]['CITY']="Irvine";`
	`$array[3]['STATE']="CA";`
	`$array[3]['ZIP']="92604";`
`$array = exe_sql(DATABASE, "select * from people where ID='2'");`	`$array['ID']="2";`
	`$array['NAME']="Sabrina Duncan";`
	`$array['CITY']="Anaheim";`
	`$array['STATE']="CA";`
	`$array['ZIP']="92604";`
`List($name)= exe_sql(DATABASE, "select NAME from people where ID='2'");`	`$name = "Sabrina Duncan";`
`exe_sql(DATABASE, "delete from people where ID='2'");`	Deletes row 3 from table

Please note that if exe_sql() is fetching data from the database, it will always return an array of data. If the query returns multiple rows of data, you'll get a multidimensional array. Otherwise, a single-dimensional array is returned.

Storing Images in a Database

It is usually better to store images in a file structure and then refer to the paths of the images in the database, but occasionally you may find the need to store images as *blobs*, or large unstructured pieces of data, directly in a database. These occasions may arise when you don't have the requisite system permissions to create a file. For example, many web administrators do not allow their webservers to create files, as a security measure. To store an image in a database, set the typecasting or variable type for the image to blob or large blob and insert the data, as shown in Listing 6-4.

```
$data_array['IMAGE_ID'] = 6;
$data_array['IMAGE'] = base64_encode(file_get_contents($file_path));
insert(DATABASE, $table, $data_array);
```

Listing 6-4: Storing an image directly in a database record

When you store a binary file, like an image, in a database, you should base64-encode the data first. Since the database assumes text or numeric data, this precaution ensures that no bit combinations will cause internal errors in the database. If you don't do this, you take the risk that some odd bit combination in the image will be interpreted as an unintended database command or special character.

Since images are—or should be—base64 encoded, you need to decode the images before you can reuse them. The script in Listing 6-5 shows how to display an image stored in a database record.

```
<!- Display an image stored in a database where the image ID is 6 -->
<img src="show_image.php?img_id=6">
```

Listing 6-5: HTML that displays an image stored in a database

Listing 6-6 shows the code to extract, decode, and present the image.

```
<?
# Get needed database library
include("LIB_mysql.php");

# Convert the variable on the URL to a new variable
$image_id=$_GET['img_id'];

# Get the base64-encoded image from the database
$sql = "select IMAGE from table where IMAGE_ID='".$image_id."'";
list($img) = exe_sql (DATABASE, $sql);

# Decode the image and send it as a file to the requester
header("Content-type: image/jpeg");
echo base64_decode($img);
exit;
?>
```

Listing 6-6: Script to query, decode, and create an image from an image record in a database

When an image tag is used in this fashion, the image src attribute is actually a function that pulls the image from the database before is sends it to the waiting web agent. This function knows which image to send because it is referenced in the query of the src attribute. In this case, that record is img_id, which corresponds with the table column IMAGE_ID. The program show_image.php actually creates a new image file each time it is executed.

Database or File?

Your decision to store information in a database or as files in a directory structure is largely dependent on your application, but because of the advantages that SQL brings to data storage, I often use databases. The one common exception to this rule is images files, which (as previously mentioned) are usually more efficiently stored as files in a directory. Nevertheless, when files are stored in local directories, it is often convenient to identify the physical address of the file you saved in a database.

Making Data Smaller

Now that you know how to store data, you'll want to efficiently store the data in ways that reduce the amount of disk spaced required, while facilitating easy retrieval and manipulation of that data. The following section explores methods for reducing the size of the data your webbots collect in these ways:

- Storing references to data
- Compressing data
- Removing unneeded formatting
- Thumbnailing or creating smaller representations of larger graphic files

Storing References to Image Files

Since your webbot and the image files it discovers share the same network, it is possible to store a network reference to the image instead of making a physical copy of it. For example, instead of downloading and storing the image north_beach.jpg from www.schrenk.com, you might store a reference to its URL, http://www.schrenk.com/north_beach.jpg, in a database. Now, instead of retrieving the file from your data structure, you could retrieve the actual file from its original location. While you can apply this technique to images, this technique is not limited to image files but also applies to HTML, JavaScript, Style Sheets, or any other networked file.

There are three main advantages to recording references to images instead of storing copies of the images. The most obvious advantage is that the reference to an image will usually consume much less space than a copy of the image file. Another advantage is that if the original image on the website changes, you will still have access to the most current version of that image—provided that the network address of the image hasn't also changed. A less obvious advantage to storing the network address of an image is that you may shield yourself from potential copyright issues when you make a copy of someone else's intellectual property.

The disadvantage of storing a reference to an image instead of the actual images is that there is no guarantee that it still references an image that's available online. When the remote image changes, your reference will be obsolete. Given the short-lived nature of online media, images can change or disappear without warning.

Compressing Data

From a webbot's perspective, compression can happen either when a web-server delivers pages or when your webbot compresses pages before it stores them for later use. Compression on inbound files will save bandwidth; the second method can save space on your hard drives. If you're ambitious, you can use both forms of compression.

Compressing Inbound Files

Many webservers automatically compress files before they serve pages to browsers. Managing your incoming data is just as important as managing the data on your hard drive.

Servers configured to serve compressed web pages will look for signals from the web client indicating that it can accept compressed pages. Like browsers, your webbots can also tell servers that they can accept compressed data by including the lines shown in Listing 6-7 in your PHP and cURL routines.

```
$header[] = "Accept-Encoding: compress, gzip";
curl_setopt($curl_session, CURLOPT_HTTPHEADER, $header);
```

Listing 6-7: Requesting compressed files from a webserver

Servers equipped to send compressed web pages won't send compressed files if they decide that the web agent cannot decompress the pages. Servers default to uncompressed pages if there's any doubt of the agent's ability to decompress compressed files. Over the years, I have found that some servers look for specific agent names—in addition to header directions—before deciding to compress outgoing data. For this reason, you won't always gain the advantage of inbound compression if your webbot's agent name is something nonstandard like *Test Webbot*. For that reason, when inbound file compression is important, it's best if your webbot emulates a common browser.[3]

Since the webserver is the final arbiter of an agent's ability to handle compressed data—and since it always defaults on the side of safety (no compressions)—you're never guaranteed to receive a compressed file, even if one is requested. If you are requesting compression from a server, it is incumbent on your webbot to detect whether or not a web page was compressed. To detect compression, look at the returned header to see if the web page is compressed and, if so, what form of compression was used (as shown in Listing 6-8).

```
if (stristr($http_header, "zip"))      // Assumes that header is in $http_header
    $compressed = TRUE;
```

Listing 6-8: Analyzing the HTTP header to detect inbound file compression

---

[3] For more information on agent name spoofing, please review Chapter 3.

If the data was compressed by the server, you can decompress the files with the function gzuncompress() in PHP, as shown in Listing 6-9.

```
$uncompressed_file = gzuncompress($compressed_file);
```

Listing 6-9: Decompressing a compressed file

Compressing Files on Your Hard Drive

PHP provides a variety of built-in functions for compressing data. Listing 6-10 demonstrates these functions. This script downloads the default HTML file from http://www.schrenk.com, compresses the file, and shows the difference between the compressed and uncompressed files. The PHP sections of this script appear in bold.

```
# Demonstration of PHP file compression

# Include cURL library
include("LIB_http.php");

# Get web page
$target         = "http://www.schrenk.com";
$ref            = "";
$method         = "GET";
$data_array     = "";
$web_page       = http_get($target, $ref, $method, $data_array, EXCL_HEAD);

# Get sizes of compressed and uncompressed versions of web page
$uncompressed_size  = strlen($web_page['FILE']);
$compressed_size    = strlen(gzcompress($web_page['FILE'], $compression_value = 9));
$noformat_size      = strlen(strip_tags($web_page['FILE']));

# Report the sizes of compressed and uncompressed versions of web page
?>
<table border="1">
    <tr>
        <th colspan="3">Compression report for <? echo $target?></th>
    </tr>
    <tr>
        <th>Uncompressed</th>
        <th>Compressed</th>
    </tr>
    <tr>
        <td align="right"><?echo $uncompressed_size?> bytes</td>
        <td align="right"><?echo $compressed_size?> bytes</td>
    </tr>
</table>
```

Listing 6-10: Compressing a downloaded file

Running the script from Listing 6-10 in a browser provides the results shown in Figure 6-6.

Before you start compressing everything your webbot finds, you should be aware of the disadvantages of file compression. In this example, compression resulted in files roughly 20 percent of the original size. While this is impressive, the biggest drawback to compression is that you can't do much with a compressed file. You can't perform searches, sorts, or comparisons on the contents of a compressed file. Nor can you modify the contents of a file while it's compressed. Furthermore, while text files (like HTML files) compress effectively, many media files like JPG, GIF, WMF, or MOV are already compressed and will not compress much further. If your webbot application needs to analyze or manipulate downloaded files, file compression may not be for you.

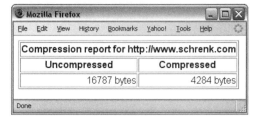

Figure 6-6: The script from Listing 6-10, showing the value of compressing files

Removing Formatting

Removing unneeded HTML formatting instructions is much more useful for reducing the size of a downloaded file than compressing it, since it still facilitates access to the useful information in the file. Formatting instructions like `<div class="font_a">` are of little use to a webbot because they only control format and not content, and because they can be removed without harming your data. Removing formatting reduces the size of downloaded HTML files while still leaving the option of manipulating the data later. Fortunately, PHP provides strip_tags_(), a built-in function that automatically strips HTML tags from a document. For example, if I add the lines shown in Listing 6-11 to the previous script, we can see the affect of stripping the HTML formatting.

```
$noformat = strip_tags($web_page['FILE']);    // Remove HTML tags
$noformat_size = strlen($noformat);           // Get size of new string
```

Listing 6-11: Removing HTML formatting using the strip_tags() function

If you run the program in Listing 6-10 again and modify the output to also show the size of the unformatted file, you will see that the unformatted web page is nearly as compact as the compressed version. The results are shown in Figure 6-7.

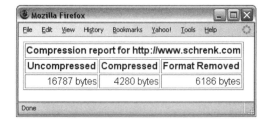

Figure 6-7: Comparison of uncompressed, compressed, and unformatted file sizes

Unlike the compressed data, the unformatted data can still be sorted, modified, and searched. You can make the file even smaller by removing excessive spaces, line feeds, and other white space with a simple PHP function called trim(), without reducing your ability to manipulate the data later. As an added benefit, unformatted pages may be easier to manipulate, since parsing routines won't confuse HTML for the content you're acting on. Remember that removing the HTML tags removes all links, JavaScript, image references, and CSS information. If any of that is important, you should extract it before removing a page's formatting.

Thumbnailing Images

The most effective method of decreasing the size of an image is to create smaller versions, or *thumbnails,* of the original. You may easily create thumbnails with the LIB_thumbnail library, which you can download from this book's website. To use this library, you will have to verify that your configuration uses the gd (revision 2.0 or higher) graphics module.[4] The script in Listing 6-12 demonstrates how to use LIB_thumbnail to create a miniature version of a larger image. The PHP sections of this script appear in bold.

```
# Demonstration of LIB_thumbnail.php

# Include libraries
include("LIB_http.php");
include("LIB_thumbnail.php");

# Get image from the Internet
$target         = "http://www.schrenk.com/north_beach.jpg";
$ref            = "";
$method         = "GET";
$data_array     = "";
$image          = http_get($target, $ref, $method, $data_array, EXCL_HEAD);

# Store captured image file to local hard drive
$handle = fopen("test.jpg", "w");
fputs($handle, $image['FILE']);
fclose($handle);

# Create thumbnail image from image that was just stored locally
$org_file = "test.jpg";
$new_file_name = "thumbnail.jpg";

# Set the maximum width and height of the thumbnailed image
$max_width = 90;
$max_height= 90;
```

---

[4] If the gd module is not installed in your configuration, please reference http://www.php.net/manual/en/ref.image.php for further instructions.

```
# Create the thumbnailed image
create_thumbnail($org_file, $new_file_name, $max_width, $max_height);
?>

Full-size image<br>
<img src="test.jpg">
<p>
Thumbnail image<br>
<img src="thumbnail.jpg">
```

Listing 6-12: Demonstration of how LIB_thumbnail may create a thumbnailed image

The script in Listing 6-12 fetches an image from the Internet, writes a copy of the original to a local file, defines the maximum dimensions of the thumbnail, creates the thumbnail, and finally displays both the original image and the thumbnail image.

The product of running the script in Listing 6-12 is shown in Figure 6-8.

The thumbnailed image shown in Figure 6-8 consumes roughly 30 percent as much space as the original file. If the original file was larger or the specification for the thumbnailed image was smaller, the savings would be even greater.

Figure 6-8: Output of Listing 6-12, making thumbnails with LIB_thumbnail

Final Thoughts

When storing information, you need to consider what is being stored and how that information will be used later. Furthermore, if the data isn't going to be used later, you need to ask yourself why you need to save it.

Sometimes it is easier to parse text before the HTML tags are removed. This is especially true with regard to data in tables, where rows and columns are parsed.

While unformatted pages are stripped of presentation, colors, and images, the remaining text is enough to represent the original file. Without the HTML, it is actually easier to characterize, manipulate, or search for the presence of keywords.

Before you continue, this is a good time to download LIB_mysql, LIB_http, and LIB_thumbnail from this book's website. You will need all of these libraries to program later examples in this book.

PART II

PROJECTS

This section expands on the concepts you learned in the previous section with simple yet demonstrative projects. Any of these projects, with further development, could be transformed from a simple webbot concept into a potentially marketable product.

Chapter 7: Price-Monitoring Webbots

The first project describes webbots that collect and analyze online prices from a mock store that exists on this book's website. The prices change periodically, creating an opportunity for your webbots to analyze and make purchase decisions based on the price of items.

Since this example store is solely for your experimentation, you'll gain confidence in testing your webbot on web pages that serve no commercial purpose and haven't changed since this book's publication. This environment also affords the freedom to make mistakes without obsessing over the crumbs your webbots leave behind in an actual online store's server log file.

Chapter 8: Image-Capturing Webbots

The image-capturing webbot leverages your knowledge of downloading and parsing web pages to create an application that copies all the images (and their directory structure) to your local hard drive. In addition to creating a useful tool, you'll also learn how to convert relative addresses into fully resolved URLs, a technique that is vital for later spidering projects.

Chapter 9: Link-Verification Webbots

Here you will have the opportunity to write a webbot that automatically verifies that all the links on a web page point to valid web pages. I'll conclude the chapter with ideas for expanding this concept into a variety of useful tools and products.

Chapter 10: Anonymous Browsing Webbots

In this chapter, I'll introduce the concept of using a webbot as a *proxy*, or intermediary agent that intercepts and modifies information flowing between a user and the Internet. The result of this project is a simple proxy webbot that allows users to surf the Internet anonymously.

Chapter 11: Search-Ranking Webbots

This project describes a simple webbot that determines how highly a search engine ranks a website, given a set of search criteria. You'll also find a host of ideas about how you can modify this concept to provide a variety of other services.

Chapter 12: Aggregation Webbots

Aggregation is a technique that gathers the contents of multiple web pages in a single location. This project introduces techniques that make it easy to exploit the availability of RSS news services.

Chapter 13: FTP Webbots

Webbots that use FTP are able to move the information they collect to an FTP server for storage or use by other applications. In this chapter, we'll explore methods for navigating on, uploading to, and downloading from FTP servers.

Chapter 14: NNTP News Webbots

While often overlooked in favor of newer, web-based sources, NNTP is still a viable protocol with an active user base. In this chapter, I'll describe methods by which you can interface your webbots to news servers, which use NNTP.

Chapter 15: Webbots That Read Email

Here you will learn how to write webbots that read and delete messages from any POP3 mail server. The ability to read email allows a webbot to interpret instructions sent by email or apply a variety of email filters.

Chapter 16: Webbots That Send Email

In this chapter, you'll learn various methods that allow your webbots to send email messages and notifications. You will also learn how to leverage what you learned in the previous chapter to create "smart email addresses" that can determine how to forward messages based on their content—without modifying anything on the mail server.

Chapter 17: Converting a Website into a Function

This project describes how you can use form emulation and parsing techniques to transform any preexisting online application into a function you can call from any PHP program.

7

PRICE-MONITORING WEBBOTS

In this chapter, we'll look at a strategic application of webbots—monitoring online prices. There are many reasons one would do this. For example, a webbot might monitor prices for these purposes:

- Notifying someone (via email or text message[1]) when a price drops below a preset threshold
- Predicting price trends by performing statistical analysis on price histories
- Establishing your company's prices by studying what the competition charges for similar items

Regardless of your reasons to monitor prices, the one thing that all of these strategies have in common is that they all download web pages containing prices and then identify and parse the data.

---

[1] Chapter 16 describes how webbots send email and text messages.

In this chapter, I will describe methods for monitoring online prices on e-commerce websites. Additionally, I will explain how to parse data from tables and prepare you for the webbot strategies revealed in Chapter 19.

The Target

The practice store, available at this book's website,[2] will be the target for our price-monitoring webbot. A screenshot of the store is shown in Figure 7-1.

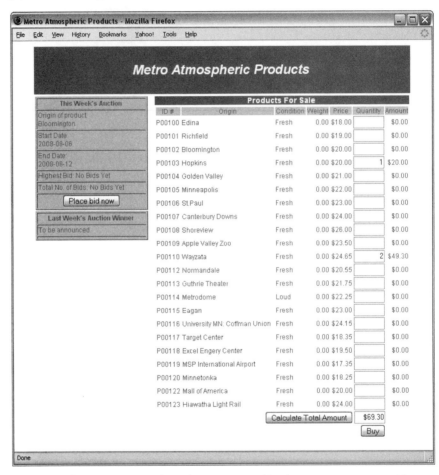

Figure 7-1: The e-commerce website that is monitored by the price-monitoring webbot

This practice store provides a controlled environment that is ideal for this exercise. For example, by targeting the example store you can do the following:

- Experiment with price-monitoring webbots without the possibility of interfering with an actual business

---

[2] The URL for this store is found at http://www.schrenk.com/nostarch/webbots.

- Control the content of this target, so you don't run the risk of someone modifying the web page, which could break the example scripts[3]

The prices change on a daily basis, so you can also use it to practice writing webbots that track and graph prices over time.

Designing the Parsing Script

Our webbot's objective is to download the target web page, parse the price variables, and place the data into an array for processing. The price-monitoring webbot is largely an exercise in parsing data that appears in tables, since useful online data usually appears as such. When tables aren't used, <div> tags are generally applied and can be parsed in a similar manner.

While we know that the test target for this example won't change, we don't know that about targets in the wild. Therefore, we don't want to be too specific when telling our parsing routines where to look for pricing information. In this example, the parsing script won't look for data in specific locations; instead, it will look for the desired data relative to easy-to-find text that tells us where the desired information is located. If the position of the pricing information on the target web page changes, our parsing script will still find it.

Let's look at a script that downloads the target web page, parses the prices, and displays the data it parsed. This script is available in its entirety from this book's website. The script is broken into sections here; however, iterative loops are simplified for clarity.

Initialization and Downloading the Target

The example script initializes by including the LIB_http and LIB_parse libraries you read about earlier. It also creates an array where the parsed data is stored, and it sets the product counter to zero, as shown in Listing 7-1.

```
# Initialization
include("LIB_http.php");
include("LIB_parse.php");
$product_array=array();
$product_count=0;

# Download the target (practice store) web page
$target = "http://www.schrenk.com/webbots/example_store";
$web_page = http_get($target, "");
```

Listing 7-1: Initializing the price-monitoring webbot

After initialization, the script proceeds to download the target web page with the get_http() function described in Chapter 3.

After downloading the web page, the script parses all the page's tables into an array, as shown in Listing 7-2.

---

[3] The example scripts are resistant to most changes in the target store.

```
# Parse all the tables on the web page into an array
$table_array = parse_array($web_page['FILE'], "<table", "</table>");
```

Listing 7-2: Parsing the tables into an array

The script does this because the product pricing data is in a table. Once we neatly separate all the tables, we can look for the table with the product data. Notice that the script uses <table, not <table>, as the leading indicator for a table. It does this because <table will always be appropriate, no matter how many table formatting attributes are used.

Next, the script looks for the first *landmark,* or text that identifies the table where the product data exists. Since the landmark represents text that identifies the desired data, that text must be exclusive to our task. For example, by examining the page's source code we can see that we cannot use the word *origin* as a landmark because it appears in both the description of this week's auction and the list of products for sale. The example script uses the words *Products for Sale,* because that phrase only exists in the heading of the product table and is not likely to exist elsewhere if the web page is updated. The script looks at each table until it finds the one that contains the landmark text, *Products for Sale,* as shown in Listing 7-3.

```
# Look for the table that contains the product information
for($xx=0; $xx<count($table_array); $xx++)
    {
    $table_landmark = "Products For Sale";
    if(stristr($table_array[$xx], $table_landmark))      // Process this table
        {
        echo "FOUND: Product table\n";
```

Listing 7-3: Examining each table for the existence of the landmark text

Once the table containing the product pricing data is found, that table is parsed into an array of table rows, as shown in Listing 7-4.

```
# Parse table into an array of table rows
$product_row_array = parse_array($table_array[$xx], "<tr", "</tr>");
```

Listing 7-4: Parsing the table into an array of table rows

Then, once an array of table rows from the product data table is available, the script looks for the product table heading row. The heading row is useful for two reasons: It tells the webbot where the data begins within the table, and it provides the column positions for the desired data. This is important because in the future, the order of the data columns could change (as part of a web page update, for example). If the webbot uses column names to identify data, the webbot will still parse data correctly if the order changes, as long as the column names remain the same.

Here again, the script relies on a landmark to find the table heading row. This time, the landmark is the word *Condition*, as shown in Listing 7-5. Once the landmark identifies the table heading, the positions of the desired table columns are recorded for later use.

```
for($table_row=0; $table_row<count($product_row_array); $table_row++)
  {
  # Detect the beginning of the desired data (heading row)
  $heading_landmark = "Condition";
  if((stristr($product_row_array[$table_row], $heading_landmark)))
    {
    echo "FOUND: Table heading row\n";

    # Get the position of the desired headings
    $table_cell_array = parse_array($product_row_array[$table_row], "<td", "</td>");
    for($heading_cell=0; $heading_cell<count($table_cell_array); $heading_cell++)
        {
        if(stristr(strip_tags(trim($table_cell_array[$heading_cell])), "ID#"))
            $id_column=$heading_cell;
        if(stristr(strip_tags(trim($table_cell_array[$heading_cell])), "Product name"))
            $name_column=$heading_cell;
        if(stristr(strip_tags(trim($table_cell_array[$heading_cell])), "Price"))
            $price_column=$heading_cell;
        }
    echo "FOUND: id_column=$id_column\n";
    echo "FOUND: price_column=$price_column\n";
    echo "FOUND: name_column=$name_column\n";

    # Save the heading row for later use

    $heading_row = $table_row;
    }
```

Listing 7-5: Detecting the table heading and recording the positions of desired columns

As the script loops through the table containing the desired data, it must also identify where the pricing data ends. A landmark is used again to identify the end of the desired data. The script looks for the landmark *Calculate*, from the form's submit button, to identify when it has reached the end of the data. Once found, it breaks the loop, as shown in Listing 7-6.

```
# Detect the end of the desired data table
$ending_landmark = "Calculate";
if((stristr($product_row_array[$table_row], $ending_landmark)))
    {
    echo "PARSING COMPLETE!\n";
    break;
    }
```

Listing 7-6: Detecting the end of the table

If the script finds the headers but doesn't find the end of the table, it assumes that the rest of the table rows contain data. It parses these table rows, using the column position data gleaned earlier, as shown in Listing 7-7.

```
# Parse product and price data
if(isset($heading_row) && $heading_row<$table_row)
    {
    $table_cell_array = parse_array($product_row_array[$table_row], "<td", "</td>");
    $product_array[$product_count]['ID'] =
            strip_tags(trim($table_cell_array[$id_column]));
    $product_array[$product_count]['NAME'] =
            strip_tags(trim($table_cell_array[$name_column]));
    $product_array[$product_count]['PRICE'] =
            strip_tags(trim($table_cell_array[$price_column]));
    $product_count++;
    echo"PROCESSED: Item #$product_count\n";
    }
```

Listing 7-7: Assigning parsed data to an array

Once the prices are parsed into an array, the webbot script can do anything it wants with the data. In this case, it simply displays what it collected, as shown in Listing 7-8.

```
# Display the collected data
for($xx=0; $xx<count($product_array); $xx++)
    {
    echo "$xx. ";
    echo "ID: ".$product_array[$xx]['ID'].", ";
    echo "NAME: ".$product_array[$xx]['NAME'].", ";
    echo "PRICE: ".$product_array[$xx]['PRICE']."\n";
    }
```

Listing 7-8: Displaying the parsed product pricing data

As shown in Figure 7-2, the webbot indicates when it finds landmarks and prices. This not only tells the operator how the webbot is running, but also provides important diagnostic information, making both debugging and maintenance easier.

Since prices are almost always in HTML tables, you will usually parse price information in a manner that is similar to that shown here. Occasionally, pricing information may be contained in other tags, (like <div> tags, for example), but this is less likely. When you encounter <div> tags, you can easily parse the data they contain into arrays using similar methods.

```
Shell                                                          - □ ×
FOUND:  Product table
FOUND:  Table heading row
FOUND:  id_column=0
FOUND:  price_column=4
FOUND:  name_column=1
PROCESSED:  Item #1
PROCESSED:  Item #2
PROCESSED:  Item #3
PROCESSED:  Item #4
PROCESSED:  Item #5
PROCESSED:  Item #6
PROCESSED:  Item #7
PROCESSED:  Item #8
PROCESSED:  Item #9
PROCESSED:  Item #10
PROCESSED:  Item #11
PROCESSED:  Item #12
PROCESSED:  Item #13
PROCESSED:  Item #14
PROCESSED:  Item #15
PROCESSED:  Item #16
PROCESSED:  Item #17
PROCESSED:  Item #18
PROCESSED:  Item #19
PROCESSED:  Item #20
PROCESSED:  Item #21
PROCESSED:  Item #22
PARSING COMPLETE!
0.  ID:  P00100,  NAME:  Edina,  PRICE:  $18.00
1.  ID:  P00101,  NAME:  Richfield,  PRICE:  $19.00
2.  ID:  P00102,  NAME:  Bloomington,  PRICE:  $20.00
3.  ID:  P00103,  NAME:  Hopkins,  PRICE:  $20.00
4.  ID:  P00104,  NAME:  Golden Valley,  PRICE:  $21.00
5.  ID:  P00105,  NAME:  Minneapolis,  PRICE:  $22.00
6.  ID:  P00106,  NAME:  St.Paul,  PRICE:  $23.00
7.  ID:  P00107,  NAME:  Canterbury Downs,  PRICE:  $24.00
8.  ID:  P00108,  NAME:  Shoreview,  PRICE:  $26.00
9.  ID:  P00109,  NAME:  Apple Valley Zoo,  PRICE:  $23.50
10.  ID:  P00110,  NAME:  Wayzata,  PRICE:  $24.65
11.  ID:  P00112,  NAME:  Normandale,  PRICE:  $20.55
12.  ID:  P00113,  NAME:  Guthrie Theater,  PRICE:  $21.75
13.  ID:  P00114,  NAME:  Metrodome,  PRICE:  $22.25
14.  ID:  P00115,  NAME:  Eagan,  PRICE:  $23.00
15.  ID:  P00116,  NAME:  University MN: Coffman Union,  PRICE:  $24.15
16.  ID:  P00117,  NAME:  Target Center,  PRICE:  $18.35
17.  ID:  P00118,  NAME:  Excel Engery Center,  PRICE:  $19.50
18.  ID:  P00119,  NAME:  MSP International Airport,  PRICE:  $17.35
19.  ID:  P00120,  NAME:  Minnetonka,  PRICE:  $18.25
20.  ID:  P00122,  NAME:  Mall of America,  PRICE:  $20.00
21.  ID:  P00123,  NAME:  Hiawatha Light Rail,  PRICE:  $24.00
```

Figure 7-2: The price-monitoring webbot, as run in a shell

Further Exploration

Now you know how to parse pricing information from a web page—what you do with this information is up to you. If you are so inclined, you can expand your experience with some of the following suggestions.

- Since the prices in the example store change on a daily basis, monitor the daily price changes for a month and save your parsed results in a database.
- Develop scripts that graph price fluctuations.
- Read about sending email with webbots in Chapter 16, and develop scripts that notify you when prices hit preset high or low thresholds.

While this chapter covers monitoring prices online, you can use similar parsing techniques to monitor and parse other types of data found in HTML tables. Consider using the techniques you learned here to monitor things like baseball scores, stock prices, weather forecasts, census data, banner ad rotation statistics,[4] and more.

---

[4] You can use webbots to perform a variety of diagnostic functions. For example, a webbot may repeatedly download a web page to gather metrics on how banner ads are rotated.

8

IMAGE-CAPTURING WEBBOTS

In this chapter, I'll describe a webbot that identifies and downloads all of the images on a web page. This webbot also stores images in a directory structure similar to the directory structure on the target website. This project will show how a seemingly simple webbot can be made more complex by addressing these common problems:

- Finding the *page base*, or the address that defines the address from which all relative addresses are referenced
- Dealing with changes to the page base, caused by page redirection
- Converting relative addresses into fully resolved URLs
- Replicating complex directory structures
- Properly downloading image files with binary formats

In Chapter 18, you'll expand on these concepts to develop a spider that downloads images from an entire website, not just one page.

Example Image-Capturing Webbot

Our image-capturing webbot downloads a target web page (in this case, the Viking Mission web page on the NASA website) and parses all references to images on the page. The webbot downloads each image, echoes the image's name and size to the console, and stores the file on the local hard drive. Figure 8-1 shows what the webbot's output looks like when executed from a shell.

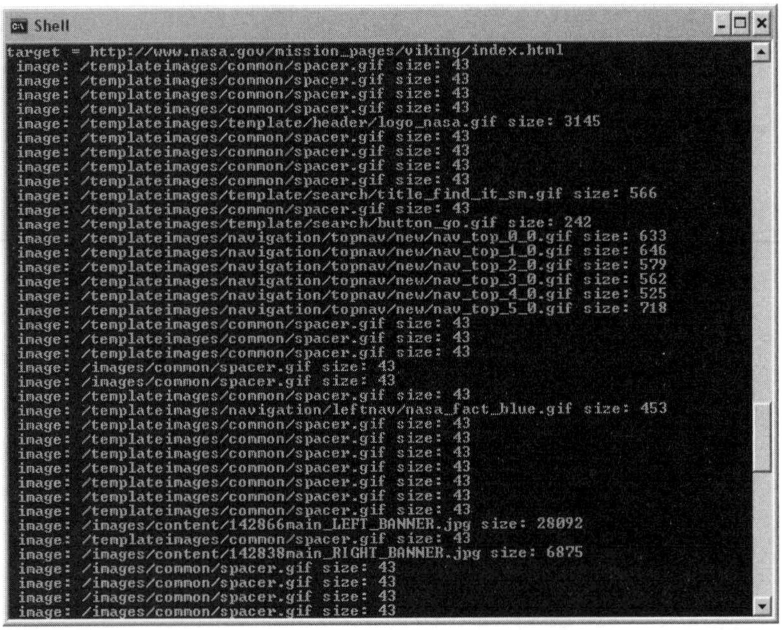

Figure 8-1: The image-capturing bot, when executed from a shell

On this website, like many others, several unique images share the same filename but have different file paths. For example, the image /templates/logo.gif may represent a different graphic than /templates/affiliate/logo.gif. To solve this problem, the webbot re-creates a local copy of the directory structure that exists on the target web page. Figure 8-2 shows the directory structure the webbot created when it saved these images it downloaded from the NASA example.

Creating the Image-Capturing Webbot

This example webbot relies on a library called LIB_download_images, which is available from this book's website. This library contains the following functions:

- download_binary_file(), which safely downloads image files
- mkpath(), which makes directory structures on your hard drive
- download_images_for_page(), which downloads all the images on a page

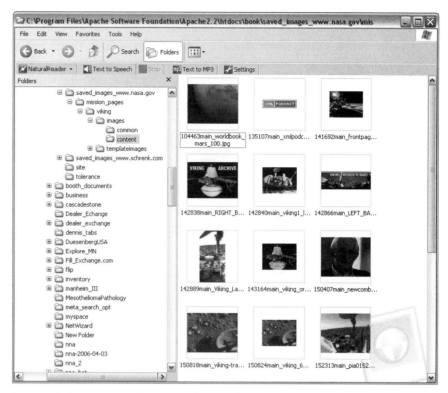

Figure 8-2: Re-creating a file structure for stored images

For clarity, I will break down this library into highlights and accompanying explanations.

The first script (Listing 8-1) shows the main webbot used in Figures 8-1 and 8-2.

```
include("LIB_download_images.php");
$target="http://www.nasa.gov/mission_pages/viking/index.html";
download_images_for_page($target);
```

Listing 8-1: Executing the image-capturing webbot

This short webbot script loads the LIB_download_images library, defines a target web page, and calls the download_images_for_page() function, which gets the images and stores them in a complementary directory structure on the local drive.

NOTE   *Please be aware that the scripts in this chapter, which are available at http://www .schrenk.com/nostarch/webbots, are created for demonstration purposes only. Although they should work in most cases, they aren't production ready. You may find long or complicated directory structures, odd filenames, or unusual file formats that will cause these scripts to crash.*

Binary-Safe Download Routine

Our image-grabbing webbot uses the function download_binary_file(), which is designed to download *binary files*, like images. Other binary files you may encounter could include executable files, compressed files, or system files. Up to this point, the only file downloads discussed have been *ASCII* (text) files, like web pages. The distinction between downloading binary and ASCII files is important because they have different formats and can cause confusion when downloaded. For example, random byte combinations in binary files may be misinterpreted as end-of-file markers in ASCII file downloads. If you download a binary file with a script designed for ASCII files, you stand a good chance of downloading a partial or corrupt file.

Even though PHP has its own, built-in *binary-safe* download functions, this webbot uses a custom download script that leverages PHP/cURL functionality to download images from SSL sites (when the protocol is HTTPS), follow HTTP file redirections, and send referer information to the server.

Sending proper referer information is crucial because many websites will stop other websites from "borrowing" images. Borrowing images from other websites (without hosting the images on your server) is bad etiquette and is commonly called *hijacking*. If your webbot doesn't include a proper referer value, its activity could be confused with a website that is hijacking images. Listing 8-2 shows the file download script used by this webbot.

```
function download_binary_file($file, $referer)
    {
    # Open a PHP/CURL session
    $s = curl_init();

    # Configure the cURL command
    curl_setopt($s, CURLOPT_URL, $file);              // Define target site
    curl_setopt($s, CURLOPT_RETURNTRANSFER, TRUE);    // Return file contents in a string
    curl_setopt($s, CURLOPT_BINARYTRANSFER, TRUE);    // Indicate binary transfer
    curl_setopt($s, CURLOPT_REFERER, $referer);       // Referer value
    curl_setopt($s, CURLOPT_SSL_VERIFYPEER, FALSE);   // No certificate
    curl_setopt($s, CURLOPT_FOLLOWLOCATION, TRUE);    // Follow redirects
    curl_setopt($s, CURLOPT_MAXREDIRS, 4);            // Limit redirections to four

    # Execute the cURL command (send contents of target web page to string)
    $downloaded_page = curl_exec($s);

    # Close PHP/CURL session and return the file
    curl_close($s);
    return $downloaded_page;
    }
```

Listing 8-2: A binary-safe file download routine, optimized for webbot use

Directory Structure

The script that creates directories (shown in Figure 8-2) is derived from a user-contributed routine found on the PHP website (http://www.php.net). Users commonly submit scripts like this one when they find something they want to share with the PHP community. In this case, it's a function that expands on mkdir() by creating complete directory structures with multiple directories at once. I modified the function slightly for our purposes. This function, shown in Listing 8-3, creates any file path that doesn't already exist on the hard drive and, if needed, it will create multiple directories for a single file path. For example, if the image's file path is images/templates/November, this function will create all three directories—*images*, *templates*, and *November*—to satisfy the entire file path.

```
function mkpath($path)
    {
    # Make sure that the slashes are all single and lean the correct way
    $path=preg_replace('/(\/){2,}|(\\\){1,}/','/',$path);

    # Make an array of all the directories in path
    $dirs=explode("/",$path);

    # Verify that each directory in path exists and create if necessary
    $path="";
    foreach ($dirs as $element)
        {
        $path.=$element."/";
        if(!is_dir($path))          // Directory verified here
            mkdir($path);           // Created if it doesn't exist
        }
    }
```

Listing 8-3: Re-creating file paths for downloaded images

This script in Listing 8-3 places all the path directories into an array and attempts to re-create that array, one directory at a time, on the local filesystem. Only nonexistent directories are created.

The Main Script

The main function for this webbot, download_images_for_page(), is broken down into highlights and explained below. As mentioned earlier, this function—and the entire LIB_download_images library—is available at this book's website.

Initialization and Target Validation

Since $target is used later for resolving the web address of the images, the $target value must be validated after the web page is downloaded. This is important because the server may redirect the webbot to an updated web page. That updated URL is the actual URL for the target page and the one that all relative files are referenced from in the next step. The script in Listing 8-4 verifies that the $target is the actual URL that was downloaded and not the product of a redirection.

```
function download_images_for_page($target)
    {
    echo "target = $target\n";
    # Download the web page
    $web_page = http_get($target, $referer="");
    # Update the target in case there was a redirection
    $target = $web_page['STATUS']['url'];
```

Listing 8-4: Downloading the target web page and responding to page redirection

Defining the Page Base

Much like the <base> HTML tag, the webbot uses $page_base to define the directory address of the target web page. This address becomes the reference for all images with relative addresses. For example, if $target is http://www.schrenk.com/april/index.php, then $page_base becomes http://www.schrenk.com/april.

This task, which is shown in Listing 8-5, is performed by the function get_base_page_address() and is actually in LIB_resolve_address and included by LIB_download_images.

```
    # Strip filename off target for use as page base
    $page_base=get_base_page_address($target);
```

Listing 8-5: Creating the page base for the target web page

As an example, if the webbot finds an image with the relative address 14/logo.gif, and the page base is http://www.schrenk.com/april, the webbot will use the page base to derive the fully resolved address for the image. In this case, the fully resolved address is http://www.schrenk.com/april/14/logo.gif. In contrast, if the image's file path is /march/14/logo.gif, the address will resolve to http://www.schrenk.com/march/14/logo.gif.

Creating a Root Directory for Imported File Structure

Since this webbot may download images from a number of domains, it creates a directory structure for each (see Listing 8-6). The root directory of each imported file structure is based on the page base.

```
    # Identify the directory where images are to be saved
    $save_image_directory = "saved_images_".str_replace("http://", "",
$page_base);
```

Listing 8-6: Creating a root directory for the imported file structure

Parsing Image Tags from the Downloaded Web Page

The webbot uses techniques described in Chapter 4 to parse the image tags from the target web page and put them into an array for easy processing.

This is shown in Listing 8-7. The webbot stops if the target web page contains no images.

```
# Parse the image tags
$img_tag_array = parse_array($web_page['FILE'], "<img", ">");
if(count($img_tag_array)==0)
    {
    echo "No images found at $target\n";
    exit;
    }
```

Listing 8-7: Parsing the image tags

The Image-Processing Loop

The webbot employs a loop, where each image tag is individually processed. For each image tag, the webbot parses the image file source and creates a fully resolved URL (see Listing 8-8). Creating a fully resolved URL is important because the webbot cannot download an image without its complete URL: the HTTP protocol identifier, the domain, the image's file path, and the image's filename.

```
$image_path = get_attribute($img_tag_array[$xx], $attribute="src");
echo " image: ".$image_path;
$image_url = resolve_address($image_path, $page_base);
```

Listing 8-8: Parsing the image source and creating a fully resolved URL

Creating the Local Directory Structure

The webbot verifies that the file path exists in the local file structure. If the directory doesn't exist, the webbot creates the directory path, as shown in Listing 8-9.

```
if(get_base_domain_address($page_base) == get_base_domain_address($image_url))
    {
    # Make image storage directory for image, if one doesn't exist
    $directory = substr($image_path, 0, strrpos($image_path, "/"));

    clearstatcache(); // Clear cache to get accurate directory status
    if(!is_dir($save_image_directory."/".$directory))      // See if dir exists
        mkpath($save_image_directory."/".$directory);       // Create if it doesn't
```

Listing 8-9: Creating the local directory structure for each image file

Downloading and Saving the File

Once the path is verified or created, the image is downloaded (using its fully resolved URL) and stored in the local file structure (see Listing 8-10).

```
# Download the image and report image size
$this_image_file =  download_binary_file($image_url, $referer=$target);
echo " size: ".strlen($this_image_file);

# Save the image
$fp = fopen($save_image_directory."/".$image_path, "w");
fputs($fp, $this_image_file);
fclose($fp);
echo "\n";
```

Listing 8-10: Downloading and storing images

The webbot repeats this process for each image parsed from the target web page.

Further Exploration

You can point this webbot at any web page, and it will generate a copy of each image that page uses, arranged in a directory structure that resembles the original. You can also develop other useful webbots based on this design. If you want to test your skills, consider the following challenges.

- Write a similar webbot that detects hijacked images.
- Improve the efficiency of the script by reworking it so that it doesn't download an image it has downloaded previously.
- Modify this webbot to create local backup copies of web pages.
- Adjust the webbot to cache movies or audio files instead of images.
- Modify the bot to monitor when images change on a web page.

Final Thoughts

If you attempt to run this webbot on a remote server, remember that your webbot must have write privileges on that server, or it won't be able to create file structures or download images.

9

LINK-VERIFICATION WEBBOTS

This webbot project solves a problem shared by all web developers—detecting broken links on web pages. Verifying links on a web page isn't a difficult thing to do, and the associated script is short.

Figure 9-1 shows the simplicity of this webbot.

Creating the Link-Verification Webbot

For clarity, I'll break down the creation of the link-verification webbot into manageable sections, which I'll explain along the way. The code and libraries used in this chapter are available for download at this book's website.

Initializing the Webbot and Downloading the Target

Before validating links on a web page, your webbot needs to load the required libraries and initialize a few key variables. In addition to LIB_http and LIB_parse, this webbot introduces two new libraries: LIB_resolve_addresses and LIB_http_codes. I'll explain these additions as I use them.

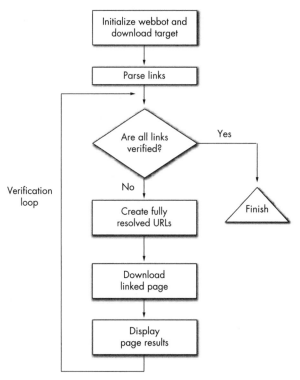

Figure 9-1: Link-verification bot flow chart

The webbot downloads the target web page with the http_get() function, which was described in Chapter 3.

```
# Include libraries
include("LIB_http.php");
include("LIB_parse.php");
include("LIB_resolve_addresses.php");
include("LIB_http_codes.php");

# Identify the target web page and the page base
$target = "http://www.schrenk.com/nostarch/webbots/
page_with_broken_links.php";
$page_base = "http://www.schrenk.com/nostarch/webbots/";

# Download the web page
$downloaded_page = http_get($target, $ref="");
```

Listing 9-1: Initializing the bot and downloading the target web page

Setting the Page Base

In addition to defining the $target, which points to a diagnostic page on the book's website, Listing 9-1 also defines a variable called $page_base. A *page base* defines the domain and server directory of the target page, which tells the webbot where to find web pages referenced with relative links.

Relative links are references to other files—relative to where the reference is made. For example, consider the relative links in Table 9-1.

Table 9-1: Examples of Relative Links

Link	References a File Located In . . .
`<a href="linked_page.html">`	Same directory as web page
`<a href="../linked_page.html">`	The page's parent directory (up one level)
`<a href="../../linked_page.html">`	The page's parent's parent directory (up 2 levels)
`<a href="/linked_page.html">`	The server's root directory

Your webbot would fail if it tried to download any of these links as is, since your webbot's reference point is the computer it runs on, and not the computer where the links where found. The page base, however, gives your webbot the same reference as the target page. You might think of it this way: The page base is to a webbot as the <base> tag is to a browser. The page base sets the reference for everything referred to on the target web page.

Parsing the Links

You can easily parse all the links and place them into an array with the script in Listing 9-2.

```
# Parse the links
$link_array = parse_array($downloaded_page['FILE'], $beg_tag="<a", $close_tag=">");
```

Listing 9-2: Parsing the links from the downloaded page

The code in Listing 9-2 uses parse_array() to put everything between every occurrence of <a and > into an array.[1] The function parse_array() is not case sensitive, so it doesn't matter if the target web page uses <a>, <A> or a combination of both tags to define links.

Running a Verification Loop

You gain a great deal of convenience when the parsed links are available in an array. The array allows your script to verify the links iteratively through one set of verification instructions, as shown in Listing 9-3. The PHP sections of this script appear in bold.

Listing 9-3 also includes some HTML formatting to create a nice-looking report, which you'll see later. Notice that the contents of the verification loop have been removed for clarity. I'll explain what happens in this loop next.

---

[1] Parsing functions are explained in Chapter 4.

```
<b>Status of links on <?echo $target?></b><br>
<table border="1" cellpadding="1" cellspacing="0">
    <tr bgcolor="#e0e0e0">
        <th>URL</th>
        <th>HTTP CODE</th>
        <th>MESSAGE</th>
        <th>DOWNLOAD TIME (seconds)</th>
    </tr>
<?
for($xx=0; $xx<count($link_array); $xx++)
    {
    // Verification and display go here
    }
```

Listing 9-3: The verification loop

Generating Fully Resolved URLs

Since the contents of the $link_array elements are actually complete anchor tags, we need to parse the value of the href attribute out of the tags before we can download and test the pages they reference.

The value of the href attribute is extracted from the anchor tag with the function get_attribute(), as shown in Listing 9-4.

```
// Parse the HTTP attribute from link
$link = get_attribute($tag=$link_array[$xx], $attribute="href");
```

Listing 9-4: Parsing the referenced address from the anchor tag

Once you have the href address, you need to combine the previously defined $page_base with the relative address to create a fully resolved URL, which your webbot can use to download pages. A *fully resolved URL* is any URL that describes not only the file to download, but also the server and directory where that file is located and the protocol required to access it. Table 9-2 shows the fully resolved addresses for the links in Table 9-1, assuming the links are on a page in the directory, http://www.schrenk.com/nostarch/webbots.

Table 9-2: Examples of Fully Resolved URLs (for links on http://www.schrenk.com/nostarch/book)

Link	Fully Resolved URL
<a href="linked_page.html">	http://www.schrenk.com/nostarch/webbots/linked_page.html
<a href="../linked_page.html">	http://www.schrenk.com/nostarch/linked_page.html
<a href="../../linked_page.html">	http://www.schrenk.com/linked_page.html
<a href="/linked_page.html">	http://www.schrenk.com/linked_page.html

Fully resolved URLs are made with the resolve_address() function (see Listing 9-5), which is in the LIB_resolve_addresses library. This library is a set of routines that converts all possible methods of referencing web pages in HTML into fully resolved URLs.

```
// Create a fully resolved URL
$fully_resolved_link_address = resolve_address($link, $page_base);
```

Listing 9-5: Creating fully resolved addresses with `resolve_address()`

Downloading the Linked Page

The webbot verifies the status of each page referenced by the links on the target page by downloading each page and examining its status. It downloads the pages with `http_get()`, just as you downloaded the target web page earlier (see Listing 9-6).

```
// Download the page referenced by the link and evaluate
$downloaded_link = http_get($fully_resolved_link_address, $target);
```

Listing 9-6: Downloading a page referenced by a link

Notice that the second parameter in `http_get()` is set to the address of the target web page. This sets the page's referer variable to the target page. When executed, the effect is the same as telling the server that someone requested the page by clicking a link from the target web page.

Displaying the Page Status

Once the linked page is downloaded, the webbot relies on the STATUS element of the downloaded array to analyze the HTTP code, which is provided by PHP/CURL. (For your future projects, keep in mind that PHP/CURL also provides total download time and other diagnostics that we're not using in this project.)

HTTP status codes are standardized, three-digit numbers that indicate the status of a page fetch.[2] This webbot uses these codes to determine if a link is broken or valid. These codes are divided into ranges that define the type of errors or status, as shown in Table 9-3.

Table 9-3: HTTP Code Ranges and Related Categories

HTTP Code Range	Category	Meaning
100–199	Informational	Not generally used
200–299	Successful	Your page request was successful
300–399	Redirection	The page you're looking for has moved or has been removed
400–499	Client error	Your web client made a incorrect or illogical page request
500–599	Server error	A server error occurred, generally associated with a bad form submission

---

[2] The official reference for HTTP codes is available on the World Wide Web Consortium's website (http://www.w3.org/Protocols/rfc2616/rfc2616-sec10.html).

The $status_code_array was created when the LIB_http_codes library was imported. When you use the HTTP code as an index into $status_code_array, it returns a human-readable status message, as shown in Listing 9-7. (PHP script is in bold.)

```
<tr>
    <td align="left"><?echo $downloaded_link['STATUS']['url']?></td>
    <td align="right"><?echo $downloaded_link['STATUS']['http_code']?></td>
    <td align="left"><?echo $status_code_array[$downloaded_link['STATUS']['http_code']]?></td>
    <td align="right"><?echo $downloaded_link['STATUS']['total_time']?></td>
</tr>
```

Listing 9-7: Displaying the status of linked web pages

As an added feature, the webbot displays the amount of time (in seconds) required to download pages referenced by the links on the target web page. This period is automatically measured and recorded by PHP/CURL when the page is downloaded. The period required to download the page is available in the array element: $downloaded_link['STATUS']['total_time'].

Running the Webbot

Since the output of this webbot contains formatted HTML, it is appropriate to run this webbot within a browser, as shown in Figure 9-2.

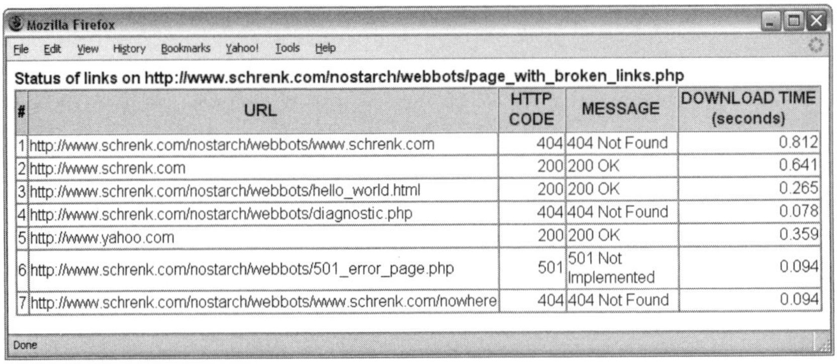

Figure 9-2: Running the link-verification webbot

This webbot counts and identifies all the links on the target website. It also indicates the HTTP code and diagnostic message describing the status of the fetch used to download the page and displays the actual amount of time it took the page to load.

Let's take this time to look at some of the libraries used by this webbot.

LIB_http_codes

The following script creates an indexed array of HTTP error codes and their definitions. To use the array, simply include the library, insert your HTTP code value into the array, and echo as shown in Listing 9-8.

```
include(LIB_http_codes.php);
echo $status_code_array[$YOUR_HTTP_CODE]['MSG']
```

Listing 9-8: Decoding an HTTP code with `LIB_http_codes`

`LIB_http_codes` is essentially a group of array declarations, with the first element being the HTTP code and the second element, `['MSG']`, being the status message text. Like the others, this library is also available for download from this book's website.

LIB_resolve_addresses

The library that creates fully resolved addresses, `LIB_resolve_addresses`, is also available for download at the book's website.

NOTE   *Before you download and examine this library, be warned that creating fully resolved URLs is a lot like making sausage—while you might enjoy how sausage tastes, you probably wouldn't like watching those lips and ears go into the grinder. Simply put, the act of converting relative links into fully resolved URLs involves awkward, asymmetrical code with numerous exceptions to rules and many special cases. This library is extraordinarily useful, but it isn't made up of pretty code.*

If you don't need to see how this conversion is done, there's no reason to look. If, on the other hand, you're intrigued by this description, feel free to download the library from the book's website and see for yourself. More importantly, if you find a cleaner solution, please upload it to the book's website to share it with the community.

Further Exploration

You can expand this basic webbot to do a variety of very useful things. Here is a short list of ideas to get you started on advanced designs.

- Create a web page with a form that allows people to enter and test the links of any web page.
- Schedule a link-verification bot to run periodically to ensure that links on web pages remain current. (For information on scheduling webbots, read Chapter 23.)
- Modify the webbot to send email notifications when it finds dead links. (More information on webbots that send email is available in Chapter 16.)
- Encase the webbot in a spider to check the links on an entire website.
- Convert this webbot into a function that is called directly from PHP. (This idea is explored in Chapter 17.)

10

ANONYMOUS BROWSING
WEBBOTS

The Internet is a public place, and as in
any other community, web surfers leave
telltale clues of where they've been and what
they've done. While many people feel anonymous
online, the fact is that server logs, cookies, and browser
caches leave little doubt to what happens on the Internet. While total online
anonymity is nearly impossible, you can cloak your activity through a specialized
webbot called a *proxybot*, or simply a *proxy*. This chapter investigates applications
for proxies and later explores a webbot proxy project that provides anonymous web browsing.

Anonymity with Proxies

A *proxy* is a special type of webbot that serves as an intermediary between
webservers and clients. Proxies have many uses including banning people
from browsing prohibited websites, blocking banner advertisements, and
inhibiting suspect scripts from running on browsers.

One of the more popular proxies is *Squid*, a web proxy that, among other things, saves bandwidth on large networks by caching frequently downloaded images.[1] Squid, along with most other proxies, also converts private network IP addresses into a single public address through a process called Network Address Translation (NAT).

A side effect of proxy use is that proxies create a potentially anonymous browsing environment because individual network addresses are pooled into a single network address. Since only the proxied network address is visible to web servers, the identities of the individual surfers remain unknown. Anonymity is the focus of this chapter, but before we start that discussion, a quick review of the liabilities of browsing in a non-proxied environment is in order.

Non-proxied Environments

In non-proxied network environments, web clients are totally exposed to the servers they access. This is important in terms of privacy because servers maintain records of requesting IP addresses, the files accessed, and the times they were accessed, as depicted in Figure 10-1.

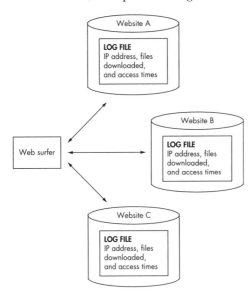

Figure 10-1: Browsing in a non-proxied network environment

Additionally, webservers may store small records of browsing activity on clients' hard drives in the form of cookies.[2] By reading cookies on a user's successive visits to the same Internet domain, webservers determine a variety of information, including previously defined browsing preferences, authentication criteria, and browsing history for that user within that domain.

---

[1] Information about Squid, a popular open source web proxy cache, is available at http://www.squid-cache.org. In addition to caching frequently downloaded images, Squid also caches DNS lookups, failed requests, and many other Internet objects.

[2] Chapters 21 and 22 describe cookies and their application to webbots in detail.

Your Online Exposure

You may think that you only expose your identity online when you formally register a username and password with a website, or that your identity is only known at sites where you've registered. However, a variety of tricks are available to monitor Internet activity, even when you don't have administration rights to a website. For example, you can learn a lot about the users of community forums, news servers, or even MySpace by uploading a *single-pixel image*, usually a transparent GIF file, to one of those services. While the single-pixel image is essentially invisible, everybody who accesses a web page containing one also downloads this seemingly innocuous little image. If things are set up correctly, each web surfer who downloads a page containing one of these single-pixel images leaves a record in a server log file, unknowingly recording his or her IP address and file access time. Here are some of the things you can learn from these log files:

- IP addresses of the web surfers accessing the page
- Frequency that someone with a specific IP address (or domain of origin) visits the page
- Time of day that web surfer visited the web page
- Total traffic the web page receives
- Indications of when traffic to the web page is heavy or light

Once you have a visitor's IP address, you could also identify his or her ISP by performing a *reverse DNS lookup*, which converts an IP address into its domain of origin. Many times, a reverse DNS lookup only reveals someone's ISP, like EarthLink or AOL. And since so many people (from all over the world) use these ISPs, that information isn't very useful. Other times, however, the domain name will give you the name of a specific corporation or organization that downloaded the web page.[3]

You can also configure the server that hosts the single-pixel image to write a cookie on the hard drive of the web surfer. With this cookie, you can determine when an individual user gains access to web pages. If you place your single-pixel image on many web pages that are visited by a specific Internet user, you can track much of that user's browsing activity.

If you think these threats to one's privacy are too theoretical, consider what happens on a larger scale with online advertising companies like MySpace, Google, DoubleClick, and SpecificClick. Given the large number of web pages on which these companies' advertisements appear, they are capable of tracking a very large percentage of your online activity. Just consider how many of the websites you visit have advertisements. Then look at your browser's cookie records (usually available in the privacy settings of your browser, as shown in Figure 10-2) to see how many of these media companies have left cookies on your computer.

---

[3] In the late 1990s, Amazon.com used a similar technique, combined with purchase data, to determine the reading lists of large corporations. For a short while, Amazon.com actually published these lists on its website. For obvious reasons, this feature was short-lived.

Figure 10-2: Viewing advertisers' cookies

Armed with what you know now, are you wondering why advertising companies write cookies to your hard drive? Are you questioning why the cookie in Figure 10-2 doesn't expire for nearly three years? I hope that this information freaks you out just a little and whets your appetite to learn more about writing anonymizing webbot proxies.

Proxied Environments

Typically, in corporate settings, proxies sit between a private network and the Internet, and all traffic that moves between the two is forced through the proxy. In the process, the proxy replaces each individual's identity with its own, and thereby "hides" the web surfer from the webserver's log files, as shown in Figure 10-3.

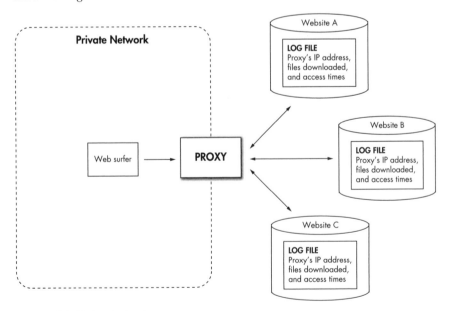

Figure 10-3: Hiding behind a proxy

Since the web surfer in Figure 10-3 is the only proxy user, no anonymity is achieved—the proxy is synonymous with the person using it. Ambiguity, and eventually anonymity, is achieved as more people use the same proxy, as in Figure 10-4.

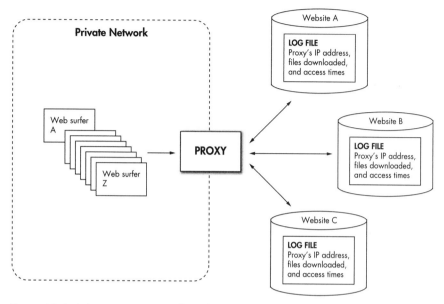

Figure 10-4: Achieving anonymity through numbers

The log files recorded by the webservers become ambiguous as more people use the proxy because the proxy's identity no longer represents a single web surfer. As the number of people using the proxy increases, the identity of individual users decreases. While anonymity is not generally an objective for proxies of this type, it is a side effect of operation, and the focus of this chapter's project.

The Anonymizer Project

In many respects, this anonymizer is like the previously described network proxies. However, this anonymizer is web-based, in contrast to most (corporate) proxies, which provide the only path from a local network to the Internet. Since all traffic between the private network and the Internet passes through these network proxies, it is simpler for them to modify traffic. Our web-based proxy, in contrast, runs on a web script and must contain the traffic within a browser. What this means is that every link passing through a web-based proxy must be modified to keep the web surfer on the anonymizer's web page, which is shown in Figure 10-5.

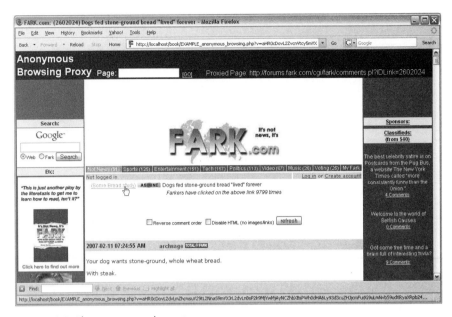

Figure 10-5: The anonymous browsing proxy

The user interface of the anonymous browsing proxy provides a place for web surfers to enter the URL of the website they wish to surf anonymously. After clicking *Go*, the page appears in the browser window, and the webserver, where the content originates, records the identity of the anonymizer. Because of the proxy, the webserver has no knowledge of the identity of the web surfer.

In order for the proxy to work, all web surfing activity must happen within the anonymizer script. If someone clicks a link, he or she must return to the anonymizer and not end up at the website referenced by the link. Therefore, before sending the web page to the browser, the anonymizer changes each link address to reference itself, while passing a Base64-encoded address of the link in a variable, as shown in the status bar at the bottom of Figure 10-5.

NOTE *This is a simple anonymizer, designed for study; it is not suitable for use in production environments. It will not work correctly on web pages that rely on forms, cookies, JavaScript, frames, or advanced web development techniques.*

Writing the Anonymizer

The following scripts describe the anonymizer's design. The complete script for the anonymizer project is available on this book's website.[4] For clarity, only script highlights are described in detail here.

---

[4] This book's website is available at http://www.schrenk.com/nostarch/webbots.

Downloading and Preparing the Target Web Page

After initializing libraries and variables, which is done in Listing 10-1, the anonymizer downloads and prepares the target web page for later processing. Note that the anonymizer makes use of the parsing and HTTP libraries described in Part I.

```
# Download the target web page
$page_array = http_get($target_webpage), $ref="", GET, $data_array="", EXCL_HEAD);

# Clean up the HTML formatting with Tidy
$web_page = tidy_html($page_array['FILE']);

# Get the base page address so we can create fully resolved addresses later
$page_base = get_base_page_address($page_array['STATUS']['url']);

# Remove JavaScript and HTML comments from web page
$web_page = remove($web_page, "<script", "</script>");
$web_page = remove($web_page, "<!--", "-->");
```

Listing 10-1: Downloading and prepping the target web page

Modifying the <base> Tag

After prepping the target web page, the <base> tag is either inserted or modified so all relative page addresses will properly resolve from the anonymizer's URL. This is shown in Listing 10-2.

```
$new_base_value = "<base href=\"".$page_base."\">";
if(!stristr($web_page, "<base"))
    {
    # If there is a <head>, insert <base> at beginning of <head></head>
    if(stristr($web_page, "<head"))
        {
        $web_page = eregi_replace("<head>", "<head>\n".$new_base_value, $web_page);
        }
    # Else insert a <head><base></head> at beginning of web page
    else
        {
        $web_page = "</head>\n".$new_base_value."\n</head>" . $web_page;
        }
    }
```

Listing 10-2: Adjusting the target page's <base> tag

Parsing the Links

The next step is to create an array of all the links on the page, which is done with the script in Listing 10-3.

```
$a_tag_array = parse_array($web_page, "<a", ">");
```

Listing 10-3: Creating an array of all the links (anchor tags)

Substituting the Links

After parsing links into an array, the code loops through each link. This loop, shown in Listing 10-4, performs the following steps:

1. Parse the hyper-reference attribute for each link.
2. Convert the hyper-reference into a fully resolved URL.
3. Convert the hyper-reference into the following format:

   anonymizer_address?v= hyper reference$^{base64\_encoded}$

4. Substitute the original hyper-reference with the URL (representing the *anonymizer_address* and the original link passed as a variable) created in the previous step.

```
for($xx=0; $xx<count($a_tag_array); $xx++)
    {
    // Get the original href value
    $original_href = get_attribute($a_tag_array[$xx], "href");
    // Convert href to a fully resolved address
    $fully_resolved_href = get_fully_resolved_address($original_href, $page_base);

    // Substitute the original href with "this_page?v=fully resolved address"
    $substitution_tag = str_replace($original_href,
                    trim($this_page."?v=".base64_encode($fully_resolved_href)),
                        $a_tag_array[$xx]);

    // Substitute the original tag with the new one
    $web_page = str_replace($a_tag_array[$xx], $substitution_tag, $web_page);
    }
```

Listing 10-4: Substituting links with coded links that re-reference the anonymizer

Displaying the Proxied Web Page

Once all the links are processed, the anonymizer sends the newly processed web page to the requesting web surfer's browser, as shown in Listing 10-5.

```
# Display the processed target web page
echo $web_page;
```

Listing 10-5: Displaying the proxied web page

That's all there is to it. The important thing is to design the anonymizer so all links displayed in the anonymizer's window re-reference the anonymizer with a $_GET variable that identifies the actual page to download. This is really not that hard to do, but as mentioned earlier, this anonymizer does not handle forms, cookies, JavaScript, frames, or more advanced web design techniques. That being said, it's a good place to start, and you should use this script to further explore the concept of anonymizing. With a few modifications, you could write web proxies that modify web content in a variety of ways.

Final Thoughts

It is important to note that anonymizers do not always provide complete anonymity. Anonymous browsing techniques rely on many users to mask the actions of individuals, and they are not foolproof. However, even simple anonymizers hide a web surfer's ISP and country of origin. Moreover, barring a disclosure of the anonymizer's server logs, users should remain anonymous; even if those logs were examined, they would still have to be referenced with the logs of ISPs to identify web surfers. Advanced anonymizers complicate issues further by making page requests from a variety of domains, which adds more confusion to server logs and users' identities. An anonymizer's access log files gain further protection if you host anonymizers on encrypted servers in countries that don't honor your home country's subpoenas for server log records.[5] (You didn't hear me make that recommendation, however.)

People argue about whether or not anonymous browsing is a good thing. On one hand, it can hamper the tracking of cyber criminals. However, anonymizers also provide freedom to people living in countries that severely limit what they can view online. I have also found anonymizers to be helpful in cases where I needed to view a website from a remote domain in order to debug security certificates. I don't have a lot of personal experience with other people's anonymizers, so I won't make any recommendations, but if these types of programs interest you, a quick Google search will reveal that many are available.

---

[5] Perhaps the most famous of these countries is Sealand, a sovereign country built on an abandoned World War II anti-aircraft platform seven miles off the coast of England. More information about Sealand is available at its official website, http://www.sealandgov.org.

11

SEARCH-RANKING WEBBOTS

Every day, millions of people find what they need online through search websites. If you own an online business, your search ranking may have far-reaching effects on that business. A higher-ranking search result should yield higher advertising revenue and more customers. Without knowing your search rankings, you have no way to measure how easy it is for people to find your web page, nor will you have a way to gauge the success of your attempts to optimize your web pages for search engines.

Manually finding your search ranking is not as easy as it sounds, especially if you are interested in the ranking of many pages with an assortment of search terms. If your web page appears on the first page of results, it's easy to find, but if your page is listed somewhere on the sixth or seventh page, you'll spend a lot of time figuring out how your website is ranked. Even searches for relatively obscure terms can return a large number of pages. (A recent Google search on the term *tapered drills*, for example, yielded over 44,000 results.) Since search engine spiders continually update their records, your search ranking may also change on a daily basis. Complicating the matter more, a web page will have a different search ranking for every search term. Manually checking web page search rankings with a browser does not make sense—webbots, however, make this task nearly trivial.

With all the search variations for each of your web pages, there is a need for an automated service to determine your web page's search ranking. A quick Internet search will reveal several such services, like the one shown in Figure 11-1.

Figure 11-1: A search-ranking service, GoogleRankings.com

This chapter demonstrates how to design a webbot that finds a search ranking for a domain and a search term. While this project's target is on the book's website, you can modify this webbot to work on a variety of available search services.[1] This example project also shows how to perform an *insertion parse*, which injects parsing tags within a downloaded web page to make parsing easier.

Description of a Search Result Page

Most search engines return two sets of results for any given search term, as shown in Figure 11-2. The most prominent search results are *paid placements*, which are purchased advertisements made to look something like search results. The other set of search results is made up of *organic placements* (or just *organics*), which are non-sponsored search results.

This chapter's project focuses on organics because they're the links that people are most likely to follow. Organics are also the search results whose visibility is improved through Search Engine Optimization.

---

[1] If you modify this webbot to work on other search services, make sure you are not violating their respective Terms of Service agreements.

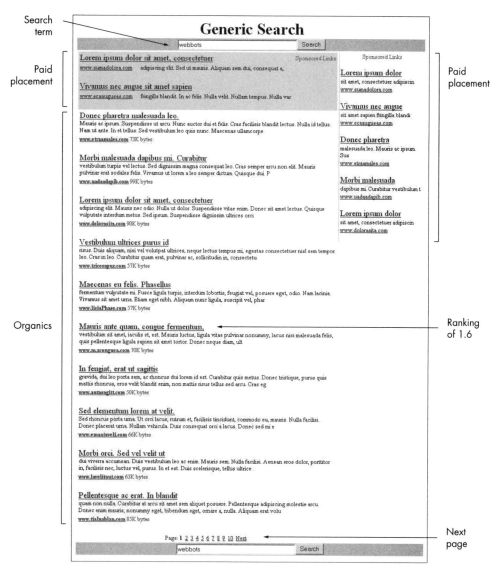

Figure 11-2: Parts of a search results page

The other part of the search result page we'll focus on is the *Next* link. This is important because it tells our webbot where to find the next page of search results.

For our purposes, the search ranking is determined by counting the number of pages in the search results until the subject web page is first found. The page number is then combined with the position of the subject web page within the organic placements on that page. For example, if a web page is the sixth organic on the first result page, it has a search ranking of 1.6. If a web page is the third organic on the second page, its search ranking is 2.3.

What the Search-Ranking Webbot Does

This webbot (actually a specialized spider) submits a search term to a search web page and looks for the subject web page in the search results. If the webbot finds the subject web page within the organic search results, it reports the web page's ranking. If, however, the webbot doesn't find the subject in the organics on that page, it downloads the next page of search results and tries again. The webbot continues searching deeper into the pages of search results until it finds a link to the subject web page. If the webbot can't find the subject web page within a specified number of pages, it will stop looking and report that it could not find the web page within the number of result pages searched.

Running the Search-Ranking Webbot

Figure 11-3 shows the output of our search-ranking webbot. In each case, there must be both a test web page (the page we're looking for in the search results) and a search term. In our test case, the webbot is looking for the ranking of http://www.loremianam.com, with a search term of *webbots*.[2] Once the webbot is run, it only takes a few seconds to determine the search ranking for this combination of web page and search term.

Figure 11-3: Running the search-ranking webbot

How the Search-Ranking Webbot Works

Our search-ranking webbot uses the process detailed in Figure 11-4 to determine the ranking of a website using a specific search term. These are the steps:

1. Initialize variables for use, including the search criteria and the subject web page.
2. Fetch the subject web page from the search engine using the search term.
3. Parse the organic search results from the advertisement and navigation text.

---

[2] Unlike a real search service, the demonstration search pages on the book's website return the same page set regardless of the search term used.

4. Determine whether or not the desired website appears in this page's search results.

    a. If the desired website is not found, keep looking deeper into the search results until the desired web page is found or the maximum number of attempts has been used.

    b. If the desired website is found, record the ranking.

5. Report the results.

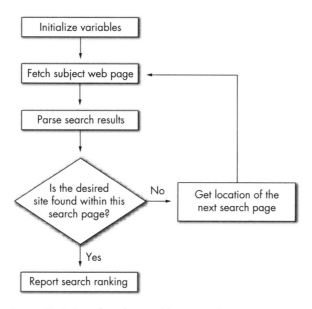

Figure 11-4: Search-ranking webbot at work

The Search-Ranking Webbot Script

The following section describes key aspects of the webbot's script. The latest version of this script is available for download at this book's website.

NOTE   *If you want to experiment with the code, you should download the webbot's script. I have simplified the scripts shown here for demonstration purposes.*

Initializing Variables

Initialization consists of including libraries and identifying the subject website and search criteria, as shown in Listing 11-1.

```
# Initialization

// Include libraries
include("LIB_http.php");
include("LIB_parse.php");
```

```
// Identify the search term and URL combination
$desired_site = "www.loremianam.com";
$search_term = "webbots";
// Initialize other miscellaneous variables
$page_index        = 0;
$url_found         = false;
$previous_target   = "";
// Define the target website and the query string for the search term
$target            = "http://www.schrenk.com/nostarch/webbots/search
$target            = $target."?q=".urlencode(trim($search_term));
# End: Initialization
```

Listing 11-1: Initializing the search-ranking webbot

The target is the page we're going to download, which in this case is a demonstration search page on this book's website. That URL also includes the search term in the query string. The webbot URL encodes the search term to guarantee that none of the characters in the search term conflict with reserved URL character combinations. For example, the PHP built-in function urlencode() changes *Karen Susan Terri* to *Karen+Susan+Terri*. If the search term contains characters that are illegal in a URL—for example, the comma or ampersand in *Karen, Susan & Terri*—it would be safely encoded to *Karen%2C+Susan+%26+Terri*.

Starting the Loop

The webbot loops through the main section of the code, which requests pages of search results and searches within those pages for the desired site, as shown in Listing 11-2.

```
# Initialize loop
while($url_found==false)
    {
    $page_index++;
    echo "Searching for ranking on page #$page_index\n";
```

Listing 11-2: Starting the main loop

Within the loop, the script removes any HTML special characters from the target to ensure that the values passed to the target web page only include legal characters, as shown in Listing 11-3. In particular, this step replaces &amp with the preferred & character.

```
// Verify that there are no illegal characters in the URLs
$target          = html_entity_decode($target);
$previous_target = html_entity_decode($previous_target);
```

Listing 11-3: Formatting characters to create properly formatted URLs

This particular step should not be confused with URL encoding, because while &amp is a legal character to have in a URL, it will be interpreted as $_GET['amp'] and return invalid results.

Fetching the Search Results

The webbot tries to simulate the action of a person who is manually looking for a website in a set of search results. The webbot uses two techniques to accomplish this trick. The first is the use of a random delay of three to six seconds between fetches, as shown in Listing 11-4.

```
sleep(rand(3, 6));
```

Listing 11-4: Implementing a random delay

Taking this precaution will make it less obvious that a webbot is parsing the search results. This a good practice for all webbots you design.

The second technique simulates a person manually clicking the *Next* button at the bottom of the search result page to see the next page of search results. Our webbot "clicks" on the link by specifying a *referer variable*, which in our case is always the target used in the previous iteration of the loop, as shown in Listing 11-5. On the initial fetch, this value is an empty string.

```
$result = http_get($target, $ref=$previous_target, GET, "", EXCL_HEAD);
$page = $result['FILE'];
```

Listing 11-5: Downloading the next page of search results from the target and specifying a referer variable

The actual contents of the fetch are returned in the FILE element of the returned $result array.

Parsing the Search Results

This webbot uses a parsing technique referred to as an *insertion parse* because it inserts special parsing tags into the fetched web page to facilitate an easy parse (and easy debug). Consider using the insertion parse technique when you need to parse multiple blocks of data that share common separators. The insertion parse is particularly useful when web pages change frequently or when the information you need is buried deep within a complicated HTML table structure. The insertion technique also makes your code much easier to debug, because by viewing where you insert your parsing tags, you can figure out where your parsing script thinks the desired data is.

Think of the text you want to parse as blocks of text surrounded by other blocks of text you don't need. Imagine that the web page you want to parse looks like Figure 11-5, where the desired text is depicted as the dark blocks. Find the beginning of the first block you want to parse. Strip away everything prior to this point and insert a <data> tag at the beginning of this block (Figure 11-6). Replace the text that separates the blocks of text you want to parse with </data> and <data> tags. Now every block of text you want to parse is sandwiched between <data> and </data> tags (see Figure 11-7). This way, the text can be easily parsed with the parse_array() function. The final <data> tag is an artifact and is ignored.

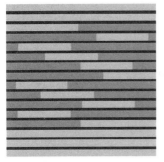

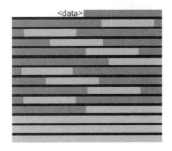

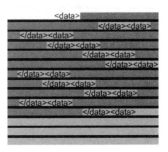

Figure 11-5: Desired data depicted in dark gray

Figure 11-6: Initiating an insertion parse

Figure 11-7: Delimiting desired text with <data> tags

The script that performs the insertion parse is straightforward, but it depends on accurately identifying the text that surrounds the blocks we want to parse. The first step is to locate the text that identifies that start of the first block. The only way to do this is to look at the HTML source code of the search results. A quick examination reveals that the first organic is immediately preceded by <!--@gap;-->.[3] The next step is to find some common text that separates each organic search result. In this case, the search terms are also separated by <!--@gap;-->.

To place the <data> tag at the beginning of the first block, the webbot uses the strops() function to determine where the first block of text begins. That position is then used in conjunction with substr() to strip away everything before the first block. Then a simple string concatenation places a <data> tag in front of the first block, as shown in Listing 11-6.

```
// We need to place the first <data> tag before the first piece
// of desired data, which we know starts with the first occurrence
// of $separator
$separator = "<!--@gap;-->";

// Find first occurrence of $separator
$beg_position = strpos($page, $separator);

// Get rid of everything before the first piece of desired data
// and insert a <data> tag before the data
$page = substr($page, $beg_position, strlen($page));
$page = "<data>".$page;
```

Listing 11-6: Inserting the initial insertion parse tag (as in Figure 11-6)

The insertion parse is completed with the insertion of the </data> and <data> tags. The webbot does this by simply replacing the block separator that we identified earlier with our insertion tags, as shown in Listing 11-7.

---

[3] Comments are common parsing landmarks, especially when web pages are created with an HTML generator like Adobe Dreamweaver.

```
$page = str_replace($separator, "</data> <data>", $page);

// Put all the desired content into an array
$desired_content_array = parse_array($page, "<data>", "</data>", EXCL);
```

Listing 11-7: Inserting the insertion delimiter tags (as in Figure 11-7)

Once the insertion is complete, each block of text is sandwiched between tags that allow the webbot to use the parse_array() function to create an array in which each array element is one of the blocks. Could you perform this parse without the insertion parse technique? Of course. However, the insertion parse is more flexible and easier to debug, because you have more control over where the delimiters are placed, and you can see where the file will be parsed before the parse occurs.

Once the search results are parsed and placed into an array, it's a simple process to compare them with the web page we're ranking, as in Listing 11-8.

```
for($page_rank=0; $page_rank<count($desired_content_array); $page_rank++)
    {
    // Look for the $subject_site to appear in one of the listings
    if(stristr($desired_content_array[$page_rank], $subject_site))
        {
        $url_found_rank_on_page = $page_rank;
        $url_found=true;
        }
    }
```

Listing 11-8: Determining if an organic matches the subject web page

If the web page we're looking for is found, the webbot records its ranking and sets a flag to tell the webbot to stop looking for additional occurrences of the web page in the search results.

If the webbot doesn't find the website in this page, it finds the URL for the next page of search results. This URL is the link that contains the string Next. The webbot finds this URL by placing all the links into an array, as shown in Listing 11-9.

```
// Create an array of links on this page
$search_links = parse_array($result['FILE'], "<a", "</a>", EXCL);
```

Listing 11-9: Parsing the page's links into an array

The webbot then looks at each link until it finds the hyperlink containing the word *Next*. Once found, it sets the referer variable with the current target and uses the new link as the next target. It also inserts a random three-to-six second delay to simulate human interaction, as shown in Listing 11-10.

```
for($xx=0; $xx<count($search_links); $xx++)
    {
    if(strstr($search_links[$xx], "Next"))
        {
        $previous_target = $target;
        $target = get_attribute($search_links[$xx], "href");

        // Remember that this path is relative to the target page, so add
        // protocol and domain
        $target = "http://www.schrenk.com/nostarch/webbots/search/".$target;
        }
    }
```

Listing 11-10: Looking for the URL for the next page of search results

Final Thoughts

Now that you know how to write a webbot that determines search rankings and how to perform an insertion parse, here are a few other things to think about.

Be Kind to Your Sources

Remember that search engines do not make money by displaying search results. The search-ranking webbot is a concept study and not a suggestion for a product that you should develop and place in a *production environment*, where the public uses it. Also—and this is important—you should not violate any search website's Terms of Service agreement when deploying a webbot like this one.

Search Sites May Treat Webbots Differently Than Browsers

Experience has taught me that some search sites serve pages differently if they think they're dealing with an automated web agent. If you leave the default setting for the agent name (in LIB_http) set to *Test Webbot*, your programs will definitely look like webbots instead of browsers.

Spidering Search Engines Is a Bad Idea

It is not a good idea to spider Google or any other search engine. I once heard (at a hacking conference) that Google limits individual IP addresses to 250 page requests a day, but I have not verified this. Others have told me that if you make the page requests too quickly, Google will stop replying after sending three result pages. Again, this is unverified, but it won't be an issue if you obey Google's Terms of Service agreement.

What I *can* verify is that I have, in other circumstances, written spiders for clients where websites *did* limit the number of daily page fetches from a particular IP address to 250. After the 251st fetch within a 24-hour period, the service ignored all subsequent requests coming from that IP address. For one such project, I put a spider on my laptop and ran it in every Wi-Fi–enabled coffee house I could find in South Minneapolis. This tactic involved drinking a lot of coffee, but it also produced a good number of unique IP addresses for my spider, and I was able to complete the job more quickly than if I had run the spider (in a limited capacity) over a period of many days in my office.

Despite Google's best attempts to thwart automated use of its search results, there are rumors indicating that MSN has been spidering Google to collect records for its own search engine.[4]

If you're interested in these issues, you should read Chapter 28, which describes how to respectfully treat your target websites.

Familiarize Yourself with the Google API

If you are interested in pursuing projects that use Google's data, you should investigate the *Google developer API*, a service (or *Application Program Interface*), which makes it easier for developers to use Google in noncommercial applications. At the time of this writing, Google provided information about its developer API at http://www.google.com/apis/index.html.

Further Exploration

Here are some other ways to leverage the techniques you learned in this chapter.

- Design another search-ranking webbot to examine the paid advertising listings instead of the organic listings.

- Write a similar webbot to run daily over a period of many days to measure how changing a web page's meta tags or content affects the page's search engine ranking.

- Design a webbot that examines web page rankings using a variety of search terms.

- Use the techniques explained in this chapter to examine how search rankings differ from search engine to search engine.

---

[4] Jason Dowdell, "Microsoft Crawling Google Results For New Search Engine?" November 11, 2004, WebProNews (http://www.webpronews.com/insiderreports/searchinsider/wpn-49-20041111MicrosoftCrawlingGoogleResultsForNewSearchEngine.html).

12

AGGREGATION WEBBOTS

If you've ever researched topics online, you've no doubt found the need to open multiple web browsers, each loaded with a different resource. The practice of viewing more than one web page at once has become so common that all major browsers now support tabs that allow surfers to easily view multiple websites at once. Another approach to simultaneously viewing more than one website is to consolidate information with an aggregation webbot.

People are doing some pretty cool things with aggregation scripts these days. To whet your appetite for what's possible with an aggregation webbot, look at the web page found at http://www.housingmaps.com. This bot combines real estate listings from http://www.craigslist.org with Google Maps. The results are maps that plot the locations and descriptions of homes for sale, as shown in Figure 12-1.

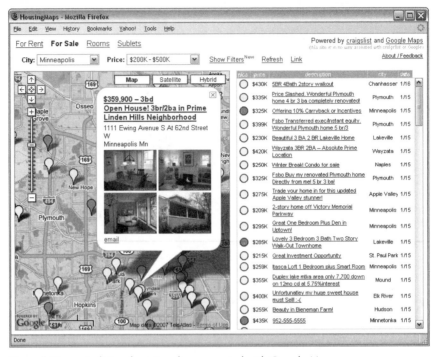

Figure 12-1: craigslist real estate ads aggregated with Google Maps

Choosing Data Sources for Webbots

Aggregation webbots can use data from a variety of places; however, some data sources are better than others. For example, your webbots can parse information directly from web pages, as you did in Chapter 7, but this should never be your first choice. Since web page content is intermixed with page formatting and web pages are frequently updated, this method is prone to error. When available, a developer should always use a non-HTML version of the data, as the creators of HousingMaps did. The data shown in Figure 12-1 came from Google Maps' Application Program Interface (API)[1] and craigslist's Real Simple Syndication (RSS) feed.

Application Program Interfaces provide access to specific applications, like Google Maps, eBay, or Amazon.com. Since APIs are developed for specific applications, the features from one API will not work in another. Working with APIs tends to be complex and often has a steep learning curve. Their complexity, however, is mitigated by the vast array of services they provide. The details of using Google's API (or any other API for that matter) are outside of the scope of this book.

In contrast to APIs, RSS provides a standardized way to access data from a variety of sources, like craigslist. RSS feeds are simple to parse and are an ideal protocol for webbot developers because, unlike unparsed web pages or site-specific APIs, RSS feeds conform to a consistent protocol. This chapter's example project explores RSS in detail.

---

[1] See http://www.google.com/apis/maps.

Example Aggregation Webbot

The webbot described in this chapter combines news from multiple sources. While the scripts in this chapter only display the data, I'll conclude with suggestions for extending this project into a webbot that makes decisions and takes action based on the information it finds.

Familiarizing Yourself with RSS Feeds

While your webbot could aggregate information from any online source, this example will combine news feeds in the RSS format. *RSS* is a standard for making online content available for a variety of uses. Originally developed by Netscape in 1997, RSS quickly became a popular means to distribute news and other online content, including blogs. After AOL and Sun Microsystems divided up Netscape, the RSS Advisory Board took ownership of the RSS specification.[2]

Today, nearly every news service provides information in the form of RSS. RSS *feeds* are actually web pages that package online content in eXtensible Markup Language (XML) format. Unlike HTML, *XML* typically lacks formatting information and surrounds data with tags that make parsing very easy. Generally, RSS feeds provide links to web pages and just enough information to let you know whether a link is worth clicking, though feeds can also include complete articles.

The first part of an RSS feed contains a header that describes the RSS data to follow, as shown in Listing 12-1.

```
<title>
    RSS feed title
</title>
<link>
    www.Link_to_web_page.com
</link>
<description>
    Description of RSS feed
</description>
<copyright>
    Copyright notice
</copyright>
<lastBuildDate>
    Date of RSS publication
</lastBuildDate>
```

Listing 12-1: The RSS feed header describes the content to follow

Not all RSS feeds start with the same set of tags, but Listing 12-1 is representative of the tags you're likely to find on most feeds. In addition to the tags shown, you may also find tags that specify the language used or define the locations of associated images.

---

[2] See http://www.rssboard.org.

Following the header is a collection of items that contains the content of the RSS feed, as shown in Listing 12-2.

```
<item>
    <title>
        Title of item
    </title>
    <link>
        URL of associated web page for item
    </link>
    <description>
        Description of item
    </description>
    <pubDate>
        Publication date of item
    </pubDate>
</item>
<item>
    Other items may follow, defined as above
</item>
```

Listing 12-2: Example of RSS item descriptions

Depending on the source, RSS feeds may also use industry-specific XML tags to describe item contents. The tags shown in Listing 12-2, however, are representative of what you should find in most RSS data.

Our project webbot takes three RSS feeds and consolidates them on a single web page, as shown in Figure 12-2.

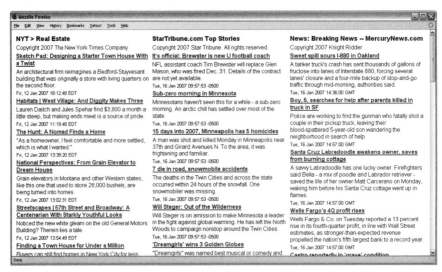

Figure 12-2: The aggregation webbot

The webbot shown in Figure 12-2 summarizes news from three sources. It always shows current information because the webbot requests the current news from each source every time the web page is downloaded.

Writing the Aggregation Webbot

This webbot uses two scripts. The main script, shown in Listing 12-3, defines which RSS feeds to fetch and how to display them. Both scripts are available at this book's website. The PHP sections of this script appear in bold.

```
<?
# Include libraries
include("LIB_http.php");
include("LIB_parse.php");
include("LIB_rss.php");
?>
<head>
  <style> BODY {font-family:arial; color: black;} </style>
</head>
<table>
  <tr>
    <td valign="top" width="33%">
        <?
        $target = "http://www.nytimes.com/services/xml/rss/nyt/RealEstate.xml";
        $rss_array = download_parse_rss($target);
        display_rss_array($rss_array);
        ?>
    </td>
    <td valign="top" width="33%">
        <?
        $target = "http://www.startribune.com/rss/1557.xml";
        $rss_array = download_parse_rss($target);
        display_rss_array($rss_array);
        ?>
    </td>
    <td valign="top" width="33%">
        <?
        $target = "http://www.mercurynews.com/mld/mercurynews/news/breaking_news/rss.xml";
        $rss_array = download_parse_rss($target);
        display_rss_array($rss_array);
        ?>
    </td>
  </tr>
</table>
```

Listing 12-3: Main aggregation webbot script, describing RSS sources and display format

As you can tell from the script in Listing 12-3, most of the work is done in the LIB_rss library, which we will explore next.

Downloading and Parsing the Target

As the name implies, the function download_parse_rss() downloads the target RSS feed and parses the results into an array for later processing, as shown in Listing 12-4.

```
function download_parse_rss($target)
    {
    # Download the RSS page
    $news = http_get($target, "");

    # Parse title and copyright notice
    $rss_array['TITLE'] = return_between($news['FILE'],
                            "<title>", "</title>", EXCL);
    $rss_array['COPYRIGHT'] = return_between($news['FILE'],
                            "<copyright>", "</copyright>", EXCL);

    # Parse the items
    $item_array = parse_array($news['FILE'], "<item>", "</item>");
    for($xx=0; $xx<count($item_array); $xx++)
        {
        $rss_array['ITITLE'][$xx] = return_between($item_array[$xx],
                            "<title>", "</title>", EXCL);
        $rss_array['ILINK'][$xx] = return_between($item_array[$xx],
                            "<link>", "</link>", EXCL);
        $rss_array['IDESCRIPTION'][$xx] = return_between($item_array[$xx],
                            "<description>", "</description>", EXCL);
        $rss_array['IPUBDATE'][$xx] = return_between($item_array[$xx],
                            "<pubDate>", "</pubDate>", EXCL);
        }

    return $rss_array;
    }
```

Listing 12-4: Downloading the RSS feed and parsing data into an array

In addition to using the http_get() function in the LIB_http library, this script also employs the return_between() and parse_array() functions to ease the task of parsing the RSS data from the XML tags.

After downloading and parsing the RSS feed, the data is formatted and displayed with the function in Listing 12-5. (PHP script appears in bold.)

```
function display_rss_array($rss_array)
    {?>
    <table border="0">
        <!-- Display the article title and copyright notice -->
        <tr>
            <td>
                <font size="+1">
                    <b><?echo strip_cdata_tags($rss_array['TITLE'])?></b>
                </font>
            </td>
        </tr>
```

```
<tr><td><?echo strip_cdata_tags($rss_array['COPYRIGHT'])?></td></tr>

<!-- Display the article descriptions and links -->
<?for($xx=0; $xx<count($rss_array['ITITLE']); $xx++)
    {?>
    <tr>
        <td>
            <a href="<?echo strip_cdata_tags($rss_array['ILINK'][$xx])?>">
                <b><?echo strip_cdata_tags($rss_array['ITITLE'][$xx])?></b>
            </a>
        </td>
    </tr>
    <tr>
        <td><?echo strip_cdata_tags($rss_array['IDESCRIPTION'][$xx])?></td>
    </tr>
    <tr>
        <td>
            <font size="-1">
                <?echo strip_cdata_tags($rss_array['IPUBDATE'][$xx])?>
            </font>
        </td>
    </tr>
    <?}?>
    </table>
<?}?>
```

Listing 12-5: Displaying the contents of $rss_array

Dealing with CDATA

It's worth noting that the function strip_cdata_tags() is used to remove
CDATA tags from the RSS data feed. XML uses *CDATA tags* to identify text
that may contain characters or combinations of characters that could confuse parsers. CDATA tells parsers that the data encased in CDATA tags should
not be interpreted as XML tags. Listing 12-6 shows the format for using
CDATA.

```
<![[   ...text goes here...   ]]>
```

Listing 12-6: format

Since parsers ignore all , the script needs to strip off the tags to make the
data displayable in a browser.

Adding Filtering to Your Aggregation Webbot

Your webbots can also modify or filter data received from RSS (or any other
source). In this chapter's news aggregator, you could filter (i.e., not use) any
stories that don't contain specific keywords or key phrases. For example, if
you only want news stories that contain the words *webbots*, *web spiders*, and
spiders, you could create a filter array like the one shown in Listing 12-7.

```
$filter_array[]="webbots";
$filter_array[]="web spiders";
$filter_array[]="spiders";
```

Listing 12-7: Creating a filter array

We can use $filter_array to select articles for viewing by modifying the download_parse_rss() function used in Listing 12-4. This modification is shown in Listing 12-8.

```
function download_parse_rss($target, $filter_array)
    {
    # Download the RSS page
    $news = http_get($target, "");

    # Parse title and copyright notice
    $rss_array['TITLE'] = return_between($news['FILE'],
                    "<title>", "</title>", EXCL);
    $rss_array['COPYRIGHT'] = return_between($news['FILE'],
                    "<copyright>", "</copyright>", EXCL);

    # Parse the items
    $item_array = parse_array($news['FILE'], "<item>", "</item>");
    for($xx=0; $xx<count($item_array); $xx++)
        {
        # Filter stories for relevance
        for($keyword=0; $keyword<count($filter_array); $keyword ++)
            {
            if(stristr($item_array[$xx], $filter_array[$keyword]))
                {
                $rss_array['ITITLE'][$xx] = return_between($item_array[$xx],
                        "<title>", "</title>", EXCL);
                $rss_array['ILINK'][$xx] = return_between($item_array[$xx],
                        "<link>", "</link>", EXCL);
                $rss_array['IDESCRIPTION'][$xx] = return_between($item_array[$xx],
                        "<description>", "</description>", EXCL);
                $rss_array['IPUBDATE'][$xx] = return_between($item_array[$xx],
                        "<pubDate>", "</pubDate>", EXCL);
                }
            }
        }
    return $rss_array;
    }
```

Listing 12-8: Adding filtering to the download_parse_rss() function

Listing 12-8 is identical to Listing 12-4, with the following exceptions:

- The filter array is passed to download_parse_rss()
- Each news story is compared to every keyword
- Only stories that contain a keyword are parsed and placed into $rss_array

The end result of the script in Listing 12-8 is an aggregator that only lists stories that contain material with the keywords in $filter_array. As configured, the comparison of stories and keywords is not case sensitive. If case sensitivity is required, simply replace stristr() with strstr(). Remember, however, that the amount of data returned is directly tied to the number of keywords and the frequency with which they appear in stories.

Further Exploration

The true power of webbots is that they can make decisions and take action with the information they find online. Here are a few suggestions for extending what you've learned to do with RSS or other data you choose to aggregate with your webbots.

- Modify the script in Listing 12-8 to accept stories that don't contain a keyword.
- Write an aggregation webbot that doesn't display information unless it finds it on two or more sources.
- Design a webbot that looks for specific keywords in news stories and sends an email notification when those keywords appear.
- Search blogs for spelling errors.
- Find an RSS feed that posts scores from your favorite sports team. Parse and store the scores in a database for later statistical analysis.
- Write a webbot that uses news stories to help you decided whether to buy or sell commodities futures.
- Devise an online clipping service that archives information about your company.
- Create an RSS feed for the example store used in Chapter 7.

13

FTP WEBBOTS

File transfer protocol (FTP) is among the oldest Internet protocols.[1] It dates from the Internet's predecessor *ARPANET*, which was originally funded by the Eisenhower administration.[2] Research centers started using FTP to exchange large files in the early 1970s, and FTP became the de facto transport protocol for email, a status it maintained until the early 1990s. Today, system administrators most commonly use FTP to allow web developers to upload and maintain files on remote webservers. Though it's an older protocol, FTP still allows computers with dissimilar technologies to share files, independent of file structure and operating system.

---

[1] The original document defining FTP can be viewed at http://www.w3.org/Protocols/rfc959.

[2] Katie Hafner and Matthew Lyon, *Where Wizards Stay Up Late: The Origins of the Internet* (New York: Simon & Schuster, 1996), 14.

Example FTP Webbot

To gain an insight for uses of an FTP-capable webbot, consider this scenario. A national retailer needs to move large sales reports from each of its stores to a centralized corporate webserver. This particular retail chain was built through acquisition, so it uses multiple protocols and proprietary computer systems. The one thing all of these systems have in common is access to an FTP server. The goal for this project is to use FTP protocols to download store sales reports and move them to the corporate server.

The script for this example project is available for study at this book's website. Just remember that the script satisfies a ficticious scenario and will not run unless you change the configuration. In this chapter, I have split it up and annotated the sections for clarity. Listing 13-1 shows the initialization for the FTP servers.

```
<?
// Define the source FTP server, file location, and authentication values
define("REMOTE_FTP_SERVER", "remote_FTP_address");  // Domain name or IP address
define("REMOTE_USERNAME", "yourUserName");
define("REMOTE_PASSWORD", "yourPassword");
define("REMOTE_DIRCTORY", "daily_sales");
define("REMOTE_FILE", "sales.txt");

// Define the corporate FTP server, file location, and authentication values
define("CORP_FTP_SERVER", "corp_FTP_address");
define("CORP_USERNAME", "yourUserName");
define("CORP_PASSWORD", "yourPassword");
define("CORP_DIRCTORY", "sales_reports");
define("CORP_FILE", "store_03_".date("Y-M-d"));
```

Listing 13-1: Initializing the FTP bot

This program also configures a routine to send a short email notification when commands fail. Automated email error notification allows the script to run autonomously without requiring that someone verify the operation manually.[3] Listing 13-2 shows the email configuration script.

```
include("LIB_MAIL.php");
$mail_addr['to'] = "admin@somedomain.com";
$mail_addr['from'] = "admin@somedomain.com";
function report_error_and_quit($error_message, $server_connection)
    {
    global $mail_addr;

    // Send error message
    echo "$error_message, $server_connection";
    formatted_mail($error_message, $error_message, $mail_addr, "text/plain");
```

---

[3] See Chapter 23 for information on how to make webbots run periodically.

```
    // Attempt to log off the server gracefully if possible
    ftp_close($server_connection);

    // It is not traditional to end a function this way, but since there is
    // nothing to return or do, it is best to exit
    exit();
    }
```

Listing 13-2: Email configuration

The next step is to make a connection to the remote FTP server. After making the connection, the script authenticates itself with its username and password, as shown in Listing 13-3.

```
// Negotiate a socket connection to the remote FTP server
$remote_connection_id = ftp_connect(REMOTE_FTP_SERVER);

// Log in (authenticate) the source server
if(!ftp_login($remote_connection_id, REMOTE_USERNAME, REMOTE_PASSWORD))
    report_error_and_quit("Remote ftp_login failed", $remote_connection_id);
```

Listing 13-3: Connecting and authenticating with the remote server

Once authenticated by the server, the script moves to the target file's directory and downloads the file to the local filesystem. After downloading the file, the script closes the connection to the remote server, as shown in Listing 13-4.

```
// Move the directory of the source file
if(!ftp_chdir($remote_connection_id, REMOTE_DIRCTORY))
    report_error_and_quit("Remote ftp_chdir failed", $remote_connection_id);

// Download the file
if(!ftp_get($remote_connection_id, "temp_file", REMOTE_FILE, FTP_ASCII))
    report_error_and_quit("Remote ftp_get failed", $remote_connection_id);

// Close connections to the remote FTP server
ftp_close($remote_connection_id);
```

Listing 13-4: Downloading the file and closing the connection

The final task, shown in Listing 13-5, uploads the file to the corporate server using techniques similar to the ones used to download the file.

```
// Negotiate a socket connection to the corporate FTP server
$corp_connection_id = ftp_connect(CORP_FTP_SERVER);

// Log in to the corporate server
if(!ftp_login($corp_connection_id, CORP_USERNAME, CORP_PASSWORD))
    report_error_and_quit("Corporate ftp_login failed", $corp_connection_id);
```

```
// Move the destination directory
if(!ftp_chdir($corp_connection_id, CORP_DIRECTORY))
    report_error_and_quit("Corporate ftp_chdir failed", $corp_connection_id);

// Upload the file
if(!ftp_put($corp_connection_id, CORP_FILE, "temp_file", FTP_ASCII))
    report_error_and_quit("Corporate ftp_put failed", $corp_connection_id);

// Close connections to the corporate FTP server
ftp_close($corp_connection_id);

// Send notification that the webbot ran successfully
formatted_mail("ftpbot ran successfully at ".time("M d,Y h:s"), "",
$mail_addr, $content_type);
?>
```

Listing 13-5: Logging in and uploading the previously downloaded file to the corporate server

PHP and FTP

PHP provides built-in functions that closely resemble standard FTP commands. In addition to transferring files, PHP allows your scripts to perform many administrative functions. Table 13-1 lists the most useful FTP commands supported by PHP.

Table 13-1: Common FTP Commands Supported by PHP

FTP Function (Where $ftp Is the FTP File Stream)	Usage
ftp_cdup($ftp);	Makes the parent directory the current directory
ftp_chdir ($ftp, "directory/path")	Changes the current directory
ftp_delete ($ftp, "file_name")	Deletes a file
ftp_get ($ftp, "local file", "remote file", MODE)	Copies the remote file to the local file where MODE indicates if the remote file is FTP_ASCII or FTP_BINARY
ftp_mkdir($ftp, "directory name")	Creates a new directory
ftp_rename($ftp, "file name")	Renames a file or a directory on the FTP server
ftp_put ($ftp, "remote file", "local file", MODE)	Copies the local file to the remote file where MODE indicates if the local file is FTP_ASCII or FTP_BINARY
ftp_rmdir($ftp, "directory/path")	Removes a directory
ftp_rawlist($ftp, "directory/path")	Returns an array with each array element containing directory information about a file

As shown in Table 13-1, the PHP FTP commands allow you to write webbots that create, delete, and rename directories and files. You may also use PHP/CURL to perform advanced FTP tasks requiring advanced authentication or encryption. Since FTP seldom uses these features, they are out of the scope of this book, but they're available for you to explore on the official PHP website available at http://www.php.net.

Further Exploration

Since FTP is often the only application-level protocol that computer systems share, it is a convenient communication bridge between new and old computer systems. Moreover, in addition to using FTP as a common path between disparate—or obsolete—systems, FTP is still the most common method for uploading files to websites. With the information in this chapter, you should be able to write webbots that update websites with information found at a variety of sources. Here are some ideas to get you started.

- Write a webbot that updates your corporate server with information gathered from sales reports.
- Develop a security webbot that uses a webcam to take pictures of your warehouse or parking lot, timestamps the images, and uploads the pictures to an archival server.
- Design a webbot that creates archives of your company's internal forums on an FTP server.
- Create a webbot that photographically logs the progress of a construction site and uploads these pictures to an FTP server. Once construction is complete, compile the individual photos into an animation showing the construction process.

If you don't have access to an FTP server on the Internet, you can still experiment with FTP bots. An FTP server is probably already on your computer if your operating system is Unix, Linux, or Mac OS X. If you have a Windows computer, you can find free FTP servers on many shareware sites. Once you locate FTP server software, you can set up your own local server by following the instructions accompanying your FTP installation.

14

NNTP NEWS WEBBOTS

Another non-web protocol your webbots can use is the *Network News Transfer Protocol (NTTP)*. Before modern applications like MySpace, Facebook, and topic-specific web forums, NNTP was used to build online communities where people with common interests exchanged information in newsgroups. Members of newsgroups contribute articles—announcements, questions, or answers relating to one of thousands of subject-specific topics. Collectively, these articles are referred to as *news*. While NNTP is an older Internet protocol, it is still in wide use today, and it provides a valuable source of information for certain webbot projects. I've recently found NNTP useful when working on projects for private investigators, the hospitality industry, and financial institutions.

NNTP Use and History

NNTP originated in 1986[1] and was designed for a network much different from the one we use today. When NNTP was conceived, broadband and always-on access to networks were virtually unheard of. To utilize the network as it existed, NNTP employed a non-centralized server configuration, similar to what email uses. Users logged in to one of the many news servers on the network where they read articles, posted new articles, and replied to old ones. Behind the scenes, NNTP servers periodically synchronized to distribute updated news to all servers hosting specific newsgroups. Today, NNTP servers exchange news so frequently that newly submitted articles appear on news servers across the world almost immediately. In 1986, however, news servers often waited until the early morning hours to synchronize, when phone (modem) calls to the network were cheapest. If the newsgroup process seems odd by today's standards, remember that NNTP was optimized for use when networks were slower and more expensive.

While HTTP has superseded many older protocols (like Gopher[2]), newsgroups have survived and are still widely used today. Most modern communication applications like Microsoft Outlook and Mozilla Thunderbird include news clients in their basic configurations (see Figure 14-1).

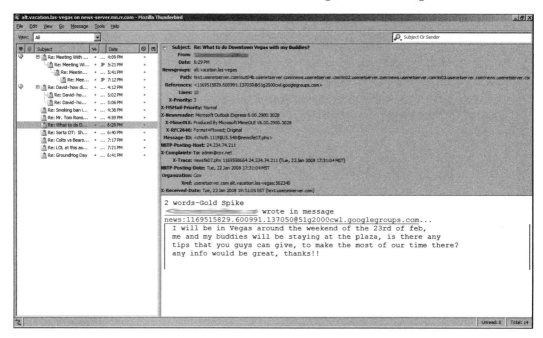

Figure 14-1: A newsgroup as viewed in Mozilla Thunderbird, a typical news reader

---

[1] RFC 977 defines the original NNTP specification (http://www.ietf.org/rfc/rfc977.txt).

[2] Gopher was a predecessor to the World Wide Web, developed at the University of Minnesota (http://www.ietf.org/rfc/rfc1436.txt).

While the number of active newsgroups is declining, there are still tens of thousands of newsgroups in use today. The news server I use (hosted by RoadRunner) subscribes to 26,365 newsgroups. Since the variety of topics covered by newsgroups is so diverse (ranging from `alt.alien.visitors` to `alt.www.software.spiders.programming`), you're apt to find one that interests you. Newsgroups are a fun source of homegrown information; however, like many sources on the Internet, you need to take what you read with a grain of salt. Newsgroups allow anyone to make anonymous contributions, and themes like conspiracy, spam, and self-promotion all thrive under those conditions.

Webbots and Newsgroups

Newsgroups are a rich source of content for webbot developers. While less convenient than websites, news servers are not hard to access, especially when you have a set of functions that do most for the work for you. All of this chapter's example scripts use the `LIB_nntp` library. Functions in this library provide easy access to articles on news servers and create many opportunities for webbots. `LIB_nntp` contains functions that list newsgroups hosted by specific news servers, list available articles within newsgroups, and download particular articles. As with all libraries used in this book, the latest version of `LIB_nntp` is available for download at the book's website.

Identifying News Servers

Before you use NNTP, you'll need to find an accessible news server. A Google search for *free news servers* will provide links to some, but keep in mind that not all news servers are equal. Since few news servers host all newsgroups, not every news server will have the group you're looking for. Many free news servers also limit the number of requests you can make in a day or suffer from poor performance. For these reasons, many people prefer to pay for access to reliable news servers. You might already have access to a premium news server through your ISP. Be warned, however, that some ISPs' news servers (like those hosted by RoadRunner and EarthLink) will not allow access if you are not directly connected to a subnet in their network.

Identifying Newsgroups

Your news bots should always verify that the group you want to access is hosted by your news server. The script in Listing 14-1 uses `get_nntp_groups()` to create an array containing all the newsgroups on a particular news server. (Remember to put the name of your news server in place of *your.news.server* below.) Putting the newsgroups in an array is handy, since it allows a webbot to examine groups iteratively.

```
include("LIB_nntp.php");
$server = "your.news.server";
$group_array= get_nntp_groups($server);
var_dump($group_array);
```

Listing 14-1: Requesting (and viewing) the newsgroups available on a news server

The result of executing Listing 14-1 is shown in Figure 14-2.

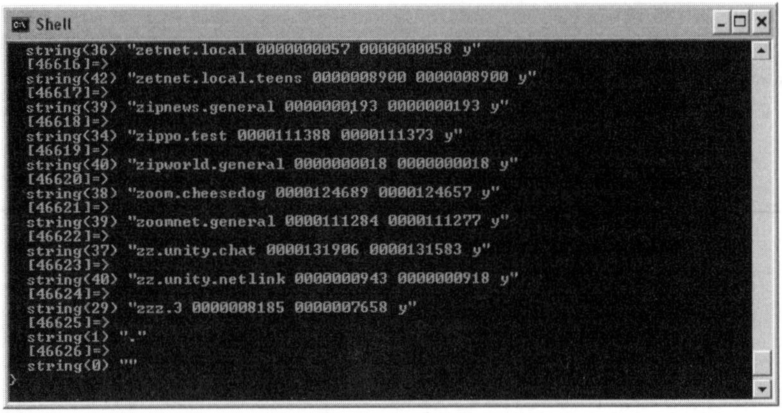

Figure 14-2: Newsgroups hosted on a news server

Notice that Figure 14-2 only shows the newsgroups that hadn't already scrolled off the screen. In this example, my news server returned 46,626 groups. (It also required 40 seconds to download them all, so expect a short delay when requesting large amounts of data.) For each group, the server responds with the name of the group, the identifier of the first article, the identifier of the last article, and a y if you can post articles to this group or an n if posting articles to this group (on this server) is prohibited.

News servers terminate messages by sending a line that contains just a period (.), which you can see in the last array element in Figure 14-2. That lone period is the only sign your webbot will receive to tell it to stop looking for data. If your webbot reads buffers incorrectly, it will either hang indefinitely or return with incomplete data. The small function shown in Listing 14-2 (found in LIB_nntp) correctly reads data from an open NNTP network socket and recognizes the end-of-message indicator.

```
function read_nntp_buffer($socket)
    {
    $this_line ="";
    $buffer ="";
      while($this_line!=".\r\n")              // Read until lone . found on line
          {
          $this_line = fgets($socket); // Read line from socket
          $buffer = $buffer . $this_line;
```

```
        }
    return $buffer;
    }
```

Listing 14-2: Reading NNTP data and identifying the end of messages

The script in Listing 14-1 uses the function get_nntp_groups() to get an array of available groups hosted by your news server. The script for that function is shown below in Listing 14-3.

```
function get_nntp_groups($server)
    {
    # Open socket connection to the mail server
    $fp = fsockopen($server, $port="119", $errno, $errstr, 30);
    if (!$fp)
        {
        # If socket error, issue error
        $return_array['ERROR'] = "ERROR: $errstr ($errno)";
        }
    else
        {
        # Else tell server to return a list of hosted newsgroups
        $out = "LIST\r\n";
        fputs($fp, $out);
        $groups = read_nntp_buffer($fp);
        $groups_array = explode("\r\n", $groups); // Convert to an array
        }
    fputs($fp, "QUIT \r\n");                      // Log out
    fclose($fp);                                  // Close socket
    return $groups_array;
    }
```

Listing 14-3: A function that finds available newsgroups on a news server

As you'll learn, all NNTP commands follow a structure similar to the one used in Listing 14-3. Most NNTP commands require that you do the following:

1.   Connect to the server (on port 119)
2.   Issue a command, like LIST (followed by a carriage return/line feed)
3.   Read the results (until encountering a line with a lone perioid)
4.   End the session with a QUIT command
5.   Close the network socket

Other NNTP commands that identify groups hosted by news servers are listed in RFC 997. You can use the basic structure of get_nntp_groups() as a guide to creating other functions that execute NNTP commands found in RFC 997.

Finding Articles in Newsgroups

As you read earlier, newsgroup articles are distributed among each of the news servers hosting a particular newsgroup and are physically located at each server hosting the newsgroup. Each article has a sequential numeric identifier that identifies the article on a particular news server. You may request the range of numeric identifiers for articles (for a given a newsgroup) with a script similar to the one in Listing 14-4.

```
include("LIB_nntp.php");
# Request article IDs
$server = "your.news.server";
$newsgroup = "alt.vacation.las-vegas";
$ids_array = get_nntp_article_ids($server, $newsgroup);

# Report Results
echo "\nInfo about articles in $newsgroup on $server\n";
echo "Code: ".                   $ids_array['RESPONSE_CODE']."\n";
echo "Estimated # of articles: ". $ids_array['EST_QTY_ARTICLES']."\n";
echo "First article ID: ".       $ids_array['FIRST_ARTICLE']."\n";
echo "Last article ID: ".        $ids_array['LAST_ARTICLE']."\n";
```

Listing 14-4: Requesting article IDs from a news server

The result of running the script in Listing 14-4 is shown in Figure 14-3.

Figure 14-3: Executing get_nntp_article_ids() and displaying the results

This function returns data in an array, with elements containing a status code,[3] the estimated quantity of articles for that group on the server, the identifier of the first article in the newsgroup, and the identifier of the last article in the newsgroup. An estimate of the number of articles is provided because some articles are deleted after submission, so not every article within the given range is actually available. It's also worth noting that each server will have its own rules for when articles become obsolete, so each server will

---

[3] There is a full list of NNTP status codes in Appendix B.

have a different number of articles for any one newsgroup. The code that actually reads the article identifiers from the server is shown in Listing 14-5.

```php
function get_nntp_article_ids($server, $newsgroup)
    {
    # Open socket connection to the mail server
    $socket = fsockopen($server, $port="119", $errno, $errstr, 30);
    if (!$socket)
        {
        # If socket error, issue error
        $return_array['ERROR'] = "ERROR: $errstr ($errno)";
        }
    else
        {
        # Else tell server which group to connect to
        fputs($socket, "GROUP ".$newsgroup." \r\n");
        $return_array['GROUP_MESSAGE']    = trim(fread($socket, 2000));

        # Get the range of available articles for this group
        fputs($socket, "NEXT \r\n");
        $res = fread($socket, 2000);
        $array = explode(" ", $res);

        $return_array['RESPONSE_CODE']     = $array[0];
        $return_array['EST_QTY_ARTICLES']  = $array[1];
        $return_array['FIRST_ARTICLE']     = $array[2];
        $return_array['LAST_ARTICLE']      = $array[3];
        }
    fputs($socket, "QUIT \r\n");
    fclose($socket);
    return $return_array;
    }
```

Listing 14-5: The function get_nntp_article_ids()

Reading an Article from a Newsgroup

Once you know the range of valid article identifiers for your newsgroup (on your news sever), you can request an individual article. For example, the script in Listing 14-6 reads article number 562340 from the group alt.vacation.las-vegas.

```php
include("LIB_nntp.php");
$server = "your.news.server";
$newsgroup = "alt.vacation.las-vegas";
$article   = read_nntp_article($server, $newsgroup, $article=562340);
echo $article['HEAD'];
echo $article['ARTICLE'];
```

Listing 14-6: Reading and displaying an article from a news server

When you execute the code in Listing 14-6, you'll see a screen similar to the one in Figure 14-4. On my news server, article 562340 is the same article displayed in the screenshot of the Thunderbird news reader, shown earlier in Figure 14-1.[4]

```
Shell                                                                    _ □ ×
C:\>php LISTING_14_6.php
HEADER:
201 free-text.usenetserver.com -- http://www.usenetserver.com/ (Tornado v1.0.6)
211 48227 514121 562347 alt.vacation.las-vegas
221 562340 <cNxth.1119$1U5.548@newsfe07.phx>
Path: text.usenetserver.com!out04b.usenetserver.com!news.usenetserver.com!in02.u
senetserver.com!news.usenetserver.com!in03.usenetserver.com!news.usenetserver.co
m!hwmnpeer01.phx!news.highwinds-media.com!hw-filter.phx!newsfe07.phx.POSTED!53ab
2750!not-for-mail
From:
Newsgroups: alt.vacation.las-vegas
References: <1169515829.600991.137050@51g2000cwl.googlegroups.com>
Subject: Re: What to do Downtown Vegas with my Buddies?
Lines: 10
X-Priority: 3
X-MSMail-Priority: Normal
X-Newsreader: Microsoft Outlook Express 6.00.2900.3028
X-MimeOLE: Produced By Microsoft MimeOLE V6.00.2900.3028
X-RFC2646: Format=Flowed; Original
Message-ID: <cNxth.1119$1U5.548@newsfe07.phx>
Date: Tue, 22 Jan 2008 16:29:29 -0800
NNTP-Posting-Host: 24.234.74.211
X-Complaints-To: admin@cox.net
X-Trace: newsfe07.phx 1169598664 24.234.74.211 (Tue, 22 Jan 2008 17:31:04 MST)
NNTP-Posting-Date: Tue, 22 Jan 2008 17:31:04 MST
Organization: Cox
Xref: usenetserver.com alt.vacation.las-vegas:562340
X-Received-Date: Tue, 22 Jan 2008 19:31:05 EST (text.usenetserver.com)

ARTICLE:
222 562340 <cNxth.1119$1U5.548@newsfe07.phx>

2 words-Gold Spike
                        wrote in message
news:1169515829.600991.137050@51g2000cwl.googlegroups.com...
>I will be in Vegas around the weekend of the 23rd of feb.
> me and my buddies will be staying at the plaza. is there any
> tips that you guys can give. to make the most of our time there?
> any info would be great. thanks!!
>

C:\>
```

Figure 14-4: Reading a newsgroup article

The first part of Figure 14-4 shows the *NTTP header*, which, like a mail or HTTP header, returns status information about the article. Following the header is the article. Notice that in the header and at the beginning of the article, it is also referred to as <cNxth.1119$1U5.548@newsfe07.phx>. Unlike the server-dependent identifier used in the previous function call, this longer identifier is universal and references this article on any news server that hosts this newsgroup.

The function called to read the news article is shown in Listing 14-7.

```
function read_nntp_article($server, $newsgroup, $article)
    {
    # Open socket connection to the mail server
    $socket = fsockopen($server, $port="119", $errno, $errstr, 30);

    if (!$socket)
        {
        # If socket error, issue error
        $return_array['ERROR'] = "ERROR: $errstr ($errno)";
        }
```

---

[4] Remember that article IDs are unique to newsgroups on each specific news server. Your article IDs are apt to be different.

```
else
    {
    # Else tell server which group to connect to
    fputs($socket, "GROUP ".$newsgroup." \r\n");

    # Request this article's HEAD
    fputs($socket, "HEAD $article \r\n");
    $return_array['HEAD'] = read_nntp_buffer($socket);

    # Request the article
    fputs($socket, "BODY $article \r\n");
    $return_array['ARTICLE'] = read_nntp_buffer($socket);
    }
fputs($socket, "QUIT \r\n");          // Sign out (newsgroup server)
fclose($socket);                      // Close socket
return $return_array;                 // Return data array
}
```

Listing 14-7: A function that reads a newsgroup article

As mentioned earlier, NNTP was designed for use on older (slower) networks. For this reason, the article headers are available separately from the actual articles. This allowed news readers to download article headers first, to show users which articles were available on their news servers. If an article interested the viewer, that article alone was downloaded, consuming minimum bandwidth.

Further Exploration

Now that you know how to use webbots to interface with newsgroups, here is a list of ideas you can use to develop news bots for your own purposes.

- Develop a newsgroup clipping service. This service could monitor numerous newsgroups for mention of specific keywords and either aggregate that information in a database or send email alerts when a keyword appears in a newsgroup.
- Build a web-based newsgroup portal, similar to http://groups.google.com.
- Create a webbot that gathers weather forecasts for Las Vegas from the National Weather Service website, and post this weather information for vacationers on alt.vacation.las-vegas.[5]
- Monitor newsgroups for unauthorized use of intellectual property.
- Create a database that archives a newsgroup.
- Write a web-based newsgroup client that allows users to read newsgroups anonymously.

---

[5] Due to the ridiculous amounts of spam on newsgroups, scripts for posting articles on newsgroups were deliberately omitted from this chapter. However, between the scripts used as examples in this chapter and the original NNTP RFC, you should be able to figure out how to post articles to newsgroups on your own.

15

WEBBOTS THAT READ EMAIL

When a webbot can read email, it's easier for it to communicate with the outside world.[1] Webbots capable of reading email can take instruction via email commands, share data with handheld devices like BlackBerries and Palm PDAs, and filter messages for content.

For example, if package-tracking information is sent to an email account that a webbot can access, the webbot can parse incoming email from the carrier to track delivery status. Such a webbot could also send email warnings when shipments are late, communicate shipping charges to your corporate accounting software, or create reports that analyze a company's use of overnight shipping.

---

[1] See Chapter 16 to learn how to send email with webbots and spiders.

The POP3 Protocol

Of the many protocols for reading email from mail servers, I selected *Post Office Protocol 3 (POP3)* for this task because of its simplicity and near-universal support among mail servers. POP3 instructions are also easy to perform in any Telnet or standard TCP/IP terminal program.[2] The ability to use Telnet to execute POP3 commands will provide an understanding of POP3 commands, which we will later convert into PHP routines that any webbot may execute.

Logging into a POP3 Mail Server

Listing 15-1 shows how to connect to a POP3 mail server though a Telnet client. Simply enter **telnet**, followed by the mail server name and the port number (which is always 110 for POP3). The mail server should reply with a message similar to the one in Listing 15-1.

```
telnet mail.server.net 110
+OK <9238.1142228@mail2.server.net>
```

Listing 15-1: Making a Telnet connection to a POP3 mail server

The reply shown in Listing 15-1 says that you've made a connection to the POP3 mail server and that it is waiting for its next command, which should be your attempt to log in. Listing 15-2 shows the process for logging in to a POP3 mail server.

```
user me@server.com
+OK
pass xxxxxxxx
+OK
```

Listing 15-2: Successful authentication to a POP3 mail server

When you try this, be sure to substitute your email account in place of *me@server.com* and the password associated with your account for *xxxxxxxx*.

If authentication fails, the mail server should return an authentication failure message, as shown in Listing 15-3.

```
-ERR authorization failed
```

Listing 15-3: POP3 authentication failure

Reading Mail from a POP3 Mail Server

Before you can download email messages from a POP3 mail server, you'll need to execute a LIST command. The mail server will then respond with the number of messages on the server.

---

[2] Telnet clients are standard on all Windows, Mac OS X, Linux, and Unix distributions.

The POP3 LIST Command

The LIST command will also reveal the size of the email messages and, more importantly, how to reference individual email messages on the server.

The response to the LIST command contains a line for every available message for the specified account. Each line consists of a sequential mail ID number, followed by the size of the message in bytes. Listing 15-4 shows the results of a LIST command on an account with two pieces of email.

```
LIST
+OK
1 2398
2 2023
.
```

Listing 15-4: Results of a POP3 LIST command

The server's reply to the LIST command tells us that there are two messages on the server for the specified account. We can also tell that message 1 is the larger message, at 2,398 bytes, and that message 2 is 2,023 bytes in length. Beyond that, we don't know anything specific about any of these messages.

The last line in the response is the end of message indicator. Servers always terminate POP3 responses with a line containing only a period.

The POP3 RETR Command

To read a specific message, enter RETR followed by a space and the mail ID received from the LIST command. The command in Listing 15-5 requests message 1.

```
RETR 1
```

Listing 15-5: Requesting a message from the server

The mail server should respond to the RETR command with a string of characters resembling the contents of Listing 15-6.

```
+OK 2398 octets
Return-Path: <returnpath@server.com>
Delivered-To: me@server.com
Received: (qmail 73301 invoked from network); 19 Feb 2006 20:55:31 -0000
Received: from mail2.server.net
          by mail1.server.net (qmail-ldap-1.03) with compressed QMQP; 19 Feb
2006 20:55:31 -0000
Delivered-To: CLUSTERHOST mail2.server.net me@server.com
Received: (qmail 50923 invoked from network); 19 Feb 2006 20:55:31 -0000
Received: by simscan 1.1.0 ppid: 50907, pid: 50912, t: 2.8647s
          scanners: attach: 1.1.0 clamav: 0.86.1/m:34/d:1107 spam: 3.0.4
Received: from web30515.mail.mud.server.com
          (envelope-sender <sender@server.com>)
          by mail2.server.net (qmail-ldap-1.03) with SMTP
          for <me@server.com>; 19 Feb 2006 20:55:28 -0000
Received: (qmail 7734 invoked by uid 60001); 19 Feb 2006 20:55:26 -0000
```

```
Message-ID: <20060219205526.7732.qmail@web30515.mail.mud.server.com>
Date: Sun, 19 Feb 2006 12:55:26 -0800 (PST)
From: mike schrenk <sender@server.com>
Subject: Hey, Can you read this email?
To: mike schrenk <me@server.com>
MIME-Version: 1.0
Content-Type: multipart/alternative; boundary="0-349883719-1140382526=:7581"
Content-Transfer-Encoding: 8bit
X-Spam-Checker-Version: SpamAssassin 3.0.4 (2005-06-05) on mail2.server.com
X-Spam-Level:
X-Spam-Status: No, score=0.9 required=17.0 tests=HTML_00_10,HTML_MESSAGE,
        HTML_SHORT_LENGTH autolearn=no version=3.0.4

--0-349883719-1140382526=:7581
Content-Type: text/plain; charset=iso-8859-1
Content-Transfer-Encoding: 8bit

This is an email sent from my Yahoo! email account.
--0-349883719-1140382526=:7581
Content-Type: text/html; charset=iso-8859-1
Content-Transfer-Encoding: 8bit

This is an email sent from my Yahoo! email account.<br><BR><BR
--0-349883719-1140382526=:7581--

.
```

Listing 15-6: A raw email message read from the server using the RETR POP3 command

As you can see, even a short email message has a lot of overhead. Most of the returned information has little to do with the actual text of a message. For example, the email message retrieved in Listing 15-6 doesn't appear until over halfway down the listing. The rest of the text returned by the mail server consists of *headers*, which tell the mail client the path the message took, which services touched it (like SpamAssassin), how to display or handle the message, to whom to send replies, and so forth.

These headers include some familiar information such as the subject header, the *to* and *from* values, and the MIME version. You can easily parse this information with the return_between() function found in the LIB_parse library (see Chapter 4), as shown in Listing 15-7.

```
$ret_path = return_between($raw_message, "Return-Path: ", "\n", EXCL );
$deliver_to = return_between($raw_message, "Delivered-To: ", "\n", EXCL );
$date = return_between($raw_message, "Date: ", "\n", EXCL );
$from = return_between($raw_message, "From: ", "\n", EXCL );
$subject = return_between($raw_message, "Subject: ", "\n", EXCL );
```

Listing 15-7: Parsing header values

The header values in Listing 15-7 are separated by their names and a \n (carriage return) character. Note that the header name must be followed by a colon (:) and a space, as these words may appear elsewhere in the raw message returned from the mail server.

Parsing the actual message is more involved, as shown in Listing 15-8.

```
$content_type = return_between($raw_message, "Content-Type: ", "\n", EXCL);
$boundary = get_attribute($content_type, "boundary");
$raw_msg = return_between($message, "--".$boundary, "--".$boundary, EXCL );
$msg_separator = $raw_msg, chr(13).chr(10).chr(13).chr(10);
$clean_msg = return_between($raw_msg, $msg_separator, $msg_separator, EXCL );
```

Listing 15-8: Parsing the actual message from a raw POP3 response

When parsing the message, you must first identify the Content-Type, which holds the boundaries describing where the message is found. The Content-Type is further parsed with the get_attribute() function, to obtain the actual boundary value.[3] Finally, the text defined within the boundaries may contain additional information that tells the client how to display the content of the message. This information, if it exists, is removed by parsing only what's within the message separator, a combination of carriage returns and line feeds.

Other Useful POP3 Commands

The DELE and QUIT (followed by the mail id) commands mark a message for deletion. Listing 15-9 shows demonstrations of both the DELE and QUIT commands.

```
DELE 8
+OK
QUIT
+OK
```

Listing 15-9: Using the POP3 DELE and QUIT commands

When you use DELE, the deleted message is only marked for deletion and not actually deleted. The deletion doesn't occur until you execute a QUIT command and your server session ends.

NOTE *If you've accidentally marked a message with the DELE function and wish to retain it when you quit, enter RSET followed by the message number. The message will not be marked for deletion when you issue the QUIT command (retention is the default condition).*

Executing POP3 Commands with a Webbot

POP3 commands can be performed with PHP's opensocket(), fputs(), and fgets() functions. The LIB_pop3 library is available for you to download from this book's website. This library contains functions for connecting to the mail server, authenticating your account on the server, finding out what mail is available for the account, requesting messages from the server, and deleting messages.

---

[3] The actual boundary, which defines the message, is prefixed with -- characters to distinguish the actual boundary from where it is defined.

The scripts in Listings 15-10 through 15-13 show how to use the LIB_pop3 library. The larger script is split up and annotated here for clarity, but it is available in its entirety on this book's website.

NOTE *Before you use the script in Listing 15-10, replace the values for SERVER, USER, and PASS with your email account information.*

```
include("LIB_pop3.php");                       // Include POP3 command library

define("SERVER", "your.mailserver.net");       // Your POP3 mailserver
define("USER",   "your@emailsccount.com ");    // Your POP3 email address
define("PASS",   "your_password");             // Your POP3 password
```

Listing 15-10: Including the LIB_pop3 library and initializing credentials

In Listing 15-11, the script makes the connection to the server and, after a successful login attempt, obtains a connection array containing the "handle" that is required for all subsequent communication with the server.

```
# Connect to POP3 server
$connection_array = POP3_connect(SERVER, USER, PASS);
$POP3_connection = $connection_array['handle'];
if($POP3_connection)
    {
    // Create an array, which is the result of a POP3 LIST command
    $list_array = POP3_list($POP3_connection);
```

Listing 15-11: Connecting to the server and making an array of available messages

The script in Listing 15-12 uses the $list_array obtained in the previous step to create requests for each email message. It displays each message along with its ID and size and then deletes the message, as shown here.

```
# Request and display all messages in $list_array
for($xx=0; $xx<count($list_array); $xx++)
    {
    // Parse the mail ID from the message size
    list($mail_id, $size) = explode(" ", $list_array[$xx]);

    // Request the message for the specific mail ID
    $message = POP3_retr($POP3_connection, $mail_id);

    // Display message and place mail ID, size, and message in an array
    echo "$mail_id, $size\n";
    $mail_array[$xx]['ID']      = $mail_id;
    $mail_array[$xx]['SIZE']    = $size;
    $mail_array[$xx]['MESSAGE'] = $message;

    // Display message in <xmp></xmp> tags to disable HTML
    // (in case script is run in a browser)
    echo "<xmp>$message</xmp>";
```

```
    // Delete the message from the server
    POP3_delete($POP3_connection, $mail_id);
    }
```

Listing 15-12: Reading, displaying, and deleting each message found on the server

Finally, after each message is read and deleted from the server, the session is closed, as shown in Listing 15-13.

```
    // End the server session
    echo POP3_quit($POP3_connection);
    }
else
    {
    echo "Login error";
    }
```

Listing 15-13: Closing the connection to the server, or noting the login error if necessary

Subsequently, if the connection wasn't originally made to the server, the script returns an error message.

Further Exploration

With a little thought, you can devise many creative uses for webbots that can access email accounts. There are two general areas that may serve as inspiration.

- Use email as a means to control webbots. For example, you could use an email message to tell a spider which domain to use as a target, or you could send an email to a procurement bot (featured in Chapter 19) to indicate which items to purchase.
- Use an email-enabled webbot to interface incompatible systems. For example, you could upload a small file to an FTP sever from a BlackBerry if the file (the contents of the email) were sent to a special webbot that, after reading the email, sent the file to the specified server. This could effectively connect a legacy system to remote users.

Email-Controlled Webbots

Here are a few ideas to get you started with email-controlled webbots.

- Design a webbot that forwards messages from a mailing list to your personal email address based upon references to a preset list of terms. (For example, the webbot could forward all messages that reference the words *robot*, *web crawler*, *webbot*, and *spider*.)
- Develop a procurement bot that automatically reconfigures your eBay bidding strategy when it receives an email from eBay indicating that someone has outbid you.

- Create a strategy that forwards an email message to a webbot that, in turn, displays the message on a 48-foot scrolling marquee that is outside your office building (assuming you have access to such a display!).

Email Interfaces

Here are a few ways you can capitalize on email-enabled webbots to interface different systems.

- Develop a webbot that automatically updates your financial records based on email you receive from PayPal.
- Create a webbot that automatically forwards all email with the word *support* in the subject line to the person working the help desk at that time.
- Write a webbot that notifies you when one of your mail servers has reached its email (size) quota.
- Write a service that interfaces shipping notification email messages from FedEx to your company's fulfillment system.
- Develop an email-to-fax service that faxes an email message to the phone number in the email's subject line. (This isn't hard to do if you have an old fax/modem from the last century lying around.)
- Write a webbot that maintains statistics about your email accounts, indicating who is sending the most email, when servers are busiest, the number of messages that are deleted without being read, when servers fail, and email addresses that are returned as undeliverable.

16

WEBBOTS THAT SEND EMAIL

In Chapter 15 you learned how to create
webbots that read email. In this chapter I'll
show you how to write webbots that can create
massive amounts of email. On that note, let's talk
briefly about email ethics.

Email, Webbots, and Spam

Spam has negatively influenced all of our email experiences.[1] It was probably
only a few years ago that every email in one's inbox had some value and
deserved to be read. Today, however, my *spam filter* (a proxy service that
examines email headers and content to determine if the email is legitimate
or a potential scam) rejects roughly 80 percent of the email I receive,

---

[1] I would like to extend my sincerest apologies to the Hormel Foods Corporation for perpetuating
the use of the word *spam* to describe unwanted email. I'd rather refer to the phenomenon of junk
email with a clever term like *eJunk* or *NetClutter*. But unfortunately, no other synonym has the
worldwide acceptance of *spam*. Hormel Foods deserves better treatment of its brand—and for this
reason I want to stress the difference between SPAM and spam. For additional information on
Hormel's take on the use of the word *spam*, please refer to http://www.spam.com/ci/ci_in.htm.

flagging it as unwanted solicitation at best and, at worst, a *phishing attack*—email that masquerades itself as legitimate and requests credit card or other personal information.

Nobody likes unsolicited email, and your webbot's effectiveness will be reduced if its messages are interpreted as spam by end readers or automated filters. When using your webbots to send volumes of mail, follow these guidelines:

Allow recipients to unsubscribe. If people can't remove themselves from a mailing list, they're subscribed involuntarily. Email that is part of a periodic mailing should include a link that allows the recipient to opt out of future mailings.[2]

Avoid multiple emails. Avoid sending multiple emails with similar content or intent to the same address.

Use a relevant subject line. Don't deceive email recipients (or try to avoid a spam filter) with misleading subject lines. If you're actually selling "herbal Via8r4," don't use a subject line like *RE: Thanks!*

Identify yourself. Don't spoof your email headers or the originator's actual email address in order to trick spam filters into delivering your email.

Obey the law. Depending where you live, laws may prohibit sending specific types of email. For example, under the *Children's Online Privacy Protection Act (COPPA)*, it is illegal in the United States to solicit personal information from children. (More information is available at the COPPA website, http://www.coppa.org.) Laws regarding email ethics change constantly. If you have questions, talk to a lawyer that specializes in online law.

NOTE   *Do not use any of the following techniques to test the resolve of people's spam filters. I recommend reading Chapter 28 and having a personal consultation with an attorney before doing anything remotely questionable.*

Sending Mail with SMTP and PHP

Outgoing email is sent using the Simple Mail Transfer Protocol (SMTP). Fortunately, PHP's built-in `mail()` function handles all SMTP socket-level protocols and handshaking for you. The `mail()` function acts as your mail client, sending email messages just as Outlook or Thunderbird might.

Configuring PHP to Send Mail

Before you can use PHP as a mail client, you must edit PHP's configuration file, php.ini, to point PHP to the mail server's location. For example, the script in Listing 16-1 shows the section of php.ini that configures PHP to work with sendmail, the Unix mail server on many networks.

---

[2] Unfortunately, many spammers rely on people opting out of mailing lists to verify that an email address is actively used. For many, opting out of a mail list ensures they will continue to receive unsolicited email.

```
[mail function]
; For Win32 only.
SMTP = localhost

; For Win32 only.
;sendmail_from = me@example.com

; For Unix only. You may supply arguments as well (default: "sendmail -t -i").
sendmail_path = /usr/sbin/sendmail -t -i
```

Listing 16-1: Configuring PHP's mail() *function*

NOTE *Notice that the configuration differs slightly for Windows and Unix installations. For example, windows servers use PHP.INI to describe the network location of the mail server you want to use. In contrast, Unix installations need the file path to your local mail server. In either case, you must have access to a mail server (preferably in the same network domain) that allows you to send email.*

Only a few years ago, you could send email through almost any mail server on the Internet using *relay host,* which enables mail servers to relay messages from mail clients in one domain to a different domain. When using relay host, one can send nearly anonymous email, because these mail servers accept commands from any mail client without needing any form of authentication.

The relay host process has been largely abandoned by system administrators because spammers can use it to send millions of anonymous commercial emails. Today, almost every mail server will ignore commands that come from a different domain or from users that are not registered as valid clients.

An "open" mail server—one that allows relaying—is obviously a dangerous thing. I once worked for a company with two corporate mail servers, one of which mistakenly allowed mail relaying. Eventually, a spammer discovered it and commandeered it as a platform for dispatching thousands of anonymous commercial emails.[3] In addition to wasting our bandwidth, our domain was reported as one that belonged to a spammer and subsequently got placed on a watch list used by spam-detection companies. Once they identified our domain as a source of spam, many important corporate emails weren't received because spam filters had rejected them. It took quite an effort to get our domain off of that list. For this reason, you will need a valid email account to send email from a webbot.

Sending an Email with mail()

PHP provides a built-in function for sending email, as shown in Listing 16-2.

```
$email_address = "some.account@someserver.com";
$email_subject = "Webbot Notification Email";
$email_message = "Your webbot found something that needs you attention";
mail($email_address, $email_subject, $email_message);
```

Listing 16-2: Sending an email with PHP's built-in mail() *function*

---

[3] Spammers write webbots to discover mail servers that allow mail relaying.

In the simplest configuration, as shown in Listing 16-2, you only need to specify the destination email address, the subject, and the message. For the reasons mentioned in the relay host discussion, however, you will need a valid account on the same server as the one specified in your php.ini file.

There are, of course, more options than those shown in Listing 16-2. However, these options usually require that you build *email headers*, which tell a mail client how to format the email and how the email should be distributed. Since the syntax for email headers is very specific, it is easy to implement them incorrectly. Therefore, I've written a small email library called LIB_mail with a function formatted_mail(), which makes it easy to send emails that are more complex than what can easily be sent with the mail() function alone. The script for LIB_mail is shown in Listing 16-3.

```
function formatted_mail($subject, $message, $address, $content_type)
    {
    # Set defaults
    if(!isset($address['cc']))        $address['cc'] = "";
    if(!isset($address['bcc']))       $address['bcc'] = "";

    # Ensure that there's a Reply-to address
    if(!isset($address['replyto']))   $address['replyto'] = $address['from'];

    # Create mail headers
    $headers = "";
    $headers = $headers . "From: ".$address['from']."\r\n";
    $headers = $headers . "Return-Path: ".$address['from']."\r\n";
    $headers = $headers . "Reply-To: ".$address['replyto']."\r\n";

    # Add Cc to header if needed
    if (strlen($address['cc'])< 0 )
        $headers = $headers . "Cc: ".$address['cc']."\r\n";

    # Add Bcc to header if needed
    if (strlen($address['bcc'])< 0 )
        $headers = $headers . "Bcc: ".$address['bcc']."\r\n";

    # Add content type
    $headers = $headers . "Content-Type: ".$content_type."\r\n";

    # Send the email
    $result = mail($address['to'], $subject, $message, $headers);

    return $result;
    }
```

Listing 16-3: Sending formatted email with LIB_mail

The main thing to take away from the script above is that the mail header is a very syntax-sensitive string that works better if it is a built-in function than if it is created repeatedly in your scripts. Also, up to six addresses are involved in sending email, and they are all passed to this routine in an array called $address. These addresses are defined in Table 16-1.

Table 16-1: Email Addresses Used by `LIB_mail`

Address	Function	Required or Optional
To:	Defines the address of the main recipient of the email	Required
Reply-to:	Defines the address where replies to the email are sent	Optional
Return-path:	Indicates where notifications are sent if the email could not be delivered	Optional
From:	Defines the email address of the party sending the email	Required
Cc:	Refers to an address of another party, who receives a *carbon copy* of the email, but is not the primary recipient of the message	Optional
Bcc:	Is similar to Cc: and stands for *blind carbon copy*; this address is hidden from the other parties receiving the same email	Optional

Configuring the Reply-to address is also important because this address is used as the address where undeliverable email messages are sent. If this is not defined, undeliverable email messages will bounce back to your system admin, and you won't know that an email wasn't delivered. For this reason, the function automatically uses the From address if a Return-path address isn't specified.

Writing a Webbot That Sends Email Notifications

Here's a simple webbot that, when run, sends an email notification if a web page has changed since the last time it was checked.[4] Such a webbot could have many practical uses. For example, it could monitor online auctions or pages on your fantasy football league's website. A modified version of this webbot could even notify you when the balance of your checking account changes. The webbot simply downloads a web page and stores a *page signature*, a number that uniquely describes the content of the page, in a database. This is also known as a *hash*, or a series of characters, that represents a test message or a file. In this case, a small hash is used to create a signature that references a file without the need to reference the entire contents of the file. If the signature of the page differs from the one in the database, the webbot saves the new value and sends you an email indicating that the page has changed. Listing 16-4 shows the script for this webbot.[5]

```
# Get libraries
include("LIB_http.php");        # include cURL library
include("LIB_mysql.php");       # include MySQL library
include("LIB_mail.php");        # include mail library

# Define parameters
$webbot_email_address       = "webbot@YourDomain.com";
$notification_email_address = "yourEmail@YourDomain.com ";
$target_web_site            = "www.trackrates.com";
```

---

[4] For information on periodic and autonomous launching of webbots, read Chapter 23.

[5] This script makes use of `LIB_mysql`. If you haven't already done so, make sure you read Chapter 6 to learn how to use this library.

```
# Download the website
$download_array = http_get($target_web_site, $ref="");
$web_page = $download_array['FILE'];

# Calculate a 40-character sha1 hash for use as a simple signature
$new_signature = sha1($web_page);

# Compare this signature to the previously stored value in a database
$sql = "select SIGNATURE from signatures where
WEB_PAGE='".$target_web_site."'";
list($old_signature) = exe_sql(DATABASE, $sql);

# If the new signature is different than the old one, update the database and
# send an email notifying someone that the web page changed.
if($new_signature != $old_signature)
    {
    // Update database
    if(isset($data_array)) unset($data_array);
    $data_array['SIGNATURE'] = $new_signature;
    update(DATABASE, $table="signatures",
        $data_array, $key_column="WEB_PAGE", $id=$target_web_site);

    // Send email
    $subject = $target_web_site." has changed";
    $message = $subject . "\n";
    $message = $message . "Old signature = ".$old_signature."\n";
    $message = $message . "New signature = ".$new_signature."\n";
    $message = $message . "Webbot ran at: ".date("r")."\n";
    $address['from']    = $webbot_email_address;
    $address['replyto'] = $webbot_email_address;
    $address['to']      = $notification_email_address;
    formatted_mail($subject, $message, $address, $content_type="text/plain");
    }
```

Listing 16-4: A simple webbot that sends an email when a web page changes

When the webbot finds that the web page's signature has changed, it sends an email like the one in Listing 16-5.

```
www.trackrates.com has changed
Old signature = baf73f476aef13ae48bd7df5122d685b6d2be2dd
New signature = baf73f476aed685b6d2be2ddf13ae48bd7df5124
Webbot ran at: Mon, 20 Mar 2007 17:08:00 -0600
```

Listing 16-5: Email generated by the webbot in Listing 16-4

Keeping Legitimate Mail out of Spam Filters

Many spam filters automatically reject any email in which the domain of the sender doesn't match the domain of the mail server used to send the message. For this reason, it is wise to verify that the domains for the From and Reply-to addresses match the outgoing mail server's domain.

The idea here is not to fool spam filters into letting you send unwanted email, but rather to ensure that legitimate email makes it to the intended Inbox and not the Junk folder, where no one will read it.

Sending HTML-Formatted Email

It's easy to send HTML-formatted email with images, hyperlinks, or any other media found in web pages. To send HTML-formatted emails with the formatted_mail() function, do the following:

- Set the $content_type variable to text/html. This will tell the routine to use the proper MIME in the email header.

- Use fully formed URLs to refer to any images or hyperlinks. Relative address references will resolve to the mail client, not the online media you want to use.

- Since you never know the capabilities of the client reading the email, use standard formatting techniques. Tables work well.

- Avoid CSS. Traditional font tags are more predictable in HTML email.

- For debugging purposes, it's a good idea to build your message in a string, as shown in Listing 16-6.

```
# Get library
include("LIB_mail.php");    # Include mail library

# Define addresses
$address['from']    = "mikeSchrenk@yahoo.com";
$address['replyto'] = $address['from'];
$address['to']      = "mikeSchrenk@yahoo.com";

# Define subject line
$subject = "Example of an HTML-formatted email";

# Define message
$message = "";
$message = $message . "<table bgcolor='#e0e0e0' border='0' cellpadding='0' cellspacing='0'>";
$message = $message .  "<tr>";
$message = $message .   "<td><img src='http://www.schrenk.com/logo.gif'><td>";
$message = $message .  "</tr>";
$message = $message .  "<tr>";
$message = $message .   "<td>";
$message = $message .    "<font face='arial'>";
$message = $message .     "Here is an example of a clean HTML-formatted email";
$message = $message .    "</font>";
$message = $message .   "<td>";
$message = $message .  "</tr>";
$message = $message .  "<tr>";
$message = $message .   "<td>";
$message = $message .    "<font face='arial'>";
$message = $message .     "with an image and a <a href='http://www.schrenk.com'>hyperlink</a>.";
```

```
$message = $message .    "</font>";
$message = $message .    "<td>";
$message = $message .    "</tr>";
$message = $message . "</table>";

echo $message;

// Send email
formatted_mail($subject, $message, $address, $content_type="text/html");
?>
```

Listing 16-6: Sending HTML-formatted email

The email sent by Listing 16-6 looks like Figure 16-1.

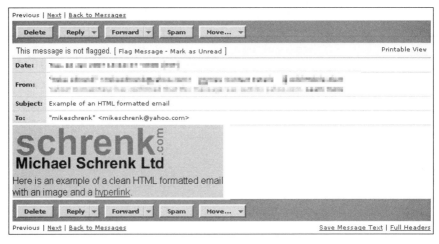

Figure 16-1: HTML-formatted email sent by the script in Listing 16-6

Be aware that not all mail clients can render HTML-formatted email. In those instances, you should send either text-only emails or a multi-formatted email that contains both HTML and unformatted messages.

Further Exploration

If you think about all the ways you use email, you'll probably be able to come up with some very creative uses for your webbots. The following concepts should serve as starting points for your own webbot development.

Using Returned Emails to Prune Access Lists

You can design an email-wielding webbot to help you identify illegitimate members of a members-only website. If someone has access to a business-to-business website but is no longer employed by a company that uses the site, that person probably also lost access to his or her corporate email address; any email sent to that account will be returned as undeliverable. You could design a webbot that periodically sends some type of report to everyone who has access to the website. Any emails that return as undeliverable will alert you to a member's email address that is no longer valid. Your webbot can then track these undeliverable emails and deactivate former employees from your list of members.

Using Email as Notification That Your Webbot Ran

It's handy to have an indication that a webbot has actually run. A simple email at the end of the webbot's session can inform you that it ran and what it did. Often, the actual content of these email notifications is not as significant as the emails themselves, which indicate that a webbot ran successfully. Similarly, you can use email notifications to tell you exactly when and how a webbot has failed.

Leveraging Wireless Technologies

Since wireless email clients like cell phones and BlackBerries allow people to use email away from their desks, your webbots can effectively use email in more situations than they could only a few years ago. Think about applications where webbots can exploit mobile email technology. For example, you could write a webbot that checks the status of your server and sends warnings to people when they're away from the office. You could also develop a webbot that sends an instant message when your company is mentioned on CNN.com.

Writing Webbots That Send Text Messages

Many wireless carriers support email interfaces for text messaging, or short message service (SMS). These messages appear as text on cell phones, and many people find them to be less intrusive than voice messages. To send a text message, you simply email the message to one of the email-to-text message addresses provided by wireless carriers—a task you could easily hand off to a webbot. Appendix C contains a list of email-to-text message addresses; if you can't find your carrier in this list, contact its customer service department to see if it provides this service.

17

CONVERTING A WEBSITE INTO A FUNCTION

Webbots are easier to use when they're packaged as functions. These functions are simply interfaces to webbots that download and parse information and return the desired data in a predefined structure. For example, the National Oceanic and Atmospheric Association (NOAA) provides weather forecasts on its website (http://www.noaa.gov). You could write a function to execute a webbot that downloads and parses a forecast. This interface could also return the forecast in an array, as shown in Listing 17-1.

```
# Get weather forecast
$forcast_array = get_noaa_forecast($zip=89109);

# Display forecast
echo $forcast_array['MONDAY']['TEMPERATURE']."<br>";
echo $forcast_array['MONDAY']['WIND_SPEED']."<br>";
echo $forcast_array['MONDAY']['WIND_DIRECTION']."<br>";
```

Listing 17-1: Simplifying webbot use by creating a function interface

While the example in Listing 17-1 is hypothetical, you can see that interfacing with a webbot in this manner conceals the dirty details of downloading or parsing web pages. Yet, the programmer has full ability to access online information and services that the webbots provide. From a programmer's perspective, it isn't even obvious that webbots are used.

When a programmer accesses a webbot from a function interface, he or she gains the ability to use the webbot both programmatically and in real time. This is a departure from the traditional method of launching webbots.[1] Customarily, you schedule a webbot to execute periodically, and if the webbot generates data, that information is stored in a database for later retrieval. With a function interface to a webbot, you don't have to wait for a webbot to run as a scheduled task. Instead, you can directly request the specific contents of a web page whenever you need them.

Writing a Function Interface

This project uses a web page that decodes ZIP codes and converts that operation into a function, which is available from a PHP program. This particular web page finds the city, county, state, and geo coordinates for the post office located in a specific ZIP code. Theoretically, you could use this function to validate ZIP codes or use the latitude and longitude information to plot locations on a map. Figure 17-1 shows the target website for this project.

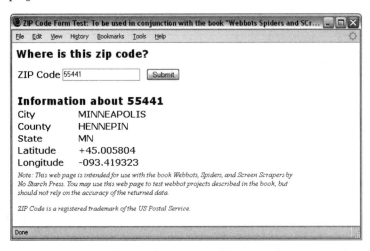

Figure 17-1: Target website, which returns information about a ZIP code

The sole purpose of the web page in Figure 17-1 is to be a target for your webbots. (A link to this page is available at this book's website.) This target web page uses a standard form to capture a ZIP code. Once you submit that form, the web page returns a variety of information about the ZIP code you entered in a table below the form.

---

[1] Traditional methods for executing webbots are described in Chapter 23.

Defining the Interface

This example function uses the interface shown in Listing 17-2, where a function named decode_zipcode() accepts a five-digit ZIP code as a input parameter and returns an array, which describes the area serviced by the ZIP code.

```
array $zipcode_array = decode_zipcode(int $zipcode);

input:
    $zipcode is a five-digit USPS ZIP code
output:
    $zipcode_array['CITY']
    $zipcode_array['COUNTY']
    $zipcode_array['STATE']
    $zipcode_array['LATITUDE']
    $zipcode_array['LONGITUDE']
```

Listing 17-2: decode_zipcode() interface

Analyzing the Target Web Page

Since this webbot needs to submit a ZIP code to a form, you will need to use the techniques you learned in Chapter 5 to emulate someone manually submitting the form. As you learned, you should always pass even simple forms through a form analyzer (similar to the one used in Chapter 5) to ensure that you will submit the form in the manner the server expects. This is important because web pages commonly insert dynamic fields or values into forms that can be hard to detect by just looking at a page.

To use the form analyzer, simply load the web page into a browser and view the source code, as shown in Figure 17-2.

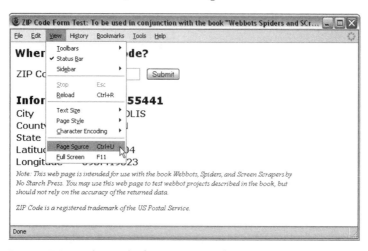

Figure 17-2: Displaying the form's source code

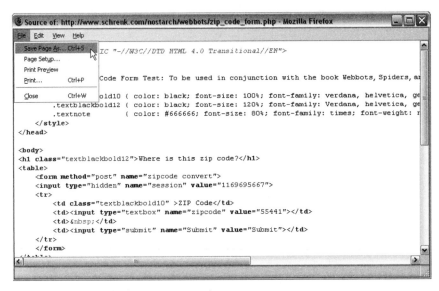

Figure 17-3: Saving the form's source code

Once you have the target's source code, save the HTML to your hard drive, as done in Figure 17-3.

Once the form's HTML is on your hard drive, you must edit it to make the form submit its content to the form analyzer instead of the target server. You do this by changing the form's action attribute to the location of the form analyzer, as shown in Figure 17-4.

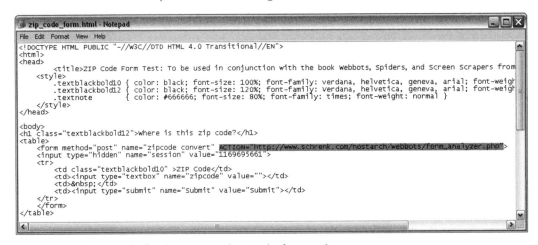

Figure 17-4: Changing the form's action attribute to the form analyzer

Now you have a copy of the target form on your hard drive, with the form's original action attribute replaced with the web address of the form analyzer. The final step is to load this local copy of the form into a browser, manually fill in the form, and submit it to the analyzer. Once submitted, you should see the analysis performed by the form analyzer, as shown in Figure 17-5.

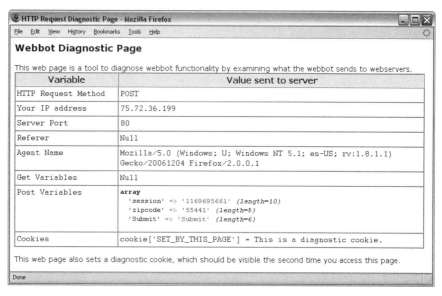

Figure 17-5: Analyzing the target form

The analysis tells us that the method is POST and that there are three required data fields. In addition to the *zipcode* field, there is also a hidden *session* field (which looks suspiciously like a Unix timestamp) and a *Submit* field, which is actually the name of the *Submit* button. To emulate the form submission, it is vitally important to correctly use all the field names (with appropriate values) as well as the same method used by the original form.

Once you write your webbot, it's a good idea to test it by using the form analyzer as a target to ensure that the webbot submits the form as the target webserver expects it to. This is also a good time to verify the agent name your webbot uses.

Using describe_zipcode()

The script that interfaces the target web page to a PHP function, called describe_zipcode(), is available in its entirety at this book's website. It is broken into smaller pieces and annotated here for clarity.

Getting the Session Value

It is uncommon to find dynamically assigned values, like the session value employed by this target, in forms. Since the session is assigned dynamically, the webbot must first make a page request to get the session value before it can submit form values. This actually mimics normal browser use, as the browser first must download the form before submitting it. The webbot captures the session variable with the script described in Listing 17-3.

```
# Start interface describe_zipcode($zipcode)
describe_zipcode($zipcode)
```

```
{
# Get required libraries and declare the target
include ("LIB_http.php");
include("LIB_parse.php");
$target = "http://www.schrenk.com/nostarch/webbots/zip_code_form.php";

# Download the target
$page = http_get($target, $ref="");

# Parse the session hidden tag from the downloaded page
#   <input type="hidden" name="session" value="xxxxxxxxxx">
$session_tag = return_between($string = $page['FILE'] ,
                              $start = "<input type=\"hidden\" name=\
                              "session\"",
                              $end   = ">",
                              $type  = EXCL
                              );
# Remove the "'s and "value=" text to reveal the session value
$session_value = str_replace("\"", "", $session_tag);
$session_value = str_replace("value=", "", $session_value);
```

Listing 17-3: Downloading the target to get the session variable

The script in Listing 17-3 is a classic screen scraper. It downloads the page and parses the session value from the form <input> tag. The str_replace() function is later used to remove superfluous quotes and the tag's value attribute. Notice that the webbot uses LIB_parse and LIB_http, described in previous chapters, to download and parse the web page.[2]

Submitting the Form

Once you know the session value, the script in Listing 17-4 may be used to submit the form. Notice the use of http_post_form() to emulate the submission of a form with the POST method. The form fields are conveniently passed to the target webserver in $data_array[].

```
$data_array['session'] = $session_value;
$data_array['zipcode'] = $zipcode;
$data_array['Submit']  = "Submit";
$form_result = http_post_form($target, $ref=$target, $data_array);
```

Listing 17-4: Emulating the form

Parsing and Returning the Result

The remaining step is to parse the desired city, county, state, and geo coordinates from the web page obtained from the form submission in the previous listing. The script that does this is shown in Listing 17-5.

```
$landmark = "Information about ".$zipcode;
$table_array = parse_array($form_result['FILE'], "<table", "</table>");
for($xx=0; $xx<count($table_array); $xx++)
```

---

[2] LIB_http and LIB_parse are described in Chapters 3 and 4, respectively.

```
    {
    # Parse the table containing the parsing landmark
    if(stristr($table_array[$xx], $landmark))
    {
    $ret['CITY'] = return_between($table_array[$xx], "CITY", "</tr>", EXCL);
    $ret['CITY'] = strip_tags($ret['CITY']);
    $ret['STATE'] = return_between($table_array[$xx], "STATE", "</tr>", EXCL);
    $ret['STATE'] = strip_tags($ret['STATE']);
    $ret['COUNTY'] = return_between($table_array[$xx], "COUNTY", "</tr>", EXCL);
    $ret['COUNTY'] = strip_tags($ret['COUNTY']);
    $ret['LATITUDE'] = return_between($table_array[$xx], "LATITUDE", "</tr>", EXCL);
    $ret['LATITUDE'] = strip_tags($ret['LATITUDE']);
    $ret['LONGITUDE'] = return_between($table_array[$xx], "LONGITUDE", "</tr>", EXCL);
    $ret['LONGITUDE'] = strip_tags($ret['LONGITUDE']);
    }
  }
# Return the parsed data
return $ret;
} # End Interface describe_zipcode($zipcode)
```

Listing 17-5: Parsing and returning the data

This script first uses parse_array() to create an array containing all the tables in the downloaded web page, which is returned in $form_result['FILE']. The script then looks for the table that contains the parsing landmark *Information about . . . .* Once the webbot finds the table that holds the data we're looking for, it parses the data using unique strings that identify the beginning and end of the desired data. The parsed data is then cleaned up with strip_tags() and returned in the array we described earlier. Once the data is parsed and placed into an array, that array is returned to the calling program.

Final Thoughts

Now that you know how to write function interfaces to a web page (or in our case, a form), you can convert the data and functionality of any web page into something your programs can use easily in real time. Here are a few more things for you to consider.

Distributing Resources

A secondary benefit of creating a function interface to a webbot is that when a webbot uses a web page on another server as a resource, it allocates bandwidth and computational power across several computers. Since more resources are deployed, you can get more done in less time. You can use this technique to spread the burden of running complex webbots to more than one computer on your local or remote networks. This technique may also be used to make page requests from multiple IP addresses (for added stealth) or to spread bandwidth across multiple Internet nodes.

Using Standard Interfaces

The interface described in this example is specific to PHP. Although scripts for Perl, Java, or C++ environments would be very similar to this one, you could not use this script directly in an environment other than PHP. You can solve this problem by returning data in a language-independent format like XML or SOAP (Simple Object Access Protocol). To learn more about these protocols, read Chapter 26.

Designing a Custom Lightweight "Web Service"

Our example assumed that the target was not under our control, so we had to live within the constraints presented by the target website. When you control the website your interface targets, however, you can design the web page in such a way that you don't have to parse the data from HTML. In these instances, the data is returned as variables that your program can use directly. These techniques are also described in detail in Chapter 26.

If you're interested in creating your own ZIP code server (with a lightweight interface), you'll need a ZIP code database. You should be able to find one by performing a Google search for *ZIP code database.*

PART III

ADVANCED TECHNICAL CONSIDERATIONS

The chapters in this section explore the finer technical aspects of webbot and spider development. In the first two chapters, I'll share some lessons I learned the hard way while writing very specialized webbots and spiders. I'll also describe methods for leveraging PHP/CURL to create webbots that manage authentication, encryption, and cookies.

Chapter 18: Spiders

This discussion of spider design starts with an exploration of simple spiders that find and follow links on specific web pages. The conversation later expands to techniques for developing advanced spiders that autonomously roam the Internet, looking for specific information and dropping payloads—performing predefined functions as they find desired information.

Chapter 19: Procurement Webbots and Snipers

In this chapter, we'll explore the design theory of writing *snipers*, webbots that automatically purchase items. Snipers are primarily used on online auctions sites, "attacking" when a specific list of criteria are met.

Chapter 20: Webbots and Cryptography

Encrypted websites are not a problem for webbots using PHP/CURL. Here we'll explore how online encryption certificates work and how PHP/CURL makes encryption easy to handle.

Chapter 21: Authentication

In this chapter on accessing authenticated (i.e., password-protected) sites, we'll explore the various methods used to protect a website from unauthorized users. You'll also learn how to write webbots that can automatically log in to these sites.

Chapter 22: Advanced Cookie Management

Advanced cookie management involves managing cookie expiration dates and multiple sets of cookies for multiple users. We'll also explore PHP/CURL's ability (and inability) to meet these challenges.

Chapter 23: Scheduling Webbots and Spiders

In the final installment in this section, we'll explore methods for periodically launching or executing a webbot. These techniques will allow your webbots to run unattended while simulating human activity.

18

SPIDERS

Spiders, also known as *web spiders, crawlers,* and *web walkers,* are specialized webbots that—unlike traditional webbots with well-defined targets—download multiple web pages across multiple websites. As spiders make their way across the Internet, it's difficult to anticipate where they'll go or what they'll find, as they simply follow links they find on previously downloaded pages. Their unpredictability makes spiders fun to write because they act as if they almost have minds of their own.

The best known spiders are those used by the major search engine companies (Google, Yahoo!, and MSN) to identify online content. And while *spiders* are synonymous with *search engines* for many people, the potential utility of spiders is much greater. You can write a spider that does anything any other webbot does, with the advantage of targeting the entire Internet. This creates a niche for developers that design specialized spiders that do very specific work. Here are some potential ideas for spider projects:

- Discover sales of original copies of 1963 *Spider-Man* comics. Design your spider to email you with links to new findings or price reductions.
- Periodically create an archive of your competitors' websites.

- Invite every MySpace member living in Cleveland, Ohio to be your friend.[1]
- Send a text message when your spider finds jobs for Miami-based fashion photographers who speak Portuguese.
- Maintain an updated version of your local newspaper on your PDA.
- Validate that all the links on your website point to active web pages.
- Perform a statistical analysis of noun usage across the Internet.
- Search the Internet for musicians that recorded new versions of your favorite songs.
- Purchase collectible Bibles when your spider detects one with a price substantially below the collectible price listed on Amazon.com.

This list could go on, but you get the idea. To a business, a well-purposed spider is like additional staff, easily justifying the one-time development cost.

How Spiders Work

Spiders begin harvesting links at the *seed URL*, the address of the initial target web page. The spider uses these links as references to the next set of pages to process, and as it downloads each of those web pages, the spider harvests more links. The first page the spider downloads is known as the first *penetration level*. In each successive level of penetration, additional web pages are downloaded as directed by the links harvested in the previous level. The spider repeats this process until it reaches the *maximum penetration level*. Figure 18-1 shows a typical spider process.

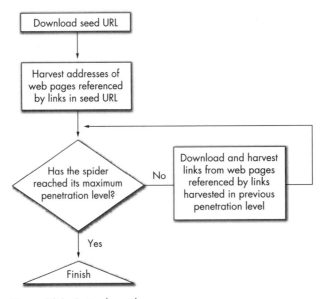

Figure 18-1: A simple spider

---

[1] This is only listed here to show the potential for what spiders can do. Please don't actually do this! Automated agents like this violate MySpace's terms of use. Develop webbots responsibly.

Example Spider

Our example spider will reuse the image harvester (described in Chapter 8) that downloads images for an entire website. The image harvester is this spider's *payload*—the task that it will perform on every web page it visits. While this spider performs a useful task, its primary purpose is to demonstrate how spiders work, so design compromises were made that affect the spider's *scalability* for use on larger tasks. After we explore this example spider, I'll conclude with recommendations for making a scalable spider suitable for larger projects.

Listings 18-1 and 18-2 are the main scripts for the example spider. Initially, the spider is limited to collecting links. Since the payload adds complexity, we'll include it after you've had an opportunity to understand how the basic spider works.

```
# Initialization
include("LIB_http.php");                  // http library
include("LIB_parse.php");                 // parse library
include("LIB_resolve_addresses.php");     // Address resolution library
include("LIB_exclusion_list.php");        // List of excluded keywords
include("LIB_simple_spider.php");         // Spider routines used by this app

set_time_limit(3600);                     // Don't let PHP time out

$SEED_URL = "http://www.YourSiteHere.com";
$MAX_PENETRATION = 1;                     // Set spider penetration depth
$FETCH_DELAY = 1;                         // Wait 1 second between page fetches
$ALLOW_OFFISTE = false;                   // Don't let spider roam from seed domain
$spider_array = array();                  // Initialize the array that holds links
```

Listing 18-1: Main spider script, initialization

The script in Listing 18-1 loads the required libraries and initializes settings that tell the spider how to operate. This project introduces two new libraries: an exclusion list (LIB_exclusion_list.php) and the spider library used for this exercise (LIB_simple_spider.php). We'll explain both of these new libraries as we use them.

In any PHP spider design, the default script time-out of 30 seconds needs to be set to a period more appropriate for spiders, since script execution may take minutes or even hours. Since spiders may have notoriously long execution times, the script in Listing 18-1 sets the PHP script time-out to one hour (3,600 seconds) with the set_time_limit(3600) command.

The example spider is configured to collect enough information to demonstrate how spiders work but not so much that the sheer volume of data distracts from the demonstration. You can set these settings differently once you understand the effects they have on the operation of your spider. For now, the maximum penetration level is set to 1. This means that the spider will harvest links from the seed URL and the pages that the links on the seed URL reference, but it will not download any pages that are more than one link away from the seed URL. Even when you tie the spider's hands—as we've done here—it still collects a ridiculously large amount of data. When limited to one penetration level, the spider still harvested 583 links when pointed at http://www.schrenk.com. This number excludes redundant links, which would otherwise raise the number of harvest links to 1,930. For demonstration purposes, the spider also rejects links that are not on the parent domain.

The main spider script, shown in Listing 18-2, is quite simple. Much of this simplicity, however, comes at the cost of storing links in an array, instead of a more scalable (and more complicated) database. As you can see, the functions in the libraries make it easy to download web pages, harvest links, exclude unwanted links, and fully resolve addresses.

```
# Get links from $SEED_URL
echo "Harvesting Seed URL\n";
$temp_link_array = harvest_links($SEED_URL);
$spider_array = archive_links($spider_array, 0, $temp_link_array);

# Spider links from remaining penetration levels
for($penetration_level=1; $penetration_level<=$MAX_PENETRATION;
$penetration_level++)
    {
    $previous_level = $penetration_level - 1;
    for($xx=0; $xx<count($spider_array[$previous_level]); $xx++)
        {
        unset($temp_link_array);
        $temp_link_array = harvest_links($spider_array[$previous_level][$xx]);
        echo "Level=$penetration_level, xx=$xx of
            ".count($spider_array[$previous_level])." \n";
        $spider_array = archive_links($spider_array, $penetration_level,
                        $temp_link_array);
        }
    }
```

Listing 18-2: Main spider script, harvesting links

When the spider uses www.schrenk.com as a seed URL, it harvests and rejects links, as shown in Figure 18-2.

Now that you've seen the main spider script, an exploration of the routines in LIB_simple_spider will provide insight to how it really works.

LIB_simple_spider

Special spider functions are found in the LIB_simple_spider library. This library provides functions that parse links from a web page when given a URL, archive harvested links in an array, identify the root domain for a URL, and identify links that should be excluded from the archive.

This library, as well as the other scripts featured in this chapter, is available for download at this book's website.

Figure 18-2: Running the simple spider from Listings 18-1 and 18-2

harvest_links()

The harvest_links() function downloads the specified web page and returns all the links in an array. This function, shown in Listing 18-3, uses the $DELAY setting to keep the spider from sending too many requests to the server over too short a period.[2]

```
function harvest_links($url)
    {
    # Initialize
    global $DELAY;
    $link_array = array();

    # Get page base for $url (used to create fully resolved URLs for the links)
    $page_base = get_base_page_address($url);

    # $DELAY creates a random delay period between 1 second and full delay period
    $random_delay = rand(1, rand(1, $DELAY));
    # Download webpage
    sleep($random_delay);
    $downloaded_page = http_get($url, "");
```

---

[2] A stealthier spider would shuffle the order of web page requests.

```
# Parse links
$anchor_tags = parse_array($downloaded_page['FILE'], "<a", "</a>", EXCL);
# Get http attributes for each tag into an array
for($xx=0; $xx<count($anchor_tags); $xx++)
    {
    $href = get_attribute($anchor_tags[$xx], "href");
    $resolved_addrses = resolve_address($href, $page_base);
    $link_array[] = $resolved_address;
    echo "Harvested: ".$resolved_addres." \n";
    }
return $link_array;
}
```

Listing 18-3: Harvesting links from a web page with the harvest_links() function

archive_links()

The script in Listing 18-4 uses the link array collected by the previous function to create an archival array. The first element of the archival array identifies the penetration level where the link was found, while the second contains the actual link.

```
function archive_links($spider_array, $penetration_level, $temp_link_array)
    {
    for($xx=0; $xx<count($temp_link_array); $xx++)
        {
        # Don't add excluded links to $spider_array
        if(!excluded_link($spider_array, $temp_link_array[$xx]))
            {
            $spider_array[$penetration_level][] = $temp_link_array[$xx];
            }
        }
    return $spider_array;
    }
```

Listing 18-4: Archiving links in $spider_array

get_domain()

The function get_domain() parses the *root domain* from the target URL. For example, given a target URL like https://www.schrenk.com/store/product_list.php, the root domain is schrenk.com.

The function get_domain() compares the root domains of the links to the root domain of the seed URL to determine if the link is for a URL that is not in the seed URL's domain, as shown in Listing 18-5.

```
function get_domain($url)
    {
    // Remove protocol from $url
    $url = str_replace("http://", "", $url);
    $url = str_replace("https://", "", $url);
```

```
// Remove page and directory references
if(stristr($url, "/"))
    $url = substr($url, 0, strpos($url, "/"));

return $url;
}
```

Listing 18-5: Parsing the root domain from a fully resolved URL

This function is only used when the configuration for $ALLOW_OFFSITE is set
to false.

exclude_link()

This function examines each link and determines if it should be included in
the archive of harvested links. Reasons for excluding a link may include the
following:

- The link is contained within JavaScript
- The link already appears in the archive
- The link contains excluded keywords are listed in the exclusion array
- The link is to a different domain

```
function excluded_link($spider_array, $link)
    {
    # Initialization
    global $exclusion_array, $ALLOW_OFFSITE;
    $exclude = false;

    // Exclude links that are JavaScript commands
    if(stristr($link, "javascript"))
        {
        echo "Ignored JavaScript function: $link\n";
        $exclude=true;
        }

    // Exclude redundant links
    for($xx=0; $xx<count($spider_array); $xx++)
        {
        $saved_link="";
        while(isset($saved_link))
            {
            $saved_link=array_pop($spider_array[$xx]);
            if($link == array_pop($spider_array[$xx]))
                {
                echo "Ignored redundant link: $link\n";
                $exclude=true;
                break;
                }
            }
        }
    }
```

```
// Exclude links found in $exclusion_array
for($xx=0; $xx<count($exclusion_array); $xx++)
    {
    if(stristr($link, $exclusion_array[$xx]))
        {
        echo "Ignored excluded link: $link\n";
        $exclude=true;
        break;
        }
    }

// Exclude offsite links if requested
if($ALLOW_OFFSITE==false)
    {
    if(get_domain($link)!=get_domain($SEED_URL))
        {
        echo "Ignored offsite link: $link\n";
        $exclude=true;
        break;
        }
    }
return $exclude;
}
```

Listing 18-6: Excluding unwanted links

There are several reasons to exclude links. For example, it's best to ignore any links referenced within JavaScript because—without a proper JavaScript interpreter—those links may yield unpredictable results. Removing redundant links makes the spider run faster and reduces the amount of data the spider needs to manage. The exclusion list allows the spider to ignore undesirable links to places like Google AdSense, banner ads, or other places you don't want the spider to go.

Experimenting with the Spider

Now that you have a general idea how this spider works, go to the book's website and download the required scripts. Play with the initialization settings, use different seed URLs, and see what happens.

Consider these three warnings before you start:

- Use a respectful $FETCH_DELAY of at least a second or two so you don't create a denial of service (DoS) attack by consuming so much bandwidth that others cannot use the web pages you target. Better yet, read Chapter 28 before you begin.

- Keep the maximum penetration level set to a low value like 1 or 2. This spider is designed for simplicity, not scalability, and if you penetrate too deeply into your seed URL, your computer will run out of memory.

- For best results, run spider scripts within a command shell, not through a browser.

Adding the Payload

The payload used by this spider is an extension of the library used in Chapter 8 to download all the images found on a web page. This time, however, we'll download all the images referenced by the entire website. The code that adds the payload to the spider is shown in Listing 18-7. You can tack this code directly onto the end of the script for the earlier spider.

```
# Add the payload to the simple spider
// Include download and directory creation lib
include("LIB_download_images.php");

// Download images from pages referenced in $spider_array
for($penetration_level=1; $penetration_level<=$MAX_PENETRATION; $penetration_level++)
    {
    for($xx=0; $xx<count($spider_array[$previous_level]); $xx++)
        {
        download_images_for_page($spider_array[$previous_level][$xx]);
        }
    }
```

Listing 18-7: Adding a payload to the simple spider

Functionally, the addition of the payload involves the inclusion of the image download library and a two-part loop that activates the image harvester for every web page referenced at every penetration level.

Further Exploration

As mentioned earlier, the example spider was optimized for simplicity, not scalability. Moreover, while it was suitable for learning about spiders, it is not suitable for use in a production environment where you want to spider many web pages. There are, however, opportunities for enhancements to improve performance and scalability.

Save Links in a Database

The single biggest limitation of the example spider is that all the links are stored in an array. Arrays can only get so big before the computer is forced to rely on *disk swapping*, a technique that expands the amount of data space by moving some of the storage task from RAM to a disk drive. Disk swapping adversely affects performance and often leads to system crashes. The other drawback to storing links in an array is that all the work your spider performed is lost as soon as the program terminates. A much better approach is to store the information your spiders harvest in a database.

Saving your spider's data in a database has many advantages. First of all, you can store more information. Not only does a database increase the number of links you can store, but it also makes it practical to cache images of the pages you download for later processing. As we'll see later, it also allows more than one spider to work on the same set of links and facilitates multiple computers to launch payloads on the data collected by the spider(s).

Separate the Harvest and Payload

The example spider performs the payload after harvesting all the links. Often, however, link harvesting and payload are two distinctly separate pieces of code, and they are often performed by two separate computers. While one script harvests links and stores them in a database, another process can query the same database to determine which web pages have not received the payload. You could, for example, use the same computer to schedule the spiders to run in the morning and the payload script to run in the evening. This assumes, of course, that you save your spidered results in a database, where the data has persistence and is available over an extended period.

Distribute Tasks Across Multiple Computers

Your spider can do more in less time if it teams with other spiders to download multiple pages simultaneously. Fortunately, spiders spend most of their time waiting for webservers to respond to requests for web pages, so there's a lot of unused computer power when a single spider process is running on a computer. You can run multiple copies of the same spider script if your spider software queries a database to identify the oldest unprocessed link. After it parses links from that web page, it can query the database again to determine whether links on the next level of penetration already exist in the database—and if not, it can save them for later processing. Once you've written one spider to operate in this manner, you can run multiple copies of the identical spider script on the same computer, each accessing the same database to complete a common task. Similarly, you can also run multiple copies of the payload script to process all the links harvested by the team of spiders.

If you run out of processing power on a single computer, you can use the same technique used to run parallel spiders on one machine to run multiple spiders on multiple computers. You can improve performance further by hosting the database on its own computer. As long as all the spiders and all the payload computers have network access to a common database, you should be able to expand this concept until the database runs out of processing power. Distributing the database, unfortunately, is more difficult than distributing spiders and payload tasks.

Regulate Page Requests

Spiders (especially the distributed types) increase the potential of overwhelming target websites with page requests. It doesn't take much computer power to completely flood a network. In fact, a vintage 33 MHz Pentium has ample resources to consume a T1 network connection. Multiple modern computers, of course, can do much more damage. If you do build a distributed spider, you should consider writing a scheduler, perhaps on the computer that hosts your database, to regulate how often page requests are made to specific domains or even to specific subnets. The scheduler could also remove redundant links from the database and perform other routine maintenance tasks. If you haven't already done so, this is a good time to read (or reread) Chapter 28.

19

PROCUREMENT WEBBOTS AND SNIPERS

A *procurement bot* is any intelligent web agent that automatically makes online purchases on a user's behalf. These webbots are improvements over manual online procurement because they not only automate the online purchasing process, but also autonomously detect events that indicate the best time to buy. Procurement bots commonly make automated purchases based on the availability of merchandise or price reductions. For other webbots, external events like low inventory levels trigger a purchase.

The advantage of using procurement bots in your business is that they identify opportunities that may only be available for a short period or that may only be discovered after many hours of browsing. Manually finding online deals can be tedious, time consuming, and prone to human error. The ability to shop automatically uncovers bargains that would otherwise go unnoticed. I've written automated procurement bots that—on a monthly basis—purchase hundreds of thousands of dollars of merchandise that would be unknown to less vigilant human buyers.

Procurement Webbot Theory

Before you begin, consider that procurement bots require both planning and in-depth investigation of target websites. These programs spend your (or your clients') money, and their success is dependent on how well you design, program, debug, and implement them. With this in mind, use the techniques described elsewhere in this book before embarking on your first procurement bot—in other words, your first webbot shouldn't be one that spends money. You can use the online test store (introduced in Chapter 7) as target practice before writing webbots that make autonomous purchases in the wild.

While procurement bots purchase a wide range of products in various circumstances, they typically follow the steps shown in Figure 19-1.

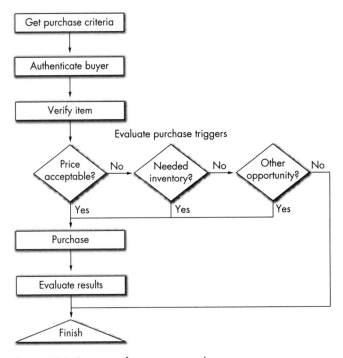

Figure 19-1: Structure of a procurement bot

While price and need govern this particular webbot in deciding when to make a purchase, you can design virtually any type of procurement bot by substituting different purchase trigger events.

Get Purchase Criteria

A procurement bot first needs to gather the *purchase criteria*, which is a description of the item or items to purchase. The purchase criteria may range from simple part numbers to item descriptions combined with complicated calculations that determine how much you want to pay for an item.

Authenticate Buyer

Once the webbot has identified the purchase criteria, it authenticates the buyer by automatically logging in to the online store as a registered user. In almost all cases, this means the webbot must know the username and password of the person it represents.[1] (For more on how webbots handle the authentication process, see Chapter 21.)

Verify Item

Prior to purchase, procurement bots should verify that requested items are still available for sale if they were selected in advance of the actual purchase. For example, if you instruct a procurement bot to buy something in an online auction, the bot should email you if the auction is canceled and the item is no longer for sale. (Chapter 16 describes how to send email from a webbot.) The procurement process should also stop at this point. This sounds obvious, but unless you program your webbot to stop when items are no longer for sale, it may attempt to purchase unavailable items.

Evaluate Purchase Triggers

Purchase triggers determine when available merchandise meets predefined purchase criteria. When those conditions are met, the purchase is made. Bear in mind that it may take days, weeks, or even months before a buying opportunity presents itself. But when it does, you'll be the first in line (unless someone who is also running a procurement bot beats you to it).[2]

Together, the purchase criteria and purchase triggers define what your procurement bot does. If you want to pick up cheap merchandise or capitalize on price reductions, you might use price as a trigger. More complicated webbots may weigh both price and inventory levels to make purchasing decisions. Other procurement bots may make purchases based on the scarcity of merchandise. Alternatively, as we'll explore later, you may write a sniper, which uses the time an auction ends as a trigger to bidding.

Make Purchase

Purchases are finalized by completing and submitting forms that collect information about the purchased product, shipping address, and payment method. Your webbot should submit these forms in the same manner as described earlier in this book. (See Chapter 5 for more on writing webbots that submit forms to websites.)

---

[1] The exceptions to this rule are instances like the eBay API, which allow third parties to act on someone's behalf without knowing that individual's username and password.

[2] Occasionally, you may find yourself in direct competition with other webbots. I've found that when this happens, it's usually best not to get overly competitive and do things like use excessive bandwidth or server connections that might identify your presence.

Evaluate Results

After making a purchase, the target server will display a web page that confirms your purchase. Your webbot should parse the page to determine that your acquisition was successful and then communicate the result of the purchase to you. Notifications of this type are usually done through email. If the procurement bot buys many items, however, it might be better to report the status of all purchases on a web page or to send an email with the consolidated results for the entire day's activity.

Sniper Theory

Of all procurement bots, snipers are the best known, largely because of their popularity on eBay. *Snipers* are procurement bots that use time as their trigger event. Snipers wait until the closing seconds of an online auction and bid just before the auction ends. The intent is to make the auction's last bid and avoid price escalation caused by bidding wars. While making the last bid is what characterizes snipers, a more important feature is that they enable people to participate in online auctions without having to dedicate their time to monitoring individual items or making bids at the most opportune moments.

While eBay is the most popular target, sniping programs can purchase products from any auction website, including Yahoo!, Overstock.com, uBid, or even official US government auction sites.

The sniping process is similar to that of the procurement bots described earlier. The main differences are that the clocks on the auction website and sniper must be synchronized, and the purchase trigger is determined by the auction's end time. Figure 19-2 shows a common sniper construction.

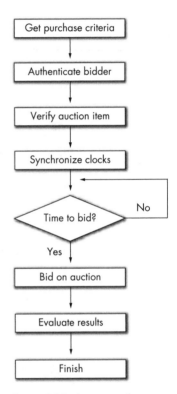

Figure 19-2: Anatomy of a sniper

Get Purchase Criteria

The purchase criteria for an auction are generally the auction identification number and the maximum price the user is willing to pay for the item. Advanced snipers, however, may periodically look for and target any auction that matches other predefined purchase criteria like the brand or age of an item.

Authenticate Buyer

Authentication of snipers is similar to other authentication practices discussed earlier. Occasionally, snipers can authenticate users without the need for a username and password, but these techniques vary depending on the auction site and the special programming interfaces it provides. The problem of disclosing login credentials to third-party sniping services is one of the reasons people often choose to write their own snipers.

Verify Item

Many auctions end prematurely due to early cancellation by the seller or to *buy-it-now purchases*, which allow a bidder to buy an item for a fixed price before the auction comes to its scheduled end. For both of these reasons, snipers must periodically verify that the auction it intends to snipe is still a valid auction. Not doing so may cause a sniper to mistakenly bid on non-existent auctions. Typically, snipers validate the auction once after collecting the purchase criteria and again just before bidding.

Synchronize Clocks

Since a sniper uses the closing time of an auction as its event trigger, the sniper and auction website must synchronize their clocks. Synchronization involves requesting the timestamp from the online auction's server and subtracting that value from the auction's scheduled end. The result is the starting value for a countdown clock. When the countdown clock approaches zero, the sniper places its bid.

A countdown clock is a more accurate method of establishing a bid time than relying on your computer's internal clock to make a bid a few seconds before the scheduled end of an auction. This is particularly true if your sniper is running on a PC, where internal clocks are notoriously inaccurate.

To guarantee synchronization of the sniper and the online auction's clock, the sniper should synchronize periodically and with increased frequency as the end of the auction nears. Periodic synchronization reduces the sniper's reliance on the accuracy of your computer's clock. Chances are, neither the clock on the auction site's server nor the one on your PC is set to the correct time, but from a sniper's perspective, the server's clock is the only one that matters.

Obtaining a server's clock value is as easy as making a header request and parsing the server's timestamp from the header, as shown in Listing 19-1.

```
// Include libraries
include("LIB_http.php");
include("LIB_parse.php");

// Identify the server you want to get local time from
$target = "http://www.schrenk.com";

// Request the httpd head
$header_array = http_header($target, $ref="");
```

```
// Parse the local server time from the header
$local_server_time = return_between($header_array['FILE'], $start="Date:",
                                    $stop="\n", EXCL);

// Convert the local server time to a timestamp
$local_server_time_ts = strtotime($local_server_time);

// Display results
echo "\nReturned header:\n";
echo $header_array['FILE']."\n";
echo "Parsed server timestamp = ".$local_server_time_ts ."\n";
echo "Formatted server time   = ".date("r", $local_server_time_ts)."\n";
```

Listing 19-1: A script that fetches and parses a server's time settings

When the script in Listing 19-1 is run, it displays a screen similar to the one in Figure 19-3. Here you can see that the script requests an HTTP header from a target server. It then parses the timestamp (which is identified by the line starting with *Date:*) from the header.

Figure 19-3: Result of running the script in Listing 19-1

It is fairly safe to assume that the target webserver's clock is the same clock that is used to time the auctions. However, as a precaution, it is worthwhile to verify that the timestamp returned from the webserver correlates to the time displayed on the auction web pages.

Once the sniper parses the server's formatted timestamp, it converts it into a *Unix timestamp*, an integer that represents the number of seconds that have elapsed since January 1, 1970. The use of the Unix timestamp is important because in order to perform the countdown, the sniper needs to know how many seconds separate the current time from the scheduled end of the auction. If you have Unix timestamps for both events, it's simply a matter of subtracting the current server timestamp value from the end of auction timestamp. Failure to convert to Unix timestamps results in some difficult calendar math. For example, without Unix timestamps, you may need to subtract 10:20 PM, September 19 from 8:12 AM, September 20 to obtain the time remaining in an auction.

Time to Bid?

A sniper needs to make one bid, close to the auction's scheduled end but just before other bidders have time to respond to it. Therefore, you will want to make your bid a few seconds before the auction ends, but not so close to the end that the auction is over before the server has time to process your bid.

Submit Bid

Your sniper will submit bids in a manner similar to the other procurement bots, but since your bid is time sensitive, your sniper will need to anticipate how long it will take to complete the forms and get responses from the target server. You should expect to fine-tune this process on live auctions.

Evaluate Results

Evaluating the results of a sniping attempt is also similar to evaluating the purchase results of other procurement bots. The only difference is that, unlike other procurement bots, there is a possibility that you were outbid or that the sniper bid too late to win the item. For these reasons, you may want to include additional diagnostic information in the results, including the final price, and whether you were outbid or the auction ended before your bid was completed. This way, you can learn what may have gone wrong and correct problems that may reappear in future sniping attempts.

Testing Your Own Webbots and Snipers

The online store you used in Chapter 7 may also be used to test your trial procurement bots and snipers. You should feel free to make your mistakes here before you commit errors with a real procurement bot that discloses a competitive advantage or causes suspension of your privileges on an actual target website. Aspects of the test store that you may find particularly useful for testing your skills include the following:

- The store requires that buyers register and authenticate themselves before making any purchase or bidding in any auction.
- The prices in the store periodically change. Use this feature to design procurement bots that capitalize on unannounced price dips.

The address of the online test store is listed on this book's website, which is available at http://www.schrenk.com/nostarch/webbots.

Further Exploration

As a developer with the skills to write procurement bots, you should ask yourself what other types of purchasing agents you can write and what other parameters you can use to make purchasing decisions. Consider mapping out your particular ideas in a flowchart as I did in Figures 19-1 and 19-2.

After you've honed your skills at the book's test store, consider the following ideas as starting points for developing your own procurement bots and snipers.

- Develop a sniper that makes counterbids as necessary.
- Design a sniper that uses scarcity of an item as criteria for purchase.
- Write a procurement bot that detects price reductions.
- Write a procurement bot that monitors the availability of tickets for upcoming concerts and sporting events. When it appears that the tickets for a concert or game will sell out in advance of the event, create a procurement bot that automatically purchases tickets for resale later. (Make sure not to conflict with local laws, of course.)

Write a procurement bot that monitors weather forecasts and makes stock or commodity purchases based on industries that are affected by inclement weather.

Final Thoughts

Purchasing agents are easier to write than to test. This is especially true when sniping high-value items like cars, jewelry, and industrial equipment, where mistakes are expensive. Obviously, when you're writing sniping agents that buy big-ticket items, you want to get things right the first time, but this is also true of procurement bots that buy cheaper merchandise. Here is some general advice for debugging procurement bots and snipers.

- Debug code in stages, only moving to the next step after validating that the prior stage works correctly.
- Assume that there are limited opportunities to test your ability to make purchases with actual trigger events. Hours, days, or even weeks may pass between purchase opportunities. Schedule ample debugging time, since the speed at which you can validate your code is directly associated with the availability of specific products to purchase.
- Assume that all *transactional websites*, sites where money is exchanged, are closely monitored. Even though your intentions are pure, the system administrator of your target webserver may confuse your coding and process errors with hackers exploiting vulnerabilities in the server. The consequences of such mistakes may lead to loss of privileges.
- Keep a low profile. Test as much as you can before communicating with the website's server, and limit the number of times you communicate with that target server.
- Make sure to read Chapters 25 and 28 before deploying any procurement bot.

20

WEBBOTS AND CRYPTOGRAPHY

Cryptography uses mathematics to secure data by applying well-known algorithms (or *ciphers*) to render the data unreadable to people who don't have the *key*, the string of bits required to unlock the code. The beauty of cryptography is that it relies on standards to secure data transmission between web clients and servers. Without these standards, it would be impossible to have consistent security across the multitude of places that require secure data transmission.

Don't confuse cryptography with obfuscation. *Obfuscation* attempts to obscure or hide data without standardized protocols—as a result, it is about as reliable as hiding your house key under the doormat. And since it doesn't rely on standard methods for "un-obfuscation," it is not suitable for applications that need to work in a variety of circumstances.

Encryption—the use of cryptography—created a commercial environment on the Internet, mostly by making it safe to pay for online purchases with credit cards. The World Wide Web didn't widely support encryption until 1995, shortly after the Netscape Navigator browser (paired with its Commerce

Server) began supporting a protocol called *Secure Sockets Layer (SSL)*. SSL is a private way to transmit personal data through an encrypted data transport layer. While Transport Layer Security (TLS) has superseded SSL, the new protocol only changes SSL slightly, and SSL is still the popular term used to describe web encryption. Today, all popular webservers and web browsers support encryption. (You can identify when a website begins to use encryption, because the protocol changes from http to https.[1]) If you design webbots that handle sensitive information, you will need to know how to download encrypted websites and make encrypted requests.

In addition to privacy, SSL also ensures the identity of websites by confirming that a *digital certificate* (what I referred to earlier as a *key*) was assigned to the website using SSL. This means, for example, that when you check your bank balance, you know that the web page you access is actually coming from your bank's server and is not the product of a *phishing attack*. This is enforced by validating the bank's certificate with the agency that assigned it to the bank's IP address. Another feature of SSL is that it ensures that web clients and servers receive all the transmitted data, because the decryption methods won't work on partial data sets.

Designing Webbots That Use Encryption

As when downloading unencrypted web pages, PHP provides choices to the webbot designer who needs to access secure servers. The following sections explore methods for requesting and downloading web pages that use encryption.

SSL and PHP Built-in Functions

In PHP version 5 or higher, you can use the standard PHP built-in functions (discussed in Chapter 3) to request and download encrypted files if you change the protocol from http: to https:. However, I wouldn't recommend using the built-in functions because they lack many features that are important to web-bot developers, like automatic forwarding, form submission, and cookie support, just to name a few.

Encryption and PHP/CURL

To download an encrypted web page in PHP/CURL, simply set the protocol to https:, as shown in Listing 20-1.

```
http_get("https://some.domain.com", $referer);
```

Listing 20-1: Requesting an encrypted web page

It's important to note that in some PHP distributions, the protocol may be case sensitive, and a protocol defined as HTTPS: will not work. Therefore, it's a good practice to be consistent and always specify the protocol in lowercase.

---

[1] Additionally, when SSL is used, the network port changes from 80 to 447.

A Quick Overview of Web Encryption

The following is a hasty overview of how web encryption works. While incomplete, it's here to provide a greater appreciation for everything PHP/CURL does and to help you be semi-literate in SSL conversations with peers, vendors, and clients.

Once a web client recognizes it is talking to a secure server, it initiates a *handshake* process, where the web client and server agree on the type of encryption to use. This is important because web clients and servers are typically capable of using several ciphers or encryption algorithms. Two commonly used encryption ciphers include Digital Encryption Standard (DES) and Message Digest Algorithm (MD5).

The server replies to the web client with a variety of data, including its *encryption certificate*, a long string of numbers used to authenticate the domain and tell the web client how to decrypt the data it gets from the server. The web client also sends the server a random string of data that the server uses to decrypt information originating from the client.

The process of creating an SSL for secure data communication should happen transparently and generally shouldn't be a concern for developers. This is regardless of the fact that creating a secure connection to a webserver requires multiple (complicated) communications between the web client and server. In the end—when set up properly—all data flowing to and from a secure website is encrypted, including all GET and POST requests and cookies. Aside from local certificates, which are explained next, that's about all webbot developers need to know about encryption. If, however, you thirst for detailed information, or you see yourself as a future Hacker Jeopardy contestant,[2] you should read the SSL specification. The full details are available at http://wp.netscape.com/eng/ssl3/ssl-toc.html.

Local Certificates

Corporate networks sometimes use local certificates to authenticate both client and server. In the vast majority of cases, however, there is no need for a local certificate—in fact, I have never been in a situation that required one. However, PHP/CURL supports local encryption certificates, and it's important to configure them even if you don't use them. Versions 7.10 and later of cURL assume that a local certificate is used and will not download any web page if the local certificate isn't defined.[3] This is counterintuitive since local certificates are seldom used; therefore, LIB_http—the library this book uses to fetch web pages and submit forms—assumes that there is no local encryption certificate and configures PHP/CURL accordingly, as shown in Listing 20-2.

---

[2] Hacker Jeopardy is a contest where contestants answer detailed questions about various Internet protocols. This game is an annual event at the hacker conference DEFCON (http://www.defcon.org).

[3] I learned this lesson the hard way when a client flew me to Palo Alto for a week to work on a project. None of my PHP/CURL routines worked on the client's server because it used a later version of cURL than I was using. After a few embarrassing moments, I discovered that the problem involved defining local certificates, even when they aren't used.

```
curl_setopt($ch, CURLOPT_SSL_VERIFYPEER, FALSE);    // No certificate
```

Listing 20-2: Telling PHP/CURL not to look for a local certificate

Later releases of cURL require this option even when no local certificate is used. For that reason, you should define this option every time you design a PHP/CURL interface.

If your webbot needs to run in a very secure network, a local certificate may be required to authenticate your webbot as a valid user of the web page or service it accesses. If you need to use a local encryption certificate, you can define one with the PHP/CURL options described in Listing 20-3.

```
curl_setopt($ch, CURLOPT_SSL_VERIFYPEER, TRUE);    // Certificate in use
curl_setopt($ch, CURLOPT_CAINFO, $file_name);      // Certificate file name
```

Listing 20-3: Telling PHP/CURL how to use a local encryption certificate

On even rarer occasions, you may have to support multiple local certificates. In those cases, you can define a directory path, instead of a filename, to tell cURL where to find the location of all your encryption certificates, as shown in Listing 20-4.

```
curl_setopt($ch, CURLOPT_SSL_VERIFYPEER, TRUE);    // Certificate in use
curl_setopt($ch, CURLOPT_CAPATH, $path);           // Directory where multiple
                                                   // certificates are stored
```

Listing 20-4: Telling PHP/CURL how to use multiple local encryption certificates

Final Thoughts

Occasionally, you can force an encrypted website into transferring unencrypted data by simply changing the protocol from https to http in the request. While this may allow you to download the web page, this technique is a bad idea because, in addition to potentially revealing confidential data, your webbot's actions will look unusual in server log files, which will destroy all attempts at stealth.

Sometimes web developers use the wrong protocol when designing web forms. It's important to remember that the default protocol for form submission is http, and unless specifically defined as https by the form's action attribute, the form is submitted without encryption, even if the form exists on a secure web page! Using the wrong network protocol is a common mistake made by inexperienced web developers. For that reason, when your webbot submits a form, you need to be sure it uses the same form-submission protocol that is defined by the downloaded form. For example, if you download an encrypted form page and the form's action attribute isn't defined, the protocol is http, not https! As wrong as it sounds, you need to use the same protocol defined by the web form, even if it is not the proper protocol to use in that specific case. If your webbot uses a protocol that is different than the one browsers use when submitting the form, you may cause the system administrator to scratch his or her head and investigate why one web client isn't using the same protocol everyone else is using.

21

AUTHENTICATION

If your webbots are going to access sensitive information or handle money, they'll need to *authenticate*, or sign in as registered users of websites. This chapter teaches you how to write webbots that access password-protected websites. As in previous chapters, you can practice what you learn with example scripts and special test pages on the book's website.

What Is Authentication?

Authentication is the processes of proving that you are who you say you are. You authenticate yourself by presenting something that only you can produce. Table 21-1 describes the three categories of things used to prove a person's identity.

Table 21-1: Things That Prove a Person's Identity

You Authenticate Yourself With . . .	Examples
Something you know	Usernames and passwords; Social Security numbers
Something you are (biometrics)	DNA samples; thumbprints; retina, voice, and facial scans
Something you have	House keys, digital certificates, encoded magnetic cards, wireless key fobs, implanted canine microchips

Types of Online Authentication

Most websites that require authentication ask for usernames and passwords (something you know). The username and password—also known as *login criteria*—are compared to records in a database. The user is allowed access to the website if the login criteria match the records in the database. Based on the login criteria, the website may optionally restrict the user to specific parts of the website or grant specific functionality.

Usernames and passwords are the most convenient way to authenticate people online because they can be authenticated with a browser and without the need for additional hardware or software.

Websites also authenticate through the use of digital certificates (something you have), which must be exchanged between client and server and validated before access to a website or service is granted. The intricacies of digital certificates are described in Chapter 20. If you skipped this chapter, this is a good time to read it. Otherwise, all you need to know is that digital certificates are files that reside on servers, or less frequently, on the hard drives of client computers. The contents of these certificate files are automatically exchanged to authenticate the computer that holds the certificate. You're most apt to encounter digital certificates when using the HTTPS protocol (also know as SSL) to access secure websites. Here, the certificate authenticates the website and facilitates the use of an encrypted data channel. Less frequently, a certificate is required on the client computer as well, to access *virtual private networks (VPNs)*, which allow remote users to access private corporate networks. PHP/CURL manages certificates automatically if you specify the *https:* protocol in the URL. PHP/CURL also facilitates the use of local certificates; in the odd circumstance that you require a client-side certificate, PHP/CURL and client-side certificates are covered in Appendix A.

Biometrics (something you are) are generally not used in online authentication and are beyond the scope of this chapter. Personally, I have only seen biometrics used to authenticate users to online services when biometric information is readily available, as in telemedicine.

Strengthening Authentication by Combining Techniques

Your webbots may encounter websites that use multiple forms of authentication, since authentication is strengthened when two or more techniques are combined. For example, ATMs require both an ATM card (something you have) and a personal identification number (PIN) (something you know). Similarly, the retailer Target experimented with an ATM-style authentication scheme when it introduced USB credit card readers that worked in conjunction with Target.com.

Authentication and Webbots

You may very well encounter certificates—and even biometrics—as a webbot developer, so the more familiar you are with the various forms of authentication, the more potential targets your webbots will have. You'll find, however, that most webbots authenticate with simple usernames and passwords. The following sections describe the most common techniques for using usernames and passwords.

Example Scripts and Practice Pages

We'll explore three types of online authentication. For each case, you'll receive examples of authentication scripts designed specifically to work with password-protected sections of this book's website. You can experiment (and make mistakes) on these practice pages before writing authenticating webbots that work on real websites. The location of the practice pages is shown in Table 21-2.

Table 21-2: Location of Authentication Practice Pages on the Book's Website

Authentication Method	Location of Practice Pages
Basic authentication	http://www.schrenk.com/nostarch/webbots/basic_authentication
Cookies sessions	http://www.schrenk.com/nostarch/webbots/cookie_authentication
Query sessions	http://www.schrenk.com/nostarch/webbots/query_authentication

For simplicity, all of the authentication examples on the book's website use the login criteria shown in Table 21-3.

Table 21-3: Login Criteria Used for All Authentication Practice Pages

Username	Password
webbot	sp1der3

Basic Authentication

The most common form of online is authentication is basic authentication. *Basic authentication* is a dialogue between the webserver and browsing agent in which the login credentials are requested and processed, as shown in Figure 21-1.

Web pages subject to basic authentication exist in what's called a realm. Generally, *realms* refer to all web pages in the current server directory as well as the web pages in sub-directories. Fortunately, browsers shield people from many of the details defined in Figure 21-1. Once you authenticate yourself with a browser, it appears that you don't re-authenticate yourself when accessing other pages within the realm. In reality, the dialogue from Figure 21-1 happens for each page downloaded within the realm. Your browser automatically resubmits your authentication credentials without asking you again for your username and password. When accessing a basic authenticated website with a webbot, you will need to send your login credentials every time the webbot requests a page within the authenticated realm, as shown later in the example script.

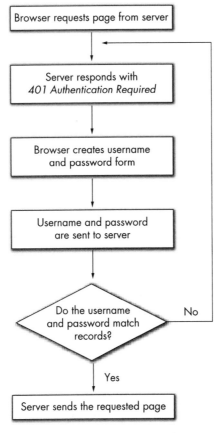

Figure 21-1: Basic authentication dialogue

Before you write an auto-authenticating webbot, you should first visit the target website and manually authenticate yourself into the site with a browser. This way you can validate your login credentials and learn about the target site before you design your webbot. When you request a web page from the book's basic authentication test area, your browser will initially present a login form for entering usernames and passwords, as shown in Figure 21-2.

Figure 21-2: Basic authentication login form

After entering your username and password, you will gain access to a simple set of practice pages (shown in Figure 21-3) for testing auto-authenticating webbots and basic authentication. You should familiarize yourself with these simple pages before reading further.

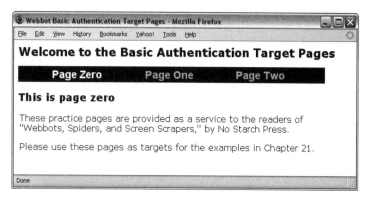

Figure 21-3: Basic authentication test pages

The commands required to download a web page with basic authentication are very similar to those required to download a page without authentication. The only change is that you need to configure the CURLOPT_USERPWD option to pass the login credentials to PHP/CURL. The format for login credentials is the username and password separated by a colon, as shown in Listing 21-1.

```
<?
# Define target page
$target = "http://www.schrenk.com/nostarch/webbots/basic_authentication/index.php";

# Define login credentials for this page
$credentials = "webbot:sp1der3";

# Create the cURL session
$ch = curl_init();
curl_setopt($ch, CURLOPT_URL, $target);          // Define target site
curl_setopt($ch, CURLOPT_USERPWD, $credentials); // Send credentials
curl_setopt($ch, CURLOPT_RETURNTRANSFER, TRUE);  // Return page in string

# Echo page
$page = curl_exec($ch);                          // Place web page into a string
echo $page;                                      // Echo downloaded page

# Close the cURL session
curl_close($ch);
?>
```

Listing 21-1: The minimal code required to access the basic authentication test pages

Once the favored form of authentication, basic authentication is losing out to other techniques because it is weaker. For example, with basic authentication, there is no way to log out without closing your browser. There is also no way to change the appearance of the authentication form because the browser creates it. Basic authentication is also not very secure, as the browser sends the login criteria to the server in cleartext. Digest authentication is an improvement over basic authentication. Unlike basic authentication, *digest authentication* sends the password to the server as an MD5 digest with 128-bit encryption. Unfortunately, support for digest authentication is spotty, especially with older browsers. If you're using PHP 5, you can use the curl_setopt() function to tell PHP/CURL which form of authentication to use. Since we're focusing on PHP 4, let's limit this discussion to basic authentication, though the process is otherwise identical with digest authentication.

Session Authentication

Unlike basic authentication, in which login credentials are sent each time a page is downloaded, *session authentication* validates users once and creates a *session value* that represents that authentication. The session values (instead of the actual username and password) are passed to each subsequent page fetch to indicate that the user is authenticated. There are two basic methods for employing session authentication—with cookies and with query strings. These methods are nearly identical in execution and work equally well. You're apt to encounter both forms of sessions as you gain experience writing webbots.

Authentication with Cookie Sessions

Cookies are small pieces of information that servers store on your hard drive. Cookies are important because they allow servers to identify unique users. With cookies, websites can remember preferences and browsing habits (within the domain), and use sessions to facilitate authentication.

How Cookies Work

Servers send cookies in HTTP headers. It is up to the client software to parse the cookie from the header and save the cookie values for later use. On subsequent fetches within the same domain, it is the client's responsibility to send the cookies back to the server in the HTTP header of the page request. In our cookie authentication example, the cookie session can be viewed in the header returned by the server, as shown in Listing 21-2.

```
HTTP/1.1 302 Found
Date: Sat, 09 Sep 2006 16:09:03 GMT
Server: Apache/2.0.58 (FreeBSD) mod_ssl/2.0.58 OpenSSL/0.9.8a PHP/4.4.2
X-Powered-By: PHP/4.4.2
Set-Cookie: authenticate=1157818143
Location: index0.php
Content-Length: 1837
Content-Type: text/html; charset=ISO-8859-1
```

Listing 21-2: Cookies returned from the server in the HTTP header

The line in bold typeface defines the name of the cookie and its value. In this case there is one cookie named authenticate with the value 1157818143.

Sometimes cookies have expiration dates, which is an indication that the server wants the client to write the cookie to a file on the hard drive. Other times, as in our example, no expiration date is specified. When no expiration date is specified, the server requests that the browser save the cookie in RAM and delete it when the browser closes. For security reasons, authentication cookies typically have no expiration date and are stored in RAM.

When authentication is done using a cookie, each successive page within the website examines the session cookie, and, based on internal rules, determines whether the web agent is authorized to download that web page. The actual value of the cookie session is of little importance to the webbot, as long as the value of the cookie session matches the value expected by the target web-server. In many cases, as in our example, the session also holds a time-out value that expires after a limited period. Figure 21-4 shows a typical cookie authentication session.

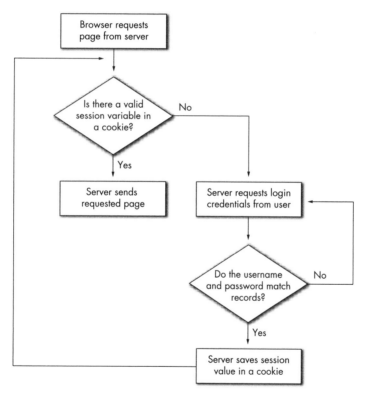

Figure 21-4: Authentication with cookie sessions

Unlike basic authentication, where the login criteria are sent in a generic (browser-dependent) form, cookie authentication uses custom forms, as shown in Figure 21-5.

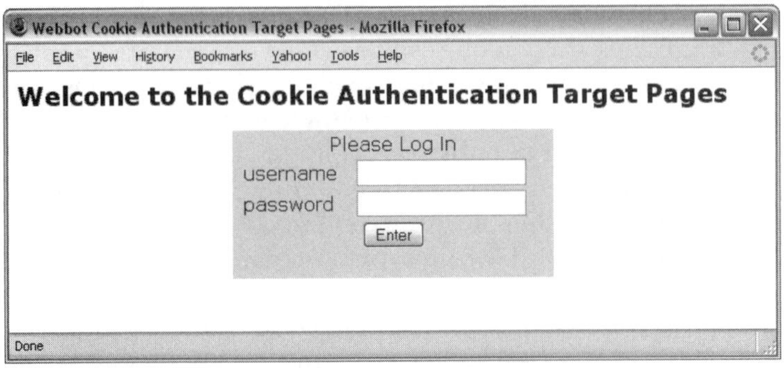

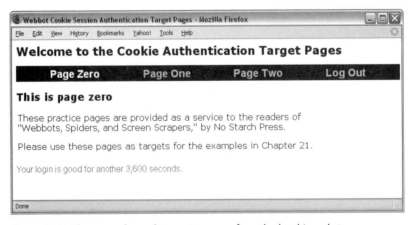

Figure 21-5: The login page for the cookie authentication example

Regardless of the authentication method used by your target web page, it's vitally important to explore your target screens with a browser before writing self-authenticating webbots. This is especially true in this example, because your webbot must emulate the login form. You should take this time to explore the cookie authentication pages on this book's website. View the source code for each page, and see how the code works. Use your browser to monitor the values of the cookies the web pages use. Now is also a good time to preview Chapter 22.

Figure 21-6 shows an example of the screens that lay beyond the login screen.

![Screenshot of the Webbot Cookie Session Authentication Target Pages in Mozilla Firefox. The page title reads "Welcome to the Cookie Authentication Target Pages" with a navigation bar containing Page Zero, Page One, Page Two, and Log Out. The content reads "This is page zero. These practice pages are provided as a service to the readers of 'Webbots, Spiders, and Screen Scrapers,' by No Starch Press. Please use these pages as targets for the examples in Chapter 21. Your login is good for another 3,600 seconds."]

Figure 21-6: The example cookie session page from the book's website

Cookie Session Example

A webbot must do the following to authenticate itself to a website that uses cookie sessions:

- Download the web page with the login form
- Emulate the form that gathers the login credentials
- Capture the cookie written by the server
- Provide the session cookie to the server on each page request

The script in Listing 21-3 first downloads the login page as a normal user would with a browser. As it emulates the form that sends the login credentials, it uses the CURLOPT_COOKIEFILE and CURLOPT_COOKIEJAR options to tell cURL where the cookies should be written and where to find the cookies that are read by the server. To most people (myself included), it seems redundant to have one set of outbound cookies and another set of inbound cookies. In every case I've seen, webbots use the same file to write and read cookies. It's important to note that PHP/CURL will always save cookies to a file, even when the cookie has no expiration date. This presents some interesting problems, which are explained in Chapter 22.

```
<?
# Define target page
$target = "http://www.schrenk.com/nostarch/webbots/cookie_authentication/index.php";

# Define the login form data
$form_data="enter=Enter&username=webbot&password=sp1der3";

# Create the cURL session
$ch = curl_init();
curl_setopt($ch, CURLOPT_URL, $target);                 // Define target site
curl_setopt($ch, CURLOPT_RETURNTRANSFER, TRUE);         // Return page in string
curl_setopt($ch, CURLOPT_COOKIEJAR, "cookies.txt");     // Tell cURL where to write cookies
curl_setopt($ch, CURLOPT_COOKIEFILE, "cookies.txt");    // Tell cURL which cookies to send
curl_setopt($ch, CURLOPT_POST, TRUE);
curl_setopt($ch, CURLOPT_POSTFIELDS, $form_data);
curl_setopt($ch, CURLOPT_FOLLOWLOCATION, TRUE);         // Follow redirects

# Execute the PHP/CURL session and echo the downloaded page
$page = curl_exec($ch);
echo $page;

# Close the cURL session
curl_close($ch);
?>
```

Listing 21-3: Auto-authentication with cookie sessions

Once the session cookie is written, your webbot should be able to download any authenticated page, as long as the cookie is presented to the website by your cURL session. Just one word of caution: Depending on your version of cURL, you may need to use a complete path when defining your cookie file.

Authentication with Query Sessions

Query string sessions are nearly identical to cookie sessions, the difference being that instead of storing the session value in a cookie, the session value is stored in the query string. Other than this difference, the process is identical to the protocol describing cookie session authentication (outlined in Figure 21-4). Query sessions create additional work for website developers, as the session value must be tacked on to all links and included in all form submissions. Yet some web developers (myself included) prefer query sessions, as some browsers and proxies restrict the use of cookies and make cookie sessions difficult to implement.

This is a good time to manually explore the test pages for query authentication on the website. Once you enter your username and password, you'll notice that the authentication session value is visible in the URL as a GET value, as shown in Figure 21-7. However, this may not be the case in all situations, as the session value could also be in a POST value and invisible to the viewer.

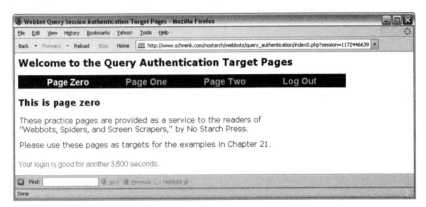

Figure 21-7: Session variable visible in the query string (URL)

Like the cookie session example, the query session example first emulates the login form. Then it parses the session value from the authenticated result and includes the session value in the query string of each page it requests. A script capable of downloading pages from the practice pages for query session authentication is shown in Listing 21-4.

```
<?
# Include libraries
include("LIB_http.php");
include("LIB_parse.php");

# Request the login page
$domain = "http://www.schrenk.com/";
$target = $domain."nostarch/webbots/query_authentication";
$page_array = http_get($target, $ref="");

echo $page_array['FILE'];        // Display the login page
sleep(2);                        // Include small delay between page fetches
echo "<hr>";

# Send the query authentication form
$login = $domain."nostarch/webbots/query_authentication/index.php";
```

```
$data_array['enter'] = "Enter";
$data_array['username'] = "webbot";
$data_array['password'] = "sp1der3";
$page_array = http_post_form($login, $ref=$target, $data_array);
echo $page_array['FILE'];   // Display first page after login page
sleep(2);                   // Include small delay between page fetches
echo "<hr>";

# Parse session variable
$session = return_between($page_array['FILE'], "session=", "\"", EXCL);

# Request subsequent pages using the session variable
$page2 = $target . "/index2.php?session=".$session;
$page_array = http_get($page2, $ref="");
echo $page_array['FILE'];   // Display page two
?>
```

Listing 21-4: Authenticating a webbot on a page using query sessions

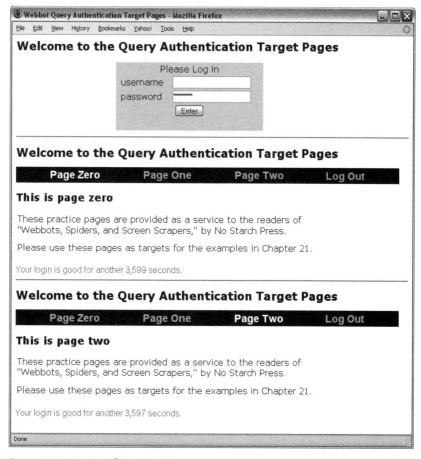

Figure 21-8: Output of Listing 21-4

Final Thoughts

Here are a few additional things to remember when writing webbots that access password-protected websites.

- For clarity, the examples in this chapter use a minimal amount of code to perform a task. In actual use, you'll want to follow the comprehensive practices mentioned elsewhere in this book for downloading pages, parsing results, emulating forms, using cURL, and writing fault-tolerant webbots.

- It's important to note that no form of online authentication is effective unless it is accompanied by encryption. After all, it does little good to authenticate users if sensitive information is sent across the network in cleartext, which can be read by anyone with a packet sniffer.[1] In most cases, authentication will be combined with encryption. For more information about webbots and encryption, revisit Chapter 20.

- If your webbot communicates with more than one domain, you need to be careful not to broadcast your login criteria when writing webbots that use basic authentication. For example, if you hard-code your username and password into a PHP/CURL routine, make sure that you don't use the same function when fetching pages from other domains. This sounds silly, but I've seen it happen, resulting in cleartext login credentials in server log files.

- Websites may use a combination of two or more authentication types. For example, an authenticated site might use both query and cookie sessions. Make sure that you account for all potential authentication schemes before releasing your webbots.

- The latest versions of all the scripts used in this chapter are available for download at this book's website.

---

[1] A *packet sniffer* is a special type of agent that lets people read raw network traffic.

22

ADVANCED COOKIE MANAGEMENT

In the previous chapter, you learned how to use cookies to authenticate webbots to access password-protected websites. This chapter further explores cookies and the challenges they present to webbot developers.

How Cookies Work

Cookies are small pieces of ASCII data that websites store on your computer. Without using cookies, websites cannot distinguish between new visitors and those that visit on a daily basis. Cookies add *persistence*, the ability to identify people who have previously visited the site, to an otherwise stateless environment. Through the magic of cookies, web designers can write scripts to recognize people's preferences, shipping address, login status, and other personal information.

There are two types of cookies. *Temporary cookies* are stored in RAM and expire when the client closes his or her browser; *permanent cookies* live on the client's hard drive and exist until they reach their expiration date (which

may be so far into the future that they'll outlive the computer they're on).
For example, consider the script in Listing 22-1, which writes one temporary
cookie and one permanent cookie that expires in one hour.

```
# Set cookie that expires when browser closes
setcookie ("TemporaryCookie", "66");

# Set cookie that expires in one hour
setcookie ("PermanentCookie", "88", time() + 3600);
```

Listing 22-1: Setting permanent and temporary cookies with PHP

Listing 22-1 shows the cookies' names, values, and expiration dates, if
required. Figures 22-1 and 22-2 show how the cookies written by the script in
Listing 22-1 appear in the privacy settings of a browser.

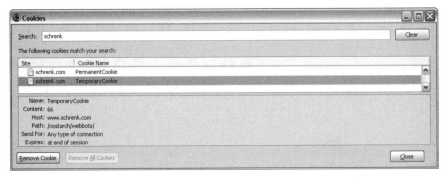

Figure 22-1: A temporary cookie written from http://www.schrenk.com, with a value of 66

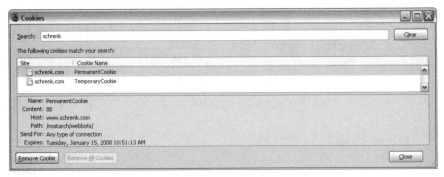

Figure 22-2: A permanent cookie written from http://www.schrenk.com, with a value of 88

Browsers and webservers exchange cookies in HTTP headers. When a
browser requests a web page from a webserver, it looks to see if it has any
cookies previously stored by that web page's domain. If it finds any, it will send
those cookies to the webserver in the HTTP header of the fetch request. When
you execute the cURL command in Figure 22-3, you can see the cookies as
they appear in the returned header.

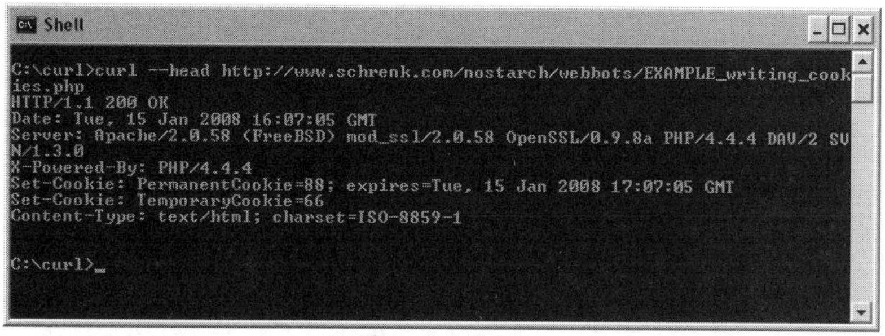

Figure 22-3: Cookies as they appear in the HTTP header sent by the server

A browser will never modify a cookie unless it expires or unless the user erases it using the browser's privacy settings. Servers, however, may write new information to cookies every time they deliver a web page. These new cookie values are then passed to the web browser in the HTTP header, along with the requested web page. According to the specification, a browser will only expose cookies to the domain that wrote them. Webbots, however, are not bound by these rules and can manipulate cookies as needed.

PHP/CURL and Cookies

You can write webbots that support cookies without using PHP/CURL, but doing so adds to the complexity of your designs. Without PHP/CURL, you'll have to read each returned HTTP header, parse the cookies, and store them for later use. You will also have to decide which cookies to send to which domains, manage expiration dates, and return everything correctly in headers of page requests. PHP/CURL does all this for you, automatically. Even with PHP/CURL, however, cookies pose challenges to webbot designers.

Fortunately, PHP/CURL does support cookies, and we can effectively use it to capture the cookies from the previous example, as shown in Listing 22-2.

```
include("LIB_http.php");
$target="http://www.schrenk.com/nostarch/webbots/EXAMPLE_writing_cookies.php";
http_get($target, "");
```

Listing 22-2: Reading cookies with PHP/CURL and the LIB_http library

LIB_http defines the file where PHP/CURL stores cookies. This declaration is done near the beginning of the file, as shown in Listing 22-3.

```
# Location of your cookie file (must be a fully resolved address)
define("COOKIE_FILE", "c:\cookie.txt");
```

Listing 22-3: Cookie file declaration, as made in LIB_http

As noted in Listing 22-3, the address for a cookie file should be a fully resolved local one. Relative addresses sometimes work, but not for all PHP/CURL distributions. When you execute the scripts in Listing 22-1 (available at this book's website), PHP/CURL writes the cookies (in Netscape Cookie Format) in the file defined in the LIB_http configuration, as shown in Listing 22-4.

```
# Netscape HTTP Cookie File
# http://www.netscape.com/newsref/std/cookie_spec.html
# This file was generated by libcurl! Edit at your own risk.

www.schrenk.com  FALSE /nostarch/webbots/  FALSE  1159120749  PermanentCookie 88
www.schrenk.com  FALSE /nostarch/webbots/  FALSE  0 TemporaryCookie  66
```

Listing 22-4: The cookie file, as written by PHP/CURL

NOTE *Each web client maintains its own cookies, and the cookie file written by PHP/CURL is not the same cookie file created by your browser.*

How Cookies Challenge Webbot Design

Webservers will not think anything is wrong if your webbots don't use cookies, since many people configure their browsers not to accept cookies for privacy reasons. However, if your webbot doesn't support cookies, you will not be able to access sites that demand their use. Moreover, if your webbot doesn't support cookies correctly, you will lose your webbot's stealthy properties. You also risk revealing sensitive information if your webbot returns cookies to servers that didn't write them.

Cookies operate transparently—as such, we may forget that they even exist. Yet the data passed in cookies is just as important as the data transferred in GET or POST methods. While PHP/CURL handles cookies for webbot developers, some instances still cause problems—most notably when cookies are supposed to expire or when multiple users (with separate cookies) need to use the same webbot.

Purging Temporary Cookies

One of the problems with the way PHP/CURL manages cookies is that as PHP/CURL writes them to the cookie file, they all become permanent, just like a cookie written to your hard drive by a browser. My experience indicates that all cookies accepted by PHP/CURL become permanent, regardless of the webserver's intention. This in itself is usually not a problem, unless your webbot accesses a website that manages authentication with temporary cookies. If you fail to purge your webbot's temporary cookies, and it accesses the same website for a year, that essentially tells the website's system administrator that you haven't closed your browser (let alone rebooted your computer!) for the same period of time. Since this is not a likely scenario, your account may receive unwanted attention or your webbot may eventually violate the website's authentication process. There is no configuration within PHP/CURL for managing cookie expiration, so you need to manually delete your cookies every so often in order to avoid these problems.

Managing Multiple Users' Cookies

In some applications, your webbots may need to manage cookies for multiple users. For example, suppose you write one of the procurement bots or snipers mentioned in Chapter 19. You may want to integrate the webbot into a website where several people may log in and specify purchases. If these people each have private accounts at the e-commerce website that the webbot targets, each user's cookies will require separate management.

Webbots can manage multiple users' cookies by employing a separate cookie file for each user. LIB_http, however, does not support multiple cookie files, so you will have to write a scheme that assigns the appropriate cookie file to each user. Instead of declaring the name of the cookie file once, as is done in LIB_http, you will need to define the cookie file each time a PHP/CURL session is used. For simplicity, it makes sense to use the person's username in the cookie file, as shown in Listing 22-5.

```
# Open a PHP/CURL session
$s = curl_init();

# Select the cookie file (based on username)
$cookie_file = "c:\bots\".$username."cookies.txt";
curl_setopt($s, CURLOPT_COOKIEFILE, $cookie_file); // Read cookie file
curl_setopt($s, CURLOPT_COOKIEJAR,  $cookie_file); // Write cookie file

# Configure the cURL command
curl_setopt($s, CURLOPT_URL, $target);             // Define target site
curl_setopt($s, CURLOPT_RETURNTRANSFER, TRUE);     // Return in string

# Indicate that there is no local SSL certificate
curl_setopt($s, CURLOPT_SSL_VERIFYPEER, FALSE);    // No certificate

curl_setopt($s, CURLOPT_FOLLOWLOCATION, TRUE);     // Follow redirections
curl_setopt($s, CURLOPT_MAXREDIRS, 4);             // Limit redirections to four

# Execute the cURL command (Send contents of target web page to string)
$downloaded_page = curl_exec($s);

# Close PHP/CURL session
curl_close($s);
```

Listing 22-5: A PHP/CURL script, capable of managing cookies for multiple users

Further Exploration

While PHP/CURL's cookie management is extremely useful to webbot developers, it has a few shortcomings. Here are some ideas for improving on what PHP/CURL already does.

- Design a script that reads cookies directly from the HTTP header and programmatically sends the correct cookies back to the server in the HTTP header of page requests. While you're at it, improve on PHP/CURL's ability to manage cookie expiration dates.

- For security reasons, sometimes administrators do not allow scripts running on hosted webservers to write local files. When this is the case, PHP/CURL is not able to maintain cookie files. Resolve this problem by writing a MySQL-based cookie management system.

- Write a webbot that pools cookies written by two or more webservers. Find a useful application for this exploit.

- Write a script that, on a daily basis, deletes temporary cookies from PHP/CURL's Netscape-formatted cookie file.

23

SCHEDULING WEBBOTS AND SPIDERS

Up to this point, all of our webbots have run only when executed directly from a command line or through a browser. In real-world situations, however, you may want to schedule your webbots and spiders to run automatically. This chapter describes methods for scheduling webbots to run unattended in a Windows environment. Most readers should have access to the scheduling tool I'll be using here.

If you are using an operating system other than Windows, don't despair. Most operating systems support scheduling software of some type. In Unix, Linux, and Mac OS X environments, you can always use the cron command, a text-based scheduling tool. Regardless of the operating system you use, there should also be a graphical interface for a scheduling tool, similar to the one Windows uses.

The Windows Task Scheduler

The *Windows Task Scheduler* is an easy-to-use graphical user interface (GUI) designed for the somewhat complex duty of scheduling tasks. You can access the Task Scheduler through the Control Panel or in the Accessories directory, under System Tools.

To see the tasks currently scheduled on your computer, simply click **Scheduled Tasks**. In addition to showing the schedule and status of these tasks, this window is also the tool you'll use to create new scheduled tasks. It will look like the one in Figure 23-1.

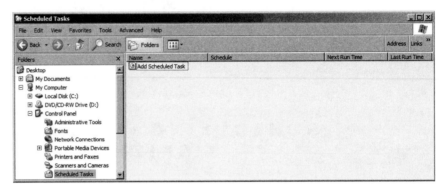

Figure 23-1: The Windows Task Scheduler

Preparing Your Webbots to Run as Scheduled Tasks

Before you schedule your webbot to run automatically, you should create a batch file that executes the webbot. It is easier to schedule a batch file than to specify the PHP file directly, because the batch file adds flexibility in defining path names and allows multiple webbots, or events, to run from the same scheduled task. Listing 23-1 shows the format for executing a PHP webbot from a batch file.

```
drive:/php_path/php drive:/webbot_path/my_webbot.php
```

Listing 23-1: Executing a local webbot from a batch file

In the batch file shown in Listing 23-1, the operating system executes the PHP interpreter, which subsequently executes my_webbot.php.

You can also use a batch file to execute a remote webbot. Listing 23-2 shows how to use cURL to execute a webbot that is on a remote webserver.

```
drive:/curl_path/curl http://www.somedomain.com/remote_webbot.php
```

Listing 23-2: Executing a remote webbot from a batch file

Scheduling a Webbot to Run Daily

To schedule a daily execution of your batch file, click **Add Scheduled Task** in the Task Scheduler window. This will initiate a wizard, which walks you through the process of creating a schedule of execution times for your application. The first step is to identify the application you want to schedule. To schedule your webbot, click the **Browse** button to locate the batch file that executes it, as shown in Figure 23-2.

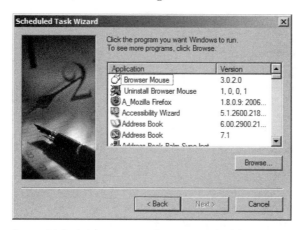

Figure 23-2: Selecting an application to schedule

Once you select the webbot you want to schedule—in this example, test_webbot.bat—the wizard asks for the *periodicity*, or the frequency of execution. Windows allows you to schedule a task to run daily, weekly, monthly, just once, when the computer starts, or when you log on, as shown in Figure 23-3.

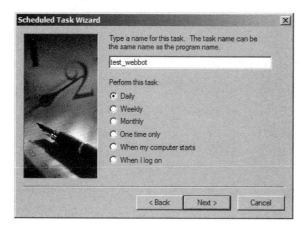

Figure 23-3: Configuring the periodicity of your webbot

After selecting a period, you will specify the time of day you want your webbot to execute. You can also specify whether the webbot will run every day or only on weekdays, as shown in Figure 23-4. You can even schedule a webbot to skip one day or more.

Additionally, you can set the entire schedule to begin sometime in the future. For example, the configuration shown in Figure 23-4 will cause the webbot to run Monday through Friday at 6:20 PM, commencing on January 16, 2008.

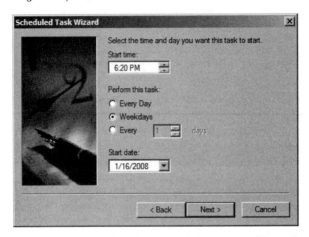

Figure 23-4: Configuring the time and days your webbot will run

The final step of the scheduling wizard is to enter your Windows username and password, as shown in Figure 23-5. This will allow your webbot to run without Windows prompting you for authentication.

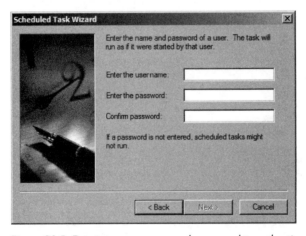

Figure 23-5: Entering a username and password to authenticate your webbot

On completing the wizard, the scheduler displays your new scheduled task, as shown in Figure 23-6.

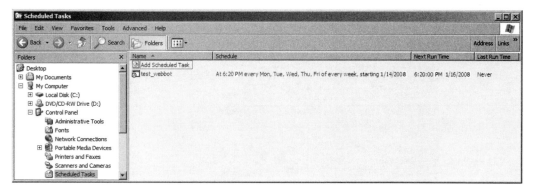

Figure 23-6: The Task Scheduler showing the status of test_webbot's schedule

Complex Schedules

There are several ways to satisfy the need for a complex schedule. The easiest solution may be to schedule additional tasks. For example, if you need to run a webbot once at 6:20 PM and again at 6:45 PM, the simplest solution is to create another task that runs the same webbot at the later time.

The Task Scheduler is also capable of managing very complex schedules. If you right-click your webbot in the Task Scheduler window, select the **Schedule** tab, and then click the **Advanced** button, you can create the schedule shown in Figure 23-7, which runs the webbot every 10 minutes from 6:20 PM to 9:10 PM, every weekday except Wednesdays, starting on January 16, 2008.

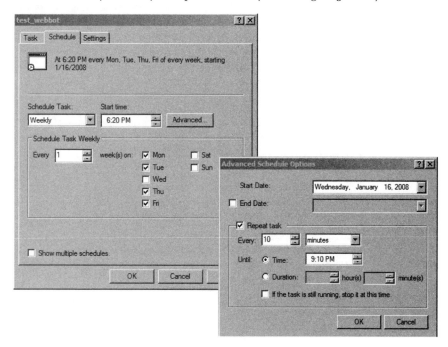

Figure 23-7: An advanced weekly schedule

If a monthly period is required, you can specify which month and days you want the webbot to run. The configuration in Figure 23-8 describes a schedule that launches a webbot on the first Wednesday of every month.

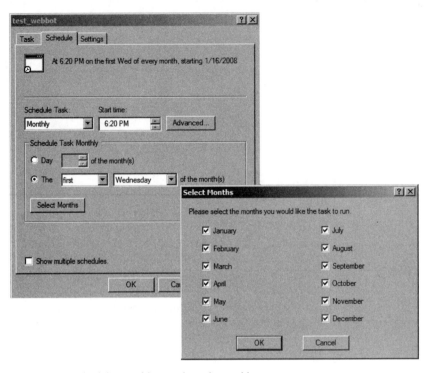

Figure 23-8: Scheduling webbots to launch monthly

Non-Calendar-Based Triggers

Calendar events, like those examined in this chapter, are not the only events that may trigger a webbot to run. However, other types of triggers usually require that a scheduled task run periodically to detect if the non-calendar event has occurred. For example, the script in the following listings uses techniques discussed in Chapter 15 to trigger a webbot to run after receiving an email with the words *Run the webbot* in the subject line.

First, the webbot initializes itself to read email and establishes the location of the webbot it will run when it receives the triggering email message, as shown in Listing 23-3.

```
// Include the POP3 command library
include("LIB_pop3.php");
define("SERVER", "your.mailserver.net");    // Your POP3 mail server
define("USER",   "your@email.com");         // Your POP3 email address
define("PASS",   "your_password");          // Your POP3 password

$webbot_path = "c:\\webbots\\view_competitor.bat";
```

Listing 23-3: Initializing the webbot that is triggered via email

Once the initialization is complete, this webbot attempts to make a connection to the mail server, as shown in Listing 23-4.

```
// Connect to POP3 server
$connection_array =  POP3_connect(SERVER, USER, PASS);
$POP3_connection = $connection_array['handle'];
```

Listing 23-4: Making a mail server connection

As shown in Figure 23-5, once a successful connection to the mail server is made, this webbot looks at each pending message to determine if it contains the trigger phrase *Run the webbot*. When this phrase is found, the webbot executes in a shell.

```
if($POP3_connection)
    {
    // Create an array of received messages
    $email_array = POP3_list($POP3_connection);

    // Examine each message in $email_array
    for($xx=0; $xx<count($email_array); $xx++)
        {
        // Get each email message
        list($mail_id, $size) = explode(" ", $email_array[$xx]);
        $message = POP3_retr($POP3_connection, $mail_id);

        // Run the webbot if email subject contains "Run the webbot"
        if(stristr($message, "Subject: Run the webbot"))
            {
            $output = shell_exec($webbot_path);
            echo "<pre>$output </pre>";

            // Delete message, so we don't trigger another event from this email
            POP3_delete($POP3_connection, $mail_id);
            }
        }
    }
```

Listing 23-5: Reading each message and executing a webbot when a specific email is received

Once the webbot runs, it deletes the triggering email message so it won't mistakenly be executed a second time on subsequent checks for email messages containing the trigger phrase.

Final Thoughts

Now that you know how to automate the task of launching webbots from both scheduled and non-scheduled events, it's time for a few words of caution.

Determine the Webbot's Best Periodicity

A common question when deploying webbots is how often to schedule a webbot to check if data has changed on a target server. The answer to this question depends on your need for stealth and how often the target data changes. If your webbot must run without detection, you should limit the number of file accesses you perform, since every file your webbot downloads leaves a clue to its existence in the server's log file. Your webbot becomes increasingly obvious as it creates more and more log entries.

The periodicity of your webbot's execution may also hinge on how often your target changes. Additionally, you may require notification as soon as a particularly important website changes. Timeliness may drive the need to run the webbot more frequently. In any case, you never want to run a webbot more often than necessary. You should read Chapter 28 before you deploy a webbot that runs frequently or consumes excessive bandwidth from a server.

I always contend that you shouldn't access a target more than what's necessary to perform a job. If that need for expedience requires that you connect to a target more than once every hour or so, you're probably hitting it too hard. Obviously, the rules change if you own the target server.

Avoid Single Points of Failure

Remember that hardware and software are both subject to unexpected crashes. If your webbot performs a mission-critical task, you should ensure that your scheduler doesn't create a single point of failure or execute a process step that may cause an entire webbot to fail if that one step crashes. Chapter 25 describes methods to ensure that your webbot does not stop working if a scheduled webbot fails to run.

Add Variety to Your Schedule

The other potential problem with scheduled tasks is that they run precisely and repeatedly, creating entries in the target's access log at the same hour, minute, and second. If you schedule your webbot to run once a month, this may not be a problem, but if a webbot runs daily at exactly the same time, it will become obvious to any competent system administrator that a webbot, and not a human, is accessing the server. If you want to schedule a webbot that emulates a human using a browser, you should continue on to Chapter 24 for more information.

PART IV

LARGER CONSIDERATIONS

As you develop webbots and spiders, you will soon learn (or wish you had learned) that there is more to webbot and spider development than mastering the underlying technologies. Beyond technology, your webbots need to coexist with society—and perhaps more importantly, they need to coexist with the system administrators of the sites you target. This section attempts to guide you through the larger considerations of webbot and spider development with the hope of keeping you out of trouble.

Chapter 24: Designing Stealthy Webbots and Spiders

Sometimes it is best if webbots are indistinguishable from normal Internet traffic. In this chapter, I'll explain when and how stealth is important to webbots and how to design and deploy webbots that look like normal browser traffic.

Chapter 25: Writing Fault-Tolerant Webbots

Since the Internet is constantly changing, it is a good idea to design webbots that will be less likely to fail if your target websites change. In this chapter, we'll focus on methods to design fault tolerance into your webbots and spiders so they will more easily adapt (or at least gracefully fail) when websites change.

Chapter 26: Designing Webbot-Friendly Websites

Here I'll explain how and why to write web pages that are easy for webbots and spiders to download and analyze, with a special focus on the needs of search engine spiders. You will also learn how to write specialized interfaces, designed specifically to transfer data from websites to webbots.

Chapter 27: Killing Spiders

In this chapter, we'll explore techniques for writing web pages that protect sensitive information from webbots and spiders, while still accommodating normal browser users.

Chapter 28: Keeping Webbots out of Trouble

Possibly the most important part of this book, this chapter discusses the possible legal issues you may encounter as a webbot developer and tells you how to avoid them.

24

DESIGNING STEALTHY WEBBOTS AND SPIDERS

This chapter explores design and implementation considerations that make webbots hard to detect. However, the inclusion of a chapter on stealth shouldn't imply that there's a stigma associated with writing webbots; you shouldn't feel self-conscious about writing webbots, as long as your goals are to create legal and novel solutions to tedious tasks. Most of the reasons for maintaining stealth have more to do with maintaining competitive advantage than covering the tracks of a malicious web agent.

Why Design a Stealthy Webbot?

Webbots that create competitive advantages for their owners often lose their value shortly after they're discovered by the targeted website's administrator. I can tell you from personal experience that once your webbot is detected, you may be accused of creating an unfair advantage for your client. This type of accusation is common against early adopters of any technology. (It is also complete bunk.) Webbot technology is available to any business that takes the time to research and implement it. Once it is discovered, however, the owner of the target site may limit or block the webbot's access to the site's resources. The other thing that can happen is that the administrator will see the value that the webbot offers and will create a similar feature on the site for everyone to use.

Another reason to write stealthy webbots is that system administrators may misinterpret webbot activity as an attack from a hacker. A poorly designed webbot may leave strange records in the log files that servers use to track web traffic and detect hackers. Let's look at the errors you can make and how these errors appear in the log files of a system administrator.

Log Files

System administrators can detect webbots by looking for odd activity in their log files, which record access to servers. There are three types of log files for this purpose: access logs, error logs, and custom logs (Figure 24-1). Some servers also deploy special monitoring software to parse and detect anomalies from normal activity within log files.

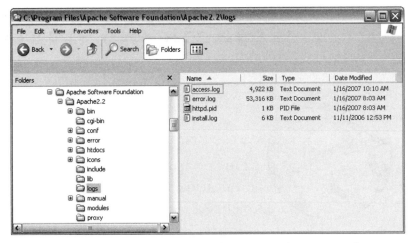

Figure 24-1: Windows' log files recording file access and errors (Apache running on Windows)

Access Logs

As the name implies, access logs record information related to the access of files on a webserver. Typical access logs record the IP address of the requestor, the time the file was accessed, the fetch method (typically GET or POST), the file requested, the HTTP code, and the size of the file transfer, as shown in Listing 24-1.

```
221.2.21.16 - - [03/Feb/2008:14:57:45 -0600] "GET / HTTP/1.1" 200 1494
12.192.2.206 - - [03/Feb/2008:14:57:46 -0600] "GET /favicon.ico HTTP/1.1" 404 283
27.116.45.118 - - [03/Feb/2008:14:57:46 -0600] "GET /apache_pb.gif HTTP/1.1" 200 2326
214.241.24.35 - - [03/Feb/2008:14:57:50 -0600] "GET /test.php HTTP/1.1" 200 41
```

Listing 24-1: Typical access log entries

Access log files have many uses, like metering bandwidth and controlling access. Know that the webserver records every file download your webbot requests. If your webbot makes 50 requests a day from a server that gets 200 hits a day, it will become obvious to even a casual system administrator that a single party is making a disproportionate number of requests, which will raise questions about your activity.

Also, remember that using a website is a privilege, not a right. Always assume that your budget of accesses per day is limited, and if you go over that limit, it is likely that a system administrator will attempt to limit your activity when he or she realizes a webbot is accessing the website. You should strive to limit the number of times your webbot accesses any site. There are no definite rules about how often you can access a website, but remember that if an individual system administrator decides your IP is hitting a site too often, his or her opinion will always trump yours.[1] If you ever exceed your bandwidth budget, you may find yourself blocked from the site.

Error Logs

Like access logs, error logs record access to a website, but unlike access logs, error logs only record errors that occur. A sampling of an actual error log is shown in Listing 24-2.

```
[Tue Mar 08 14:57:12 2008] [warn] module mod_php4.c is already added, skipping
[Tue Mar 08 15:48:10 2008] [error] [client 127.0.0.1] File does not exist:
c:/program files/apache group/apache/htdocs/favicon.ico
[Tue Mar 08 15:48:13 2008] [error] [client 127.0.0.1] File does not exist:
c:/program files/apache group/apache/htdocs/favicon.ico
[Tue Mar 08 15:48:37 2008] [error] [client 127.0.0.1] File does not exist:
c:/program files/apache group/apache/htdocs/t.gif
```

Listing 24-2: Typical error log entries

The errors your webbot is most likely to make involve requests for unsupported methods (often HEAD requests) or requesting files that aren't on the website. If your webbot repeatedly commits either of these errors, a system administrator will easily determine that a webbot is making the erroneous page requests, because it is almost impossible to cause these errors when manually surfing with a browser. Since error logs tend to be smaller than access logs, entries in error logs are very obvious to system administrators.

However, not all entries in an error log indicate that something unusual is going on. For example, it's common for people to use expired bookmarks or to follow broken links, both of which could generate *File not found* errors.

At other times, errors are logged in access logs, not error logs. These errors include using a GET method to send a form instead of a POST (or visa versa), or emulating a form and sending the data to a page that is not a valid action address. These are perhaps the worst errors because they are impossible for someone using a browser to commit—therefore, they will make your webbot stand out like a sore thumb in the log files.

---

[1] There may also be legal implications for hitting a website too many times. For more information on this subject, see Chapter 28.

These are the best ways to avoid strange errors in log files:

- Debug your webbot's parsing software on web pages that are on your own server before releasing it into the wilderness
- Use a form analyzer, as described in Chapter 5, when emulating forms
- Program your webbot to stop if it is looking for something specific but cannot find it

Custom Logs

Many web administrators also keep detailed custom logs, which contain additional data not found in either error or access logs. Information that may appear in custom logs includes the following:

- The name of the web agent used to download a file
- A fully resolved domain name that resolves the requesting IP address
- A coherent list of pages a visitor viewed during any one session
- The referer to get to the requested page

The first item on the list is very important and easy to address. If you call your webbot *test webbot*, which is the default setting in LIB_http, the web administrator will finger your webbot as soon as he or she views the log file. Sometimes this is by design; for example, if you want your webbot to be discovered, you may use an agent name like *See www.myWebbot.com for more details*. I have seen many webbots brand themselves similarly.

If the administrator does a reverse DNS lookup to convert IP addresses to domain names, that makes it very easy to trace the origin of traffic. You should always assume this is happening and restrict the number of times you access a target.

Some metrics programs also create reports that show which pages specific visitors downloaded on sequential visits. If your webbot always downloads the same pages in the same order, you're bound to look odd. For this reason, it's best to add some variety (or randomness, if applicable) to the sequence and number of pages your webbots access.

Log-Monitoring Software

Many system administrators use monitoring software that automatically detects strange behavior in log files. Servers using monitoring software may automatically send a notification email, instant message, or even page to the system administrator upon detection of critical errors. Some systems may even automatically shut down or limit accessibility to the server.

Some monitoring systems can have unanticipated results. I once created a webbot for a client that made HEAD requests from various web pages. While the use of the HEAD request is part of the web specification, it is rarely used, and this particular monitoring software interpreted the use of the HEAD request as malicious activity. My client got a call from the system administrator, who demanded that we stop hacking his website. Fortunately, we all discussed what we were doing and left as friends, but that experience taught me that many administrators are inexperienced with webbots; if you approach situations like this with confidence and knowledge, you'll generally be respected. The other thing I learned from this experience is that when you want to analyze a header, you should request the entire page instead of only the header, and then parse the results on your hard drive.

Stealth Means Simulating Human Patterns

Webbots that don't draw attention to themselves are ones that behave like people and leave normal-looking records in log files. For this reason, you want your webbot to simulate normal human activity. In short, stealthy webbots don't act like machines.

Be Kind to Your Resources

Possibly the worst thing your webbot can do is consume too much bandwidth from an individual website. To limit the amount of bandwidth a webbot uses, you need to restrict the amount of activity it has at any one website. Whatever you do, don't write a webbot that frequently makes requests from the same source. Since your webbot doesn't read the downloaded web pages and click links as a person would, it is capable of downloading pages at a ridiculously fast rate. For this reason, your webbot needs to spend most of its time waiting instead of downloading pages.

The ease of writing a stealthy webbot is directly correlated with how often your target data changes. In the early stages of designing your webbot, you should decide what specific data you need to collect and how often that data changes. If updates of the target data happen only once a day, it would be silly to look for it more often than that.

System administrators also use various methods and traps to deter webbots and spiders. These concepts are discussed in detail in Chapter 27.

Run Your Webbot During Busy Hours

If you want your webbot to generate log records that look like normal browsing, you should design your webbot so that it makes page requests when everyone else makes them. If your webbot runs during busy times, your log records will be intermixed with normal traffic. There will also be more records separating your webbot's access records in the log file. This will not reduce the total percentage of requests coming from your webbot, but it will make your webbot slightly less noticeable.

Running webbots during high-traffic times is slightly counterintuitive, since many people believe that the best time to run a webbot is in the early morning hours—when the system administrator is at home sleeping and you're not interfering with normal web traffic. While the early morning may be the best time to go out in public without alerting the paparazzi, on the Internet, there is safety in numbers. ,

Don't Run Your Webbot at the Same Time Each Day

If you have a webbot that needs to run on a daily basis, it's best not to run it at exactly same time every day, because doing so would leave suspicious-looking records in the server log file. For example, if a system administrator notices that someone with a certain IP address access the same file at 7:01 AM every day, he or she will soon assume that the requestor is either a highly compulsive human or a webbot.

Don't Run Your Webbot on Holidays and Weekends

Obviously, your webbot shouldn't access a website over a holiday or weekend if it would be unusual for a person to do the same. For example, I've written procurement bots (see Chapter 19) that buy things from websites only used by businesses. It would have been odd if the webbot checked what was available for purchase at a time when businesses are typically closed. This is, unfortunately, an easy mistake to make, because few task-scheduling programs track local holidays. You should read Chapter 23 for more information on this issue.

Use Random, Intra-fetch Delays

One sure way to tell a system administrator that you've written a webbot is to request pages faster than humanly possible. This is an easy mistake to make, since computers can make page requests at lightening speeds. For this reason, it's imperative to insert delays between repeated page fetches on the same domain. Ideally, the delay period should be a random value that mimics human browsing behavior.

Final Thoughts

A long time ago—before I knew better—I needed to gather some information for a client from a government website (on a Saturday, no less). I determined that in order to collect all the data I needed by Monday morning, my spider would have to run at full speed for most of the weekend (another bad idea). I started in the morning, and everything was going well; the spider was downloading pages, parsing information, and storing the results in my database at a blazing rate.

While only casually monitoring the spider, I used the idle time to browse the website I was spidering. To my horror, I found that the welcome page explicitly stated that the website did not, under any circumstances, allow webbots to gather information from it.

Furthermore, the welcome page stated that any violation of this policy was considered a felony, and violators would be prosecuted fully. Since this was a government website, I assumed it had the lawyers to follow through with a threat like this. In retrospect, the phrase *full extent of the law* was probably more of a fear tactic than an indication of eminent legal action. Since all the data I collected was in the public domain, and the funding of the site's servers came from public money (some of it mine), I couldn't possibly have done anything wrong, could I?

My fear was that since I was hitting the server very hard, the department would file a *trespass-to-chattels*[2] case against me. Regardless, it had my attention, and I questioned the wisdom of what I was doing. An activity that seemed so innocent only moments earlier suddenly had the potential of becoming a criminal offense. I wasn't sure what the department's legal rights were, nor was I sure to what extent a judge would have agreed with its arguments, since there were no applicable warnings on the pages I was spidering. Nevertheless, it was obvious that the government would have more lawyers at its disposal than I would, if it came to that.

Just as I started to contemplate my future in jail, the spider suddenly stopped working. Fearing the worst, I pointed my browser at the page I had been spidering and felt the blood drain from my face as I read a web page similar to the one shown in Figure 24-2.

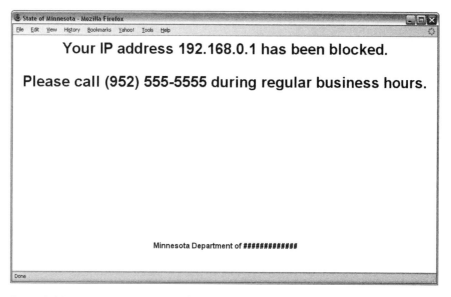

Figure 24-2: A government warning that my IP address had been blocked

I knew I had no choice but to call the number on the screen. This website obviously had monitoring software, and it detected that I was operating outside of stated policies. Moreover, it had my IP address, so someone could easily discover who I was by tracing my IP address back to my ISP.[3] Once the department knew who my ISP was, it could subpoena billing and log files to use as evidence. I was busted—not by some guy with a server, but by the full force and assets (i.e., lawyers) of the State of Minnesota. My paranoia was magnified by the fact that it was only late Saturday morning, and I had all weekend to think about my situation before I could call the number on Monday morning.

When Monday finally came, I called the number and was very apologetic. Realizing that they already knew what I was doing, I gave them a full confession.

---

[2] See Chapter 28 for more information about trespass to chattels.

[3] You can find the owner of an IP address at http://www.arin.net.

Moreover, I noted that I had read the policy on the main page *after* I started spidering the site and that there were no warnings on the pages I was spidering.

Fortunately, the person who answered the phone was not the department's legal counsel (as I feared), but a friendly system administrator who was mostly concerned about maintaining a busy website on a limited budget. She told me that she'd unblock my IP address if I promised not to hit the server more than three times a minute. Problem solved. (Whew!)

The embarrassing part of this story is that I should have known better. It only takes a small amount of code between page requests to make a webbot's actions look more human. For example, the code snippet in Listing 24-3 will cause a random delay between 20 and 45 seconds.

```
$minumum_delay_seconds = 20;
$maximum_delay_seconds = 45;
sleep($minumum_delay_seconds, $maximum_delay_seconds);
```

Listing 24-3: Creating a random delay

You can summarize the complete topic of stealthy webbots in a single concept: Don't do anything with a webbot that doesn't look like something one person using a browser would do. In that regard, think about how and when people use browsers, and try to write webbots that mimic that activity.

25

WRITING FAULT-TOLERANT WEBBOTS

The biggest complaint users have about webbots is their unreliability: Your webbots will suddenly and inexplicably fail if they are not *fault tolerant,* or able to adapt to the changing conditions of your target websites. This chapter is devoted to helping you write webbots that are tolerant to network outages and unexpected changes in the web pages you target.

Webbots that don't adapt to their changing environments are worse than nonfunctional ones because, when presented with the unexpected, they may perform in odd and unpredictable ways. For example, a non-fault-tolerant webbot may not notice that a form has changed and will continue to emulate the nonexistent form. When a webbot does something that is impossible to do with a browser (like submit an obsolete form), system administrators become aware of the webbot. Furthermore, it's usually easy for system administrators to identify the owner of a webbot by tracing an IP address or matching a user to a username and password. Depending on what your webbot does and which website it targets, the identification of a webbot can lead to possible banishment from the website and the loss of a competitive advantage for your business. It's better to avoid these issues by designing fault-tolerant webbots that anticipate changes in the websites they target.

Fault tolerance does not mean that everything will always work perfectly. Sometimes changes in a targeted website confuse even the most fault-tolerant webbot. In these cases, the proper thing for a webbot to do is to abort its task and report an error to its owner. Essentially, you want your webbot to fail in the same manner a person using a browser might fail. For example, if a webbot is buying an airline ticket, it should not proceed with a purchase if a seat is not available on a desired flight. This action sounds silly, but it is exactly what a poorly programmed webbot may do if it is expecting an available seat and has no provision to act otherwise.

Types of Webbot Fault Tolerance

For a webbot, fault tolerance involves adapting to changes to URLs, HTML content (which affect parsing), forms, cookie use, and network outages and congestion). We'll examine each of these aspects of fault tolerance in the following sections.

Adapting to Changes in URLs

Possibly the most important type of webbot fault tolerance is *URL tolerance*, or a webbot's ability to make valid requests for web pages under changing conditions. URL tolerance ensures that your webbot does the following:

- Download pages that are available on the target site
- Follow header redirections to updated pages
- Use referer values to indicate that you followed a link from a page that is still on the website

Avoid Making Requests for Pages That Don't Exist

Before you determine that your webbot downloaded a valid web page, you should verify that you made a valid request. Your webbot can verify successful page requests by examining the *HTTP code*, a status code returned in the header of every web page. If the request was successful, the resulting HTTP code will be in the 200 series—meaning that the HTTP code will be a three-digit number beginning with a two. Any other value for the HTTP code may indicate an error. The most common HTTP code is 200, which says that the request was valid and that the requested page was sent to the web agent. The script in Listing 25-1 shows how to use the LIB_http library's http_get() function to validate the returned page by looking at the returned HTTP code. If the webbot doesn't detect the expected HTTP code, an error handler is used to manage the error and the webbot stops.

```
<?
include("LIB_http.php");
# Get the web page
$page = http_get($target="www.schrenk.com", $ref="");
# Vector to error handler if error code detected
if($page['STATUS']['http_code']!="200")
    error_handler("BAD RESULT", $page['STATUS']['http_code']);
?>
```

Listing 25-1: Detecting a bad page request

Before using the method described in Listing 25-1, review a list of HTTP codes and decide which codes apply to your situation.[1]

If the page no longer exists, the fetch will return a *404 Not Found* error. When this happens, it's imperative that the webbot stop and not download any more pages until you find the cause of the error. Not proceeding after detecting an error is a far better strategy than continuing as if nothing is wrong.

Web developers don't always remove obsolete web pages from their websites—sometimes they just link to an updated page without removing the old one. Therefore, webbots should start at the web page's home page and verify the existence of each page between the home page and the actual targeted web page. This process does two things. It helps your webbot maintain stealth, as it simulates the browsing habits of a person using a browser. Moreover, by validating that there are links to subsequent pages, you verify that the pages you are targeting are still in use. In contrast, if your webbot targets a page within a site without verifying that other pages still link to it, you risk targeting an obsolete web page.

The fact that your webbot made a valid page request does not indicate that the page you've downloaded is the one you intended to download or that it contains the information you expected to receive. For that reason, it is useful to find a *validation point*, or text that serves as an indication that the newly downloaded web page contains the expected information. Every situation is different, but there should always be some text on every page that validates that the page contains the content you're expecting. For example, suppose your webbot submits a form to authenticate itself to a website. If the next web page contains a message that welcomes the member to the website, you may wish to use the member's name as a validation point to verify that your webbot successfully authenticated, as shown in Listing 25-2.

```
$username = "GClasemann";
$page = http_get($target, $ref="");
if(!stristr($page['FILE'], "$username")
    {
    echo "authentication error";
    error_handler("BAD AUTHENTICATION for ".$username, $target);
    }
```

Listing 25-2: Using a username as a validation point to confirm the result of submitting a form

---

[1] A full list of HTTP codes is available in Appendix B.

The script in Listing 25-2 verifies that a validation point, in this case a username, exists as anticipated on the fetched page. This strategy works because the only way that the user's name would appear on the web page is if he or she had been successfully authenticated by the website. If the webbot doesn't find the validation point, it assumes there is a problem and it reports the situation with an error handler.

Follow Page Redirections

Page redirections are instructions sent by the server that tell a browser that it should download a page other than the one originally requested. Web developers use page redirection techniques to tell browsers that the page they're looking for has changed and that they should download another page in its place. This allows people to access correct pages even when obsolete addresses are bookmarked by browsers or listed by search engines. As you'll discover, there are several methods for redirecting browsers. The more web redirection techniques your webbots understand, the more fault tolerant your webbot becomes.

Header redirection is the oldest method of page redirection. It occurs when the server places a Location: *URL* line in the HTTP header, where *URL* represents the web page the browser should download (in place of the one requested). When a web agent sees a header redirection, it's supposed to download the page defined by the new location. Your webbot could look for redirections in the headers of downloaded pages, but it's easier to configure PHP/CURL to follow header redirections automatically.[2] Listing 25-3 shows the PHP/CURL options you need to make automatic redirection happen.

```
curl_setopt($curl_session, CURLOPT_FOLLOWLOCATION, TRUE);   // Follow redirects
curl_setopt($curl_session, CURLOPT_MAXREDIRS, 4);           // Only follow 4 redirects
```

Listing 25-3: Configuring PHP/CURL to follow up to four header redirections

The first option in Listing 25-3 tells PHP/CURL to follow all page redirections as they are defined by the target server. The second option limits the number of redirections your webbot will follow. Limiting the number of redirections defeats *webbot traps* where servers redirect agents to the page they just downloaded, causing an endless number of requests for the same page and an endless loop.

In addition to header redirections, you should also be prepared to identify and accommodate page redirections made between the <head> and </head> tags, as shown in Listing 25-4.

```
<html>
  <head>
    <meta http-equiv="refresh" content="0; URL=http://www.nostarch.com">
  </head>
</html >
```

Listing 25-4: Page redirection between the <head> and </head> tags

---

[2] LIB_http does this for you.

In Listing 25-4, the web page tells the browser to download http://www.nostarch.com instead of the intended page. Detecting these kinds of redirections is accomplished with a script like the one in Listing 25-5. This script looks for redirections between the <head> and </head> tags in a test page on the book's website.

```
<?
# Include http, parse, and address resolution libraries
include("LIB_http.php");
include("LIB_parse.php");
include("LIB_resolve_addresses.php");

# Identify the target web page and the page base
$target = "http://www.schrenk.com/nostarch/webbots/head_redirection_test.php";
$page_base = "http://www.schrenk.com/nostarch/webbots/";

# Download the web page
$page = http_get($target, $ref="");

# Parse the <head></head>
$head_section = return_between($string=$page['FILE'], $start="<head>", $end="</head>",
                               $type=EXCL);

# Create an array of all the meta tags
$meta_tag_array = parse_array($head_section, $beg_tag="<meta", $close_tag=">");

# Examine each meta tag for a redirection command
for($xx=0; $xx<count($meta_tag_array); $xx++)
    {
    # Look for http-equiv attribute
    $meta_attribute = get_attribute($meta_tag_array[$xx], $attribute="http-equiv");
    if(strtolower($meta_attribute)=="refresh")
        {
        $new_page = return_between($meta_tag_array[$xx], $start="URL", $end=">", $type=EXCL);
        # Clean up URL
        $new_page = trim(str_replace("", "", $new_page));
        $new_page = str_replace("=", "", $new_page);
        $new_page = str_replace("\"", "", $new_page);
        $new_page = str_replace("'", "", $new_page);
        # Create fully resolved URL
        $new_page = resolve_address($new_page, $page_base);
        }
    break;
    }

# Echo results of script
echo "HTML Head redirection detected<br>";
echo "Redirect page = ".$new_page;
?>
```

Listing 25-5: Detecting redirection between the <head> and </head> tags

Listing 25-5 is also an example of the need for good coding practices as part of writing fault-tolerant webbots. For instance, in Listing 25-5 notice how these practices are followed:

- The script looks for the redirection between the `<head>` and `</head>` tags, and not just anywhere on the web page
- The script looks for the `http-equiv` attribute only within a meta tag
- The redirected URL is converted into a fully resolved address
- Like a browser, the script stops looking for redirections when it finds the first one

The last—and most troublesome—type of redirection is that done with JavaScript. These instances are troublesome because webbots typically lack JavaScript parsers, making it difficult for them to interpret JavaScript. The simplest redirection of this type is a single line of JavaScript, as shown in Listing 25-6.

```
<script>document.location = 'http://www.schrenk.com'; </script>
```

Listing 25-6: A simple JavaScript page redirection

Detecting JavaScript redirections is also tricky because JavaScript is a very flexible language, and page redirections can take many forms. For example, consider what it would take to detect a page redirection like the one in Listing 25-7.

```
<html>
    <head>
        <script>
            function goSomeWhereNew(URL)
                {
                location.href = URL;
                }
        </script>
        <body onLoad=" goSomeWhereNew('http://www.schrenk.com')">
        </body>
</html>
```

Listing 25-7: A complicated JavaScript page redirection

Fortunately, JavaScript page redirection is not a particularly effective way for a web developer to send a visitor to a new page. Some people turn off JavaScript in their browser configuration, so it doesn't work for everyone; therefore, JavaScript redirection is rarely used. Since it is difficult to write fault-tolerant routines to handle JavaScript, you may have to tough it out and rely on the error-detection techniques addressed later in this chapter.

Maintain the Accuracy of Referer Values

The last aspect of verifying that you're using correct URLs is ensuring that your referer values correctly simulate followed links. You should set the referer to the last target page you requested. This is important for several reasons. For example, some image servers use the referer value to verify that a request for an image is preceded by a request for the entire web page. This defeats *bandwidth hijacking*, the practice of sourcing images from other people's domains. In addition, websites may defeat *deep linking*, or linking to a website's inner pages, by examining the referer to verify that people followed a prescribed succession of links to get to a specific point within a website.

Adapting to Changes in Page Content

Parse tolerance is your webbot's ability to parse web pages when your webbot downloads the correct page, but its contents have changed. The following paragraphs describe how to write parsing routines that are tolerant to minor changes in web pages. This may also be a good time to review Chapter 4, which covers general parsing techniques.

Avoid Position Parsing

To facilitate fault tolerance when parsing web pages, you should avoid all attempts at *position parsing*, or parsing information based on its position within a web page. For example, it's a bad idea to assume that the information you're looking for has these characteristics:

- Starts x characters from the beginning of the page and is y characters in length
- Is in the xth table in a web page
- Is at the very top or bottom of a web page

Any small change in a website can effect position parsing. There are much better ways of finding the information you need to parse.

Use Relative Parsing

Relative parsing is a technique that involves looking for desired information relative to other things on a web page. For example, since many web pages hold information in tables, you can place all the tables into an array, identifying which table contains a *landmark* term that identifies the correct table. Once a webbot finds the correct table, the data can be parsed from the correct cell by finding the cell relative to a specific column name within that table. For an example of how this works, look at the parsing techniques performed in Chapter 7 in which a webbot parses prices from an online store.

Table column headings may also be used as landmarks to identify data in tables. For example, assume you have a table like Table 25-1, which presents statistics for three baseball players.

Table 25-1: Use Table Headers to Identify Data Within Columns

Player	Team	Hits	Home Runs	Average
Zoe	Marsupials	78	15	.327
Cullen	Wombats	56	16	.331
Kade	Wombats	58	17	.324

In this example you could parse all the tables from the web page and isolate the table containing the landmark *Player Statistics*. In that table, your webbot could then use the column names as secondary landmarks to identify players and their statistics.

Look for Landmarks That Are Least Likely to Change

You achieve additional fault tolerance when you choose landmarks that are least likely to change. From my experience, the things in web pages that change with the lowest frequency are those that are related to server applications or back-end code. In most cases, names of form elements and values for hidden form fields seldom change. For example, in Listing 25-8 it's very easy to find the names and breeds of dogs because the form handler needs to see them in a well-defined manner. Webbot developers generally don't look for data values in forms because they aren't visible in rendered HTML. However, if you're lucky enough to find the data values you're looking for within a form definition, that's where you should get them, even if they appear in other visible places on the website.

```
<form method="POST" action="dog_form.php">
  <input type="hidden" name="Jackson" value="Jack Russell Terrier">
  <input type="hidden" name="Xing" value="Shepherd Mix">
  <input type="hidden" name="Buster" value="Maltese">
  <input type="hidden" name="Bare-bear" value="Pomeranian">
</form>
```

Listing 25-8: Finding data values in form variables

Similarly, you should avoid landmarks that are subject to frequent changes, like dynamically generated content, HTML comments (which Macromedia Dreamweaver and other page-generation software programs automatically insert into HTML pages), and information that is time or calendar derived.

Adapting to Changes in Forms

Form tolerance defines your webbot's ability to verify that it is sending the correct form information to the correct form handler. When your webbot detects that a form has changed, it is usually best to terminate your webbot, rather than trying to adapt to the changes on the fly. Form emulation is complicated, and it's too easy to make embarrassing mistakes—like submitting nonexistent forms. You should also use the form diagnostic page on the book's website (described in Chapter 5) to analyze forms before writing form emulation scripts.

Before emulating a form, a webbot should verify that the form variables it plans to submit are still in use in the submitted form. This check should verify the data pair names submitted to the form handler and the form's method and action. Listing 25-9 parses this information on a test page on the book's website. You can use similar scripts to isolate individual form elements, which can be compared to the variables in form emulation scripts.

```
<?
# Import libraries
include("LIB_http.php");
include("LIB_parse.php");
include("LIB_resolve_addresses.php");

# Identify location of form and page base address
$page_base ="http://www.schrenk.com/nostarch/webbots/";
$target = "http://www.schrenk.com/nostarch/webbots/easy_form.php";
$web_page = http_get($target, "");

# Find the forms in the web page
$form_array = parse_array($web_page['FILE'], $open_tag="<form", $close_tag="</form>");

# Parse each form in $form_array
for($xx=0; $xx<count($form_array); $xx++)
    {
    $form_beginning_tag = return_between($form_array[$xx], "<form", ">", INCL);
    $form_action = get_attribute($form_beginning_tag, "action");

    // If no action, use this page as action
    if(strlen(trim($form_action))==0)
        $form_action = $target;
    $fully_resolved_form_action = resolve_address($form_action, $page_base);

    // Default to GET method if no method specified
    if(strtolower(get_attribute($form_beginning_tag, "method")=="post"))
        $form_method="POST";
    else
        $form_method="GET";

    $form_element_array = parse_array($form_array[$xx], "<input", ">");
    echo "Form Method=$form_method<br>";
    echo "Form Action=$fully_resolved_form_action<br>";
    # Parse each element in this form
    for($yy=0; $yy<count($form_element_array); $yy++)
        {
        $element_name = get_attribute($form_element_array[$yy], "name");
        $element_value = get_attribute($form_element_array[$yy], "value");
        echo "Element Name=$element_name, value=$element_value<br>";
        }
    }
?>
```

Listing 25-9: Parsing form values

Listing 25-9 finds and parses the values of all forms in a web page. When run, it also finds the form's method and creates a fully resolved URL for the form action, as shown in Figure 25-1.

Figure 25-1: Results of running the script in Listing 25-9

Adapting to Changes in Cookie Management

Cookie tolerance involves saving the cookies written by websites and making them available when fetching successive pages from the same website. Cookie management should happen automatically if you are using the LIB_http library and have the COOKIE_FILE pointing to a file your webbots can access.

One area of concern is that the LIB_http library (and PHP/CURL, for that matter) will not delete expired cookies or cookies without an expiration date, which are supposed to expire when the browser is closed. In these cases, it's important to manually delete cookies in order to simulate new browser sessions. If you don't delete expired cookies, it will eventually look like you're using a browser that has been open continuously for months or even years, which can look pretty suspicious.

Adapting to Network Outages and Network Congestion

Unless you plan accordingly, your webbots and spiders will hang, or become nonresponsive, when a targeted website suffers from a network outage or an unusually high volume of network traffic. Webbots become nonresponsive when they request and wait for a page that they never receive. While there's nothing you can do about getting data from nonresponsive target websites, there's also no reason your webbot needs to be hung up when it encounters one. You can avoid this problem by inserting the command shown in Listing 25-10 when configuring your PHP/CURL sessions.

```
curl_setopt($curl_session, CURLOPT_TIME, $timeout_value);
```

Listing 25-10: Setting time-out values in PHP/CURL

CURLOPT_TIME defines the number of seconds PHP/CURL waits for a targeted website to respond. This happens automatically if you use the LIB_http library featured in this book. By default, page requests made by LIB_http wait a maximum of 25 seconds for any target website to respond. If there's no response within the allotted time, the PHP/CURL session returns an empty result.

While on the subject of time-outs, it's important to recognize that PHP, by default, will time-out if a script executes longer than 30 seconds. In normal use, PHP's time-out ensures that if a script takes too long to execute, the webserver will return a server error to the browser. The browser, in turn, informs the user that a process has timed-out. The default time-out works great for serving web pages, but when you use PHP to build webbot or spider scripts, PHP must facilitate longer execution times. You can extend (or eliminate) the default PHP script-execution time with the commands shown in Listing 25-11.

You should exercise extreme caution when eliminating PHP's time-out, as shown in the second example in Listing 25-11. If you eliminate the time-out, your script may hang permanently if it encounters a problem.

```
set_time_limit(60);    // Set PHP time-out to 60 seconds
set_time_limit(0);     // Completely remove PHP script time-out
```

Listing 25-11: Adjusting the default PHP script time-out

Always try to avoid time-outs by designing webbots that execute quickly, even if that means your webbot needs to run more than once to accomplish a task. For example, if a webbot needs to download and parse 50 web pages, it's usually best to write the bot in such a way that it can process pages one at a time and know where it left off; then you can schedule the webbot to execute every minute or so for an hour. Webbot scripts that execute quickly are easier to test, resemble normal network traffic more closely, and use fewer system resources.

Error Handlers

When a webbot cannot adjust to changes, the only safe thing to do is to stop it. Not stopping your webbot may otherwise result in odd performance and suspicious entries in the target server's access and error log files. It's a good idea to write a routine that handles all errors in a prescribed manner. Such an error handler should send you an email that indicates the following:

- Which webbot failed
- Why it failed
- The date and time it failed

A simple script like the one in Listing 25-12 works well for this purpose.

```
function webbot_error_handler($failure_mode)
    {
    # Initialization
    $email_address = "your.account@someserver.com";
    $email_subject = "Webbot Failure Notification";

    # Build the failure message
    $email_message = "Webbot T-Rex encountered a fatal error <br>";
    $email_message = $email_message . $failure_more . "<br>";
    $email_message = $email_message . "at".date("r") . "<br>";

    # Send the failure message via email
    mail($email_address, $email_subject, $email_message);
    # Don't return, force the webbot script to stop
    exit;
    }
```

Listing 25-12: Simple error-reporting script

The trick to effectively using error handlers is to anticipate cases in which things may go wrong and then test for those conditions. For example, the script in Listing 25-13 checks the size of a downloaded web page and calls the function in the previous listing if the web page is smaller than expected.

```
# Download web page
$target = "http://www.somedomain.com/somepage.html";
$downloaded_page = http_get($target, $ref="");
$web_page_size = strlen($downloaded_page['FILE']);
if($web_page_size < 1500)
    webbot_error_handler($target." smaller than expected, actual size=".$web_page_size);
```

Listing 25-13: Anticipating and reporting errors

In addition to reporting the error, it's important to turn off the scheduler when an error is found if the webbot is scheduled to run again in the future. Otherwise, your webbot will keep bumping up against the same problem, which may leave odd records in server logs. The easiest way to disable a scheduler is to write error handlers that record the webbot's status in a database. Before a scheduled webbot runs, it can first query the database to determine if an unaddressed error occurred earlier. If the query reveals that an error has occurred, the webbot can ignore the requests of the scheduler and simply terminate its execution until the problem is addressed.

26

DESIGNING WEBBOT-FRIENDLY WEBSITES

I'll start this chapter with suggestions that help make web pages accessible to the most widely used webbots—the spiders that download, analyze, and rank web pages for search engines, a process often called *search engine optimization (SEO)*.

Finally, I'll conclude the chapter by explaining the occasional importance of special-purpose web pages, formatted to send data directly to webbots instead of browsers.

Optimizing Web Pages for Search Engine Spiders

The most important thing to remember when designing a web page for SEO is that spiders rely on you, the developer, to provide context for the information they find. This is important because web pages using HTML mix content with display format commands. To add complexity to the spider's task, a spider has to examine words in the web page's content to determine how relevant the words are to the web page's main topic. You can improve a spider's ability to *index* and *rank* your web pages, as well as improve your search ranking by predictably using a few standard HTML tags. The topic of SEO is vast and many books are entirely dedicated to it. This chapter only scratches the surface, but it should get you on your way.

Well-Defined Links

Search engines generally associate the number of links to a web page with the web page's popularity and importance. In fact, getting other websites to link to your web page is probably the best way to improve your web page's search ranking. Regardless of where the links originate, it's always important to use descriptive hyper-references when making links. Without descriptive links, search engine spiders will know the linked URL, but they won't know the importance of the link. For example, the first link in Listing 26-1 is much more useful to search spiders than the second link.

```
<!- Example of a descriptive link -->
<a href="http://www.schrenk.com/js">JavaScript Animation Tutorial</a>

<!- Example of a nondescriptive link -->
<a href="http://www.schrenk.com/js">Click here</a> for a JavaScript tutorial
```

Listing 26-1: Descriptive and nondescriptive links

Google Bombs and Spam Indexing

Google bombing is an example of how search rankings are affected by the terms used to describe links. *Google bombing* (also known as *spam indexing*) is a technique where people conspire to create many links, with identical link descriptions, to a specific web page. As Google (or any other search engine) indexes these web pages, the link descriptions become associated with the targeted web page. As a result, when people enter the link descriptions as search terms, the targeted pages are highly ranked in the results. Google bombing is occasionally used for political purposes to place a targeted politician's website as the highest ranked result for a derogatory search term. For example, depending on the search engine you use, a search for the phrase *miserable failure* may return the official biography of George W. Bush as the top result. Similarly, a search for the word *waffles* may produce the official web page of Senator John Kerry. While Google has adapted its rankings to account for a few well-known instances of this gamesmanship, Google bombing is still possible, and it remains an unresolved challenge for all search engines.

Title Tags

The HTML title tag helps spiders identify the main topic of a web page. Each web page should have a unique title that describes the general purpose of the page, as shown in Listing 26-2.

```
<title>Official Website: Webbots, Spiders, and Screen Scrapers</title>
```

Listing 26-2: Describing a web page with a title tag

Meta Tags

You can think of meta tags as extensions of the title tag. Like title tags, meta tags explain the main topic of the web page. However, unlike title tags, they allow for detailed descriptions of the content on the web page and the search terms people may use to find the page. For example, Listing 26-3 shows meta tags that may accompany the title tag used in the previous example.

```
<!- The meta:author defines the author of the web page -->
<meta name="Author" content="Michael Schrenk">

<!- The meta:description is how search engines describe the page in search results-->
<meta name="Description" content="Official Website: Webbots, Spiders, and Screen Scrapers">

<!- The meta:keywords are a list of search terms that may lead people to your web page-->
<meta name="Keywords" content="Webbot, Spider, Webbot Development, Spider Development">
```

Listing 26-3: Describing a web page in detail with meta tags

There are many misconceptions about meta tags. Many people insist on using every conceivable keyword that may apply to a web page, using *the more, the better* theory. In reality, you should limit your selection of keywords to the six or eight keywords that best describe the content of your web page. It's important to remember that the keywords represent potential search terms that people may use to find your web page. Moreover, for each additional keyword you use, your web page becomes less specific in the eyes of search engines. As you increase the number of keywords, you also increase the competition for use of those keywords. When this happens, other pages containing the same keywords dilute your position within search rankings. There are also rumors that some search engines ignore web pages that have excessive numbers of keywords as a measure to avoid *keyword spamming*, or the overuse of keywords. Whether these rumors are true or not, it still makes sense to use fewer, but better quality, keywords. For this reason, there is usually no need to include regular plurals[1] in keywords.

NOTE *The more unique your keywords are, the higher your web page will rank in search results when people use those keywords in web searches. Once thing to watch out for is when your keyword is part of another, longer word. For example, I once worked for a company called Entolo. We had difficulty getting decent rankings on search engines because the word* Entolo *is a subset of the word* Scientology *(sciENTOLOgy). Since there were many more heavily linked web pages dedicated to Scientology, our website seldom registered highly with any search services.*

Header Tags

In addition to making web pages easier to read, header tags help search engines identify and locate important content on web pages. For example, consider the example in Listing 26-4.

---

[1] A regular plural is the singular form of a word followed by the letter *s*.

```
<h1 class="main_header">North American Wire Packaging</h1>
In North America, large amounts of wire are commonly shipped on spools...
```

Listing 26-4: Using header tags to identify key content on a web page

In the past, web designers strayed from using header tags because they only offer a small availability of font selections. But now, with the wide acceptance of style sheets, there is no reason not to use HTML header tags to describe important sections of your web pages.

Image alt Attributes

Long ago, before everyone had graphical browsers, web designers used the alt attribute of the HTML <img> tag to describe images to people with text-based browsers. Today, with the increasing popularity of image search tools, the alt attribute helps search engines interpret the content of images, as shown below in Listing 26-5.

```
<img src="mydog.jpg" alt="Jackson the wonder dog">
```

Listing 26-5: Using the alt attribute to identify the content of an image

Web Design Techniques That Hinder Search Engine Spiders

There are common web design techniques that inhibit search engine spiders from properly indexing web pages. You don't have to avoid using these techniques altogether, but you should avoid using them in situations where they obscure links and ASCII text from search engine spiders. There is no single set of standards or specifications for SEO. Search engine companies also capriciously change their techniques for compiling search results. The concepts mentioned here, however, are a good set of suggestions for you to consider as you develop your own best practice policies.

JavaScript

Since most webbots and spiders lack JavaScript interpreters, there is no guarantee that a spider will understand hyper-references made with JavaScript. For example, the second hyper-reference in Listing 26-6 stands a far better chance of being indexed by a spider than the first one.

```
<-- Example of a non-optimized hyper-reference -->
<script>
    function linkToPage(url)
```

```
        {
        document.location=url;
        }
</script>

<-- Example of an easy-to-index hyper-reference -->
<a href="http://www.MySpace.com/haxtor">My home page</a>
```

Listing 26-6: JavaScript links are hard for search spiders to interpret.

Non-ASCII Content

Search engine spiders depend on ASCII characters to identify what's on a web page. For that reason, you should avoid presenting text in images or Flash movies. It is particularly important not to design your website's navigation scheme in Flash, because it will not be visible outside of the Flash movie, and it will be completely hidden from search pages. Not only will your Flash pages fail to show up in search results, but other pages will also not be able to deep link directly to the pages within Flash movies. In short, websites done entirely in Flash kill any and all attempts at SEO and will receive less traffic than properly formatted HTML websites.

Designing Data-Only Interfaces

Often, the express purpose of a web page is to deliver data to a webbot, another website, or a stand-alone desktop application. These web pages aren't concerned about how people will read them in a browser. Rather, they are optimized for efficiency and ease of use by other computer programs. For example, you might need to design a web page that provides real-time sales information from an e-commerce site.

XML

Today, the eXtensible Markup Language (XML) is considered the de facto standard for transferring online data. XML describes data by wrapping it in HTML-like tags. For example, consider the sample sales data from an e-commerce site, shown in Table 26-1.

When converted to XML, the data in Table 26-1 looks like Listing 26-7.

Table 26-1: Sample Sales Information

Brand	Style	Color	Size	Price
Gordon LLC	Cotton T	Red	XXL	19.95
Ava St	Girlie T	Blue	S	19.95

```
<ORDER>
    <SHIRT>
        <BRAND>Gordon LLC</BRAND>
        <STYLE>Cotton T</STYLE >
        <COLOR>Red</COLOR>
        <SIZE>XXL</SIZE>
        <PRICE>19.95</PRICE>
    </SHIRT>
    <SHIRT>
        <BRAND>Ava St</BRAND>
        <STYLE>Girlie T</STYLE >
        <COLOR>Blue</COLOR>
        <SIZE>S</SIZE>
        <PRICE>19.95</PRICE>
    </SHIRT>
</ORDER>
```

Listing 26-7: An XML version of the data in Table 26-1

XML presents data in a format that is not only easy to parse, but, in some applications, it may also tell the client computer what to do with the data. The actual tags used to describe the data are not terribly important, as long as the XML server and client agree to their meaning. The script in Listing 26-8 downloads and parses the XML represented in the previous listing.

```
# Include libraries
include("LIB_http.php");
include("LIB_parse.php");

# Download the order
$url = "http://www.schrenk.com/nostarch/webbots/26_1.php";
$download = http_get($url, "");

# Parse the orders
$order_array = return_between($download ['FILE'], "<ORDER>", "</ORDER>", $type=EXCL);

# Parse shirts from order array
$shirts = parse_array($order_array, $open_tag="<SHIRT>", $close_tag="</SHIRT>");
for($xx=0; $xx<count($shirts); $xx++)
    {
    $brand[$xx] = return_between($shirts[$xx], "<BRAND>", "</BRAND>", $type=EXCL);
    $color[$xx] = return_between($shirts[$xx], "<COLOR>", "</COLOR>", $type=EXCL);
    $size[$xx]  = return_between($shirts[$xx], "<SIZE>",  "</SIZE>",  $type=EXCL);
    $price[$xx] = return_between($shirts[$xx], "<PRICE>", "</PRICE>", $type=EXCL);
    }

# Echo data to validate the download and parse
for($xx=0; $xx<count($color); $xx++)
    echo "BRAND=".$brand[$xx]."<br>
          COLOR=".$color[$xx]."<br>
          SIZE=".$size[$xx]."<br>
          PRICE=".$price[$xx]."<hr>";
```

Listing 26-8: A script that parses XML data

Lightweight Data Exchange

As useful as XML is, it suffers from *overhead* because it delivers much more protocol than data. While this isn't important with small amounts of XML, the problem of overhead grows along with the size of the XML file. For example, it may take a 30KB XML file to present 10KB of data. Excess overhead needlessly consumes bandwidth and CPU cycles, and it can become expensive on extremely popular websites. In order to reduce overhead, you may consider designing lightweight interfaces. *Lightweight interfaces* deliver data more efficiently by presenting data in variables or arrays that can be used directly by the webbot. Granted, this is only possible when you define both the web page delivering the data and the client interpreting the data.

How *Not* to Design a Lightweight Interface

Before we explore proper methods for passing data to webbots, let's explore what can happen if your design doesn't take the proper security measures. For example, consider the order data from Table 26-1, reformatted as variable/ value pairs, as shown in Listing 26-9.

```
$brand[0]="Gordon LLC";
$style[0]="Cotton T";
$color[0]="red";
$size[0]="XXL";
$price[0]=19.95;
$brand[1]="Ava LLC";
$style[0]="Girlie T";
$color[1]="blue";
$size[1]="S";
$price[1]=19.95;
```

Listing 26-9: Data sample available at http://www.schrenk.com/nostarch/webbots/ 26_2.php

The webbot receiving this data could convert this string directly into variables with PHP's eval() function, as shown in Listing 26-10.

```
# Include libraries
include("LIB_http.php");
$url = "http://www.schrenk.com/nostarch/webbots/26_2.php";
$download = http_get($url, "");
# Convert string received into variables
eval($download['FILE']);

# Show imported variables and values
for($xx=0; $xx<count($color); $xx++)
    echo "BRAND=".$brand[$xx]."<br>
          COLOR=".$color[$xx]."<br>
          SIZE=".$size[$xx]."<br>
          PRICE=".$price[$xx]."<hr>";
```

Listing 26-10: Incorrectly interpreting variable/value pairs

While this seems very efficient, there is a severe security problem associated with this technique. The eval() function, which interprets the variable settings in Listing 26-10, is also capable of interpreting any PHP command. This opens the door for malicious code that can run directly on your webbot!

A Safer Method of Passing Variables to Webbots

An improvement on the previous example would verify that only data variables are interpreted by the webbot. We can accomplish this by slightly modifying the variable/value pairs sent to the webbot (shown in Listing 26-11) and adjusting how the webbot processes the data (shown in Listing 26-12). Listing 26-11 shows a new lightweight test interface that will deliver information directly in variables for use by a webbot.

```
brand[0]="Gordon LLC";
style[0]="Cotton T";
color[0]="red";
size[0]="XXL";
price[0]=19.95;
brand[1]="Ava LLC";
style[0]="Girlie T";
color[1]="blue";
size[1]="S";
price[1]=19.95;
```

Listing 26-11: Data sample used by the script in Listing 26-12

The script in Listing 26-12 shows how the lightweight interface in Listing 26-11 is interpreted.

```
# Get http library
include("LIB_http.php");

# Define and download lightweight test interface
$url = "http://www.schrenk.com/nostarch/webbots/26_3.php";
$download = http_get($url, "");

# Convert the received lines into array elements
$raw_vars_array = explode(";", $download['FILE']);

# Convert each of the array elements into a variable declaration
for($xx=0; $xx<count($raw_vars_array)-1; $xx++)
    {
    list($variable, $value)=explode("=", $raw_vars_array[$xx]);
    $eval_string="$".trim($variable)."="."\"".trim($value)."\".";";
    eval($eval_string);
    }

# Echo imported variables
for($xx=0; $xx<count($color); $xx++)
    {
    echo "BRAND=".$brand[$xx]."<br>
        COLOR=".$color[$xx]."<br>
```

```
        SIZE=".$size[$xx]."<br>
        PRICE=".$price[$xx]."<hr>";
    }
```

Listing 26-12: A safe method for directly transferring values from a website to a webbot

The technique shown in Figure 26-12 safely imports the variable/data pairs from Listing 26-11 because the eval() command is explicitly directed to only set a variable to a value and not to execute arbitrary code.

This lightweight interface actually has another advantage over XML, in that the data does not have to appear in any particular order. For example, if you rearranged the data in Listing 26-11, the webbot would still interpret it correctly. The same could not be said for the XML data. And while the protocol is slightly less platform independent than XML, most computer programs are still capable of interpreting the data, as done in the example PHP script in Listing 26-12.

SOAP

No discussion of machine-readable interfaces is complete without mentioning the Simple Object Access Protocol (SOAP). SOAP is designed to pass instructions and data between specific types of web pages (known as *web services*) and scripts run by webbots, webservers, or desktop applications. SOAP is the successor of earlier protocols that make remote application calls, like Remote Procedure Call (RPC), Distributed Component Object Model (DCOM), and Common Object Request Broker Architecture (CORBA).

SOAP is a web protocol that uses HTTP and XML as the primary protocols for passing data between computers. In addition, SOAP also provides a layer (or two) of abstraction between the functions that make the request and receive the data. In contrast to XML, where the client needs to make a fetch and parse the results, SOAP facilitates functions that (appear to) directly execute functions on remote services, which return data in easy-to-use variables. An example of a SOAP call is shown in Listing 26-13.

In typical SOAP calls, the SOAP interface and client are created and the parameters describing requested web services are passed in an array. With SOAP, using a web service is much like calling a local function.

If you'd like to experiment with SOAP, consider creating a free account at Amazon Web Services. Amazon provides SOAP interfaces that allow you to access large volumes of data at both Amazon and Alexa, a web-monitoring service (http://www.alexa.com). Along with Amazon Web Services, you should also review the PHP-specific Amazon SOAP tutorial at Dev Shed, a PHP developers' site (http://www.devshed.com).

PHP 5 has built-in support for SOAP. If you're using PHP 4, however, you will need to use the appropriate PHP Extension and Application Repository (PEAR, http://www.pear.php.net) libraries, included in most PHP distributions. The PHP 5 SOAP client is faster than the PEAR libraries, because SOAP support in PHP 5 is compiled into the language; otherwise both versions are identical.

```
include("inc/PEAR/SOAP");       // Import SOAP client

# Define the request
$params = array(
                'manufacturer' => "XYZ CORP",
                'mode'      => 'development',
                'sort'      => '+product',
                'type'      => 'heavy',
                'userkey' => $ACCESS_KEY
                )

# Create the SOAP object
$WSDL       = new SOAP_WSDL($ADDRESS_OF_SOAP_INTERFACE);

# Instantiate the SOAP client
$client     = $WSDL->getProxy();

# Make the request
$result_array = $client->SomeGenericSOAPRequest($params);
```

Listing 26-13: A SOAP call

Advantages of SOAP

SOAP interfaces to web services provide a common protocol for requesting and receiving data. This means that web services running on one operating system can communicate with a variety of computers, PDAs, or cell phones using any operating system, as long as they have a SOAP client.

Disadvantages of SOAP

SOAP is a very heavy interface. Unlike the interfaces explored earlier, SOAP requires many layers of protocols. In traffic-heavy applications, all this overhead can result in sluggish performance. SOAP applications can also suffer from a steep learning curve, especially for developers accustomed to lighter data interfaces. That being said, SOAP and web services are the standard for exchanging online data, and SOAP instructions are something all webbot developers should know how to use. The best way to learn SOAP is to use it. In that respect, if you'd like to explore SOAP further, you should read the previously mentioned Dev Shed tutorial on using PHP to access the Amazon SOAP interface. This will provide a gradual introduction that should make complex interfaces (like eBay's SOAP API) easier to understand.

27

KILLING SPIDERS

Thus far, we have talked about how to create effective, stealthy, and smart webbots. However, there is also a market for developers who create countermeasures that defend websites from webbots and spiders. These opportunities exist because sometimes website owners want to shield their sites from webbots and spiders for these purposes:

- Protect intellectual property
- Shield email addresses from spammers
- Regulate how often the website is used
- Create a level playing field for all users

The first three items in this list are fairly obvious, but the fourth is more complicated. Believe it or not, creating a level playing field is one of the main reasons web developers cite for attempting to ban webbots from their sites. Online companies often try to be as impartial as possible when wholesaling items to resellers or awarding contracts to vendors. At other times, websites deny access to all webbots to create an assumption of fairness or parity, as is the case with MySpace. This is where the conflict exists. Businesses that seek to use the Internet to gain competitive advantages are not interested in parity. They want a strategic advantage.

Successfully defending websites from webbots is more complex than simply blocking all webbot activity. Many webbots, like those used by search engines, are beneficial, and in most cases they should be able to roam sites at will. It's also worth pointing out that, while it's more expensive, people with browsers can gather corporate intelligence and make online purchases just as effectively as webbots can. Rather than barring webbots in general, it's usually preferable to just ban certain behavior.

Let's look at some of the things people do to attempt to block webbots and spiders. We'll start with the simplest (and least effective) methods and graduate to more sophisticated practices.

Asking Nicely

Your first approach to defending a website from webbots is to request nicely that webbots and spiders do not use your resources. This is your first line of defense, but if used alone, it is not very effective. This method doesn't actually keep webbots from accessing data—it merely states your desire for such—and it may or may not express the actual rights of the website owner. Though this strategy is limited in its effectiveness, you should always ask first, using one of the methods described below.

Create a Terms of Service Agreement

The simplest way to ask webbots to avoid your website is to create a site policy or *Terms of Service agreement*, which is a list of limitations on how the website should be used by all parties. A website's Terms of Service agreement typically includes a description of what the website does with data it collects, a declaration of limits of liability, copyright notifications, and so forth. If you don't want webbots and spiders harvesting information or services from your website, your Terms of Service agreement should prohibit the use of automated web agents, spiders, crawlers, and screen scapers. It is a good idea to provide a link to the usage policy on every page of your website. Though some webbots will honor your request, others surely won't, so you should never rely solely on a usage policy to protect a website from automated agents.

Although an official usage policy probably won't keep webbots and spiders away, it is your opportunity to state your case. With a site policy that specifically forbids the use of webbots, it's easier to make a case if you later decide to play hardball and file legal action against a webbot or spider owner.

You should also recognize that a written usage policy is for humans to read, and it will not be understood by automated agents. There are, however, other methods that convey your desires in ways that are easy for webbots to detect.

Use the robots.txt File

The robots.txt file,[1] or *robot exclusion file,* was developed in 1994 after a group of webmasters discovered that search engine spiders indexed sensitive parts of their websites. In response, they developed the robots.txt file, which instructs web agents to access only certain parts of a site. According to the robots.txt specification, a webbots should first look for the presence of a file called *robots.txt* in the website's root directory before it downloads anything else from the website. This file defines how the webbot should access files in other directories.[2]

The robots.txt file borrows its Unix-type format from permissions files. A typical robots.txt file is shown in Figure 27-1.

Figure 27-1: A typical robots.txt file, disallowing all user agents from selected directories

In addition to what you see in Figure 27-1, a robots.txt file may disallow different directories for specific web agents. Some robots.txt files even specify the amount of time that webbots must wait between fetches, though these parameters are not part of the actual specification. Make sure to read the specification[3] before implementing a robots.txt file.

There are many problems with robots.txt. The first problem is that no recognized body, such as the World Wide Web Consortium (W3C) or a corporation, governs the specification. The robots exclusion file is actually the result of a "consensus of opinion" of members of a now-defunct robots mailing list. The lack of a recognized organizing body has left the specification woefully out of date. For example, the specification did not anticipate agent name spoofing, so unless a robots.txt file disallows all webbots, any webbot can comply with the imposed restrictions by changing its name. In fact, a robots.txt file may actually direct a webbot to sensitive areas of a website or otherwise hidden directories. A much better tactic is to secure your confidential information through authentication or even obfuscation. Perhaps the most serious problem with the robots.txt specification is that there is no enforcement mechanism. Compliance is strictly voluntary.

---

[1] The filename *robots.txt* is case sensitive. It must always be lowercase.

[2] Each website should have only one robots.txt file.

[3] The robots.txt specification is available at http://www.robotstxt.org,

However futile the attempt, you should still use the robots.txt file if for no other reason than to mark your turf. If you are serious about securing your site from webbots and spiders, however, you should use the the tactics described later in this chapter.

Use the Robots Meta Tag

Like the robots.txt file, the intent of the robots meta tag[4] is to warn spiders to stay clear of your website. Unfortunately, this tactic suffers from many of the same limitations as the robots.tx file, because it also lacks an enforcement mechanism. A typical robots meta tag is shown in Listing 27-1.

```
<head>
    <meta name="robots" content="noindex, nofollow">
</head>
```

Listing 27-1: The robots meta tag

There are two main commands for this meta tag: noindex and nofollow. The first command tells spiders not to index the web page in search results. The second command tells spiders not to follow links from this web page to other pages. Conversely, index and follow commands are also available, and they achieve the opposite effect. These commands may be used together or independently.

The problem with site usage policies, robots.txt files, and meta tags is that the webbots visiting your site must voluntarily honor your requests. On a good day, this *might* happen. On its own, a Terms of Service policy, a robots.txt file, or a robots meta tag is something short of a social contract, because a contract requires at least two willing parties. There is no enforcing agency to contact when someone doesn't honor your requests. If you want to deter webbots and spiders, you should start by asking nicely and then move on to the tougher approaches described next.

Building Speed Bumps

Better methods of deterring webbots are ones that make it difficult for a webbot to operate on a website. Just remember, however, that a determined webbot designer may overcome these obstacles.

Selectively Allow Access to Specific Web Agents

Some developers may be tempted to detect their visitors' web agent names and only serve pages to specific browsers like Internet Explorer or Firefox. This is largely ineffective because a webbot can pose as any web agent it chooses.[5]

---

[4] The specification for the robots meta tag is available at http://www.robotstxt.org/wc/meta_user.html

[5] Read Chapter 3 if you are interested in browser spoofing.

However, if you insist on implementing this strategy, make sure you use a server-side method of detecting the agent, since you can't trust a webbot to interpret JavaScript.

Use Obfuscation

As you learned in Chapter 20, obfuscation is the practice of hiding something through confusion. For example, you could use HTML special characters to obfuscate an email link, as shown in Listing 27-2.

```
Please email me at:
<a href="mailto:&#109;&#101;&#64;<s></s>&#97;&#100;&#100;&#114;&#46;&#99;&#111;&#109;">
        &#109;&#101;<b></b>&#64;&#97;&#100;&#100;&#114; <u></u>&#46;&#99;&#111;&#109;
</a>
```

Listing 27-2: Obfuscating the email address me@addr.com with HTML special characters

While the special characters are hard for a person to read, a browser has no problem rendering them, as you can see in Figure 27-2.

You shouldn't rely on obfuscation to protect data because once it is discovered, it is usually easily defeated. For example, in the previous illustration, the PHP function htmlspecialchars() can be used to convert the codes into characters. There is no effective way to protect HTML through obfuscation. Obfuscation will slow determined webbot developers, but it is not apt to stop them, because obfuscation is not the same as encryption. Sooner or later, a determined webbot designer is bound to decode any obfuscated text.[6]

Figure 27-2: A browser rendering of the obfuscated script in Listing 27-2

Use Cookies, Encryption, JavaScript, and Redirection

Lesser webbots and spiders have trouble handling cookies, encryption, and page redirection, so attempts to deter webbots by employing these methods may be effective in some cases. While PHP/CURL resolves most of these issues, webbots still stumble when interpreting cookies and page redirections written in JavaScript, since most webbots lack JavaScript interpreters. Extensive use of JavaScript can often effectively deter webbots, especially if JavaScript creates links to other pages or if it is used to create HTML content.

---

[6] To learn the difference between obfuscation and encryption, read Chapter 20.

Authenticate Users

Where possible, place all confidential information in password-protected areas. This is your best defense against webbots and spiders. However, authentication only affects people without login credentials; it does not prevent authorized users from developing webbots and spiders to harvest information and use services within password-protected areas of a website. You can learn about writing webbots that access password-protected websites in Chapter 21.

Update Your Site Often

Possibly the single most effective way to confuse a webbot is to change your site on a regular basis. A website that changes frequently is more difficult for a webbot to parse than a static site. The challenge is to change the things that foul up webbot behavior without making your site hard for people to use. For example, you may choose to randomly take one of the following actions:

- Change the order of form elements
- Change form methods
- Rename files in your website
- Alter text that may serve as convenient parsing reference points, like form variables

These techniques may be easy to implement if you're using a high-quality content management system (CMS). Without a CMS, though, it will take a more deliberate effort.

Embed Text in Other Media

Webbots and spiders rely on text represented by HTML codes, which are nothing more than numbers capable of being matched, compared, or manipulated with mathematical precision. However, if you place important text inside images or other non-textual media like Flash, movies, or Java applets, that text is hidden from automated agents. This is different from the obfuscation method discussed earlier, because embedding relies on the reasoning power of a human to react to his or her environment. For example, it is now common for authentication forms to display text embedded in an image and ask a user to type that text into a field before it allows access to a secure page. While it's possible for a webbot to process text within an image, it is quite difficult. This is especially true when the text is varied and on a busy background, as shown in Figure 27-3. This technique is called a *Completely Automated Public Turing test to tell Computers and Humans Apart (CAPTCHA).*[7] You can find more information about CAPTCHA devices at this book's website.

Before embedding all your website's text in images, however, you need to recognize the downside. When you put text in images, beneficial spiders, like those used by search engines, will not be able to index your web pages. Placing text within images is also a very inefficient way to render text.

---

[7] Completely Automated Public Turing test to tell Computers and Humans Apart (CAPTCHA) is a registered trademark of Carnegie Mellon University.

Figure 27-3: Text within an image is hard for a webbot to interpret

Setting Traps

Your strongest defenses against webbots are techniques that detect webbot behavior. Webbots behave differently because they are machines and don't have the reasoning ability of people. Therefore, a webbot will do things that a person won't do, and a webbot lacks information that a person either knows or can figure out by examining his or her environment.

Create a Spider Trap

A *spider trap* is a technique that capitalizes on the behavior of a spider, forcing it to identify itself without interfering with normal human use. The spider trap in the following example exploits the spider behavior of indiscriminately following every hyperlink on a web page. If some links are either invisible or unavailable to people using browsers, you'll know that any agent that follows the link is a spider. For example, consider the hyperlinks in Listing 27-3.

```
<a href="spider_trap.php"><a>
<a href="spider_trap.php"><img src="spacer.gif" width="0" height="0"><a>
```

Listing 27-3: Two spider traps

There are many ways to trap a spider. Some other techniques include image maps with hot spots that don't exist and hyperlinks located in invisible frames without width or height attributes.

Fun Things to Do with Unwanted Spiders

Once unwanted guests are detected, you can treat them to a variety of services.

Identifying a spider is the first step in dealing with it. Moreover, with browser-spoofing techniques, a spider trap becomes a necessity in determining which traffic is automated and which is human. What you do once you detect a spider is up to you, but Table 27-1 should give you some ideas. Just remember to act within commonsense legal guidelines and your own website policies.

Table 27-1: Strategies for Responding When You Identify a Spider

Strategy	Implementation
Banish	Record the IP addresses of spiders that reach the spider trap and configure the webserver to ignore future requests from these addresses.
Limit access	Record the IP addresses of the spiders in the spider trap and limit the pages they can access on their next visit.
Mislead	Depending on the situation, you could redirect known (unwanted) spiders with an alternate set of misleading web pages. As much as I love this tactic, you should consult with an attorney before implementing this idea.
Analyze	Analyze the IP address and find out where the spider comes from, who might own it, and what it is up to. A good resource for identifying IP addresses registered in the United States is http://www.arin.net. You could even create a special log that tracks all activity from known hostile spiders. You can also use this technique to learn whether or not a spider is part of a distributed attack.
Ignore	The default option is to just ignore any automated activity on your website.

Final Thoughts

Before website owners decide to expend their resources on deterring webbots, they should ask themselves a few questions.

- What can a webbot do with your website that a person armed with a browser cannot do?

- Are your deterrents keeping desirable spiders (like search engines) from accessing your web pages?

- Does an automated agent (that you want to thwart) pose an actual threat to your website? Is it possible that it may even provide a benefit, as a procurement bot might?

- If your website contains information that needs to be protected from webbots, should that information really be online in the first place?

- If you put information in a public place, do you really have the right to bar certain methods of reading it?

If you still insist on banning webbots from your website, keep in mind that unless you deliberately develop measures like the ones near the end of this chapter, you will probably have little luck in defending your site from rogue webbots.

28

KEEPING WEBBOTS OUT OF TROUBLE

By this point, you know how to access, download, parse, and process any of the 76 million websites on the Internet.[1] Knowing how to do something, however, does not give you the right to do it. While I have cast warnings throughout the book, I haven't, until now, focused on the consequences of designing webbots or spiders that act selfishly and without regard to the rights of website owners or related infrastructure.[2]

Since many businesses rely on the performance of their websites to conduct business, you should consider interfering with a corporate website equivalent to interfering with a physical store or factory. When deploying a webbot or spider, remember that someone else is paying for hosting, bandwidth, and development for the websites you target. Writing webbots and spiders that consume irresponsible amounts of bandwidth, guess passwords, or capriciously reuse intellectual property may well be a violation of someone's rights and will

---

[1] This estimate of the number of websites on the Internet as of February 2006 comes from http://news.netcraft.com/archives/web_server_survey.html.

[2] If you interfere with the operation of one site, you may also affect other, non-targeted websites if they are hosted on the same (virtual) server.

eventually land you in trouble. Back in the day—that is, before the populariza-tion of the Internet—programmers had to win their stripes before they earned the confidence of their peers and gained access to networks or sensitive infor-mation. At that time, people who had access to data networks were less likely to abuse them because they had a stake in the security of data and the per-formance of networks. One of the outcomes of the Internet's free access to information, open infrastructure, and apparent anonymous browsing is that it is now easier than ever to act irresponsibly. A free dial-up account gives anyone and everyone access to (and the opportunity to compromise) servers all over the world. With worldwide access to data centers and the ability to download quick exploits, it's easy for people without a technical background (or a vested interest in the integrity of the Internet) to access confidential infor-mation or launch attacks that render services useless to others.

The last thing I want to do is pave a route for people to create havoc on the Internet. The purpose of this book is to help Internet developers think beyond the limitations of the browser and to develop webbots that do new and useful things. Webbot development is still virgin territory and there are still many new and creative things to do. You simply lack creativity if you can't develop webbots that do interesting things without violating someone's rights.

Webbots (and their developers) generally get into trouble when they make unauthorized use of copyrighted information or use an excessive amount of a website's infrastructure (bandwidth, servers, administration, etc.). This chapter addresses both of these areas. We'll also explore the requests webmasters make to limit webbot use on their websites.

NOTE *This chapter introduces warnings that all webbot and spider writers should understand and consider before embarking on webbot projects. I'm not dispensing legal advice, so don't even think of blaming me if you misbehave and are sued or find the FBI knocking at your door. This is my attempt to identify a few (but not all) issues related to developing webbots and spiders. Perhaps with this information, you will be able to at least ask an attorney intelligent questions. To reiterate, I am not a lawyer, and this is not legal advice. My responsibility is to tell you that, if misused, automated web agents can get you into deep trouble. In turn, you're obligated to take responsibility for your own actions and to consult an attorney who is aware of local laws before doing anything that even remotely violates the rights of someone else. I urge you to think before you act.*

It's All About Respect

Your career as a webbot developer will be short-lived if you don't respect the rights of those who own, maintain, and rely upon the web servers your webbots and spiders target. Remember that websites are designed for people using browsers and that often a website's profit model is dependent on those traffic patterns. In a matter of seconds, a single webbot can create as much web traffic as a thousand web surfers, without the benefit of generating commerce or ad revenue, or extending a brand. It's helpful to think of webbots as "super browsers," as webbots have increased abilities. But in order to walk among mere browsers, webbots and spiders need to comply with the norms and customs of the rest of the web agents on the Internet.

In Chapter 27 you read about website polices, robots.txt files, robots meta tags, and other tools server administrators use to regulate webbots and spiders. It's important to remember, however, that obeying a webmaster's webbot restrictions does not absolve webbot developers from responsibility. For example, even if a webbot doesn't find any restrictions in the website's Terms of Service agreement, robots.txt file, or meta tags, the webbot developer still doesn't have permission to violate the website's intellectual property rights or use inordinate amounts of the webserver's bandwidth.

Copyright

One way to keep your webbots out of trouble is to obey *copyright*, the set of laws that protects intellectual property owners. Copyright allows people and organizations to claim the exclusive right to use specific text, images, media, and control the manner in which they are published. All webbot developers need to have an awareness of copyright. Ignoring copyright can result in banishment from websites and even lawsuits.

Do Consult Resources

Before you venture off on your own (or assume that what you're reading here applies to your situation), you should check out a few other resources. For basic copyright information, start with the website of the United States Copyright Office, http://www.copyright.gov. Another resource, which you might find more readable, is http://www.bitlaw.com/copyright, maintained by Daniel A. Tysver of Beck & Tysver, a firm specializing in intellectual property law. Of course, these websites only apply to US laws. If you're outside the United States, you'll need to consult other resources.

Don't Be an Armchair Lawyer

Mitigating factors and varying interpretations affect copyright law enforcement. There seems to be an exception to every rule. If you have specific questions about copyright law, the smartest thing to do is to consult an attorney. Since the Internet is relatively new, intellectual property law—as it applies to the Internet—is somewhat fluid and open to interpretation. Ultimately, courts interpret the law. While it is not within the scope of this book to cover copyright in its entirety, the following sections identify common copyright issues that webbot developers may find interesting.

Copyrights Do Not Have to Be Registered

In the United States, you do not have to officially register a copyright with the Copyright Office to have the protection of copyright laws. The US Copyright office states that copyrights are granted automatically, as soon as an original work is created. As the Copyright Office describes on its website:

> Copyright is secured automatically when the work is created, and a work is "created" when it is fixed in a copy or phonorecord for the first time. "Copies" are material objects from which a work can be read or visually perceived either directly or with the aid of a machine or device, such as books, manuscripts, sheet music, film, videotape, or microfilm. "Phonorecords" are material objects embodying fixations of sounds (excluding, by statutory definition, motion picture soundtracks), such as cassette tapes, CDs, or LPs. Thus, for example, a song (the "work") can be fixed in sheet music ("copies") or in phonograph disks ("phonorecords"), or both. If a work is prepared over a period of time, the part of the work that is fixed on a particular date constitutes the created work as of that date.[3]

Notice that online content isn't specifically mentioned in the above paragraph, while there are specific references to original works "fixed in copy" through books, sheet music, videotape, CDs, and LPs. While there is no specific mention of websites, one may assume that references to works that may be "perceived either directly or through the aid of a machine or device" also covers content on webservers. The important thing for webbot developers to remember is that it is dangerous to assume that something is free to use if it is not expressly copyrighted.

If you don't need to register a copyright, why do people still do it? People file for specific copyrights to strengthen their ability to defend their rights in court. If you are interested in registering a copyright for a website, the US Copyright Office has a special publication for you.[4]

Assume "All Rights Reserved"

If you hold (or claim to hold) a copyright, you don't need to explicitly add the phrase *all rights reserved* to the copyright notice. For example, if a movie script does not indicate that all rights are reserved, you are not free to assume that you can legally produce an online cartoon based on the movie. Similarly, if a web page doesn't explicitly state that the site owner reserves all rights, don't assume that a webbot can legally use the site's images in an unrelated project. The habit of stating *all rights reserved* in a copyright notice stems from old intellectual property treaties that required it. If a work is unmarked, assume that all rights are reserved.

---

[3] US Copyright Office, "Copyright Office Basics," July 2006 (http://www.copyright.gov/circs/circ1.html).

[4] US Copyright Office, "Copyright Registration for Online Works (Circular 66)," July 2006 (http://www.copyright.gov/circs/circ66.html).

You Cannot Copyright a Fact

The US Copyright Office website explains that copyright protects the way one expresses oneself and that no one has exclusive rights to facts, as stated below:

> Copyright protects the particular way an author has expressed himself; it does not extend to any ideas, systems, or factual information conveyed in the work.[5]

How would you interpret this? You might conclude that someone cannot copy the manner or style in which someone else publishes facts, but that the facts themselves are not copyrightable. What happens if a business announces on its website that it has 83 employees? Does the head count for that company become a fact that is not protected by copyright laws? What if the website also lists prices, phone numbers, addresses, or historic dates?

You might be safe if you write a webbot that only collects pure facts.[6] But that doesn't prevent someone else from having a differing opinion and challenging you in court.

You Can Copyright a Collection of Facts if Presented Creatively

In the previous excerpt from the US Copyright Office website, we learned that copyright law protects the "particular way" in which someone expresses him or herself and that facts themselves are not protected by copyright. One way to think of this is that while you cannot copyright a fact, you *might* be able to copyright a collection of facts—if they are presented creatively. For example, a phone company cannot copyright a phone number, but it can copyright an entire phone directory website, if the phone numbers are presented in an *original and creative way.*

It appears that courts are serious when they say copyright only applies to collections of facts when they are presented in new and creative ways. For example, in one case a phone company republished the names and phone numbers (subscriber information) from another phone company's directory.[7] A dispute over intellectual property rights erupted between the two companies, and the case went to court. The fact that the original phone book contained phone numbers from a selected area and listed them in alphabetical order was not enough creativity to secure copyright protection. The judge ruled that the original phone directory lacked originality and was not protected by copyright law—even though the publication had a registered copyright. If nothing else, this indicates that intellectual property law is open to interpretation and that individuals' interpretations of the law are less important than court decisions.

---

[5] US Copyright Office, "Fair Use," July 2006 (http://www.copyright.gov/fls/fl102.html).

[6] Consult your attorney for clarification on your legal rights to collect specific information.

[7] *Feist Publications, Inc. v. Rural Telephone Service Co.*, 499 U.S. 340, 1991.

You Can Use Some Material Under Fair Use Laws

United States copyright law also allows for *fair use*, a set of exclusions from copyright for material used within certain limits. The scope of what falls into the fair use category is largely dependent on the following:

- Nature of the copyrighted material
- Amount of material used
- Purpose for which the material is used
- Market effect of the new work upon the original

Copyrighted material commonly falls under fair use if a limited amount of the material is used for scholastic or archival purposes. Fair use also protects the right to use selections of copyrighted material for parody, in short quotations, or in reviews. Generally speaking, you can quote a small amount of copyrighted material if you include a reference to the original source. However, you may become a target for a lawsuit if you profit from selling shirts featuring a catchphrase from a movie, even though you are only quoting a small part of a larger work, as it will likely interfere with the market for legitimate T-shirts.

The US Copyright Office says the following regarding fair use:

> Under the *fair use* doctrine of the U.S. copyright statute, it is permissible to use limited portions of a work including quotes, for purposes such as commentary, criticism, news reporting, and scholarly reports. There are no legal rules permitting the use of a specific number of words, a certain number of musical notes, or percentage of a work. Whether a particular use qualifies as fair use depends on all the circumstances.[8]

As you may guess, fair use exclusions are often abused and frequently litigated. A famous case surrounding fair use was Kelly v. Arriba Soft.[9] In this case, Leslie A. Kelly conducted an online business of licensing copyrighted images. The Arriba Soft Corporation, in contrast, created an image-management program that used webbots and spiders to search the Internet for new images to add to its library. Arriba Soft failed to identify the sources of the images it found and gave the general impression that the images it found were available under fair use statutes. While Kelly eventually won her case against Arriba Soft, it took five years of charges, countercharges, rulings, and appeals. Much of the confusion in settling the suit was caused by applying pre-Internet laws to determine what constituted fair use of intellectual property published online.

Trespass to Chattels

In addition to copyright, the other main concept that you should be aware of is trespass to chattels. Unlike traditional trespass, which refers to unauthorized use of real property (land or real estate), *trespass to chattels*

---

[8] US Copyright Office, "Can I Use Someone Else's Work? Can Someone Else Use Mine? (FAQ)," July 12, 2006 (http://www.copyright.gov/help/faq/faq-fairuse.html#howmuch).

[9] If you Google *Kelly v. Arriba*, you'll find a wealth of commentary and court rulings for this saga.

prevents or impairs an owner's use of or access to personal property. The trespass-to-chattels laws were written before the invention of the Internet, but in certain instances, they still protect access to personal property. Consider the following examples of trespass to chattels:

- Blocking access to someone's boat with a floating swim platform
- Preventing the use of a fax machine by continually spamming it with nuisance or junk faxes
- Erecting a building that blocks someone's ocean view

From your perspective as a webbot or spider developer, violation of trespass to chattels may include:

- Consuming so much bandwidth from a target server that you affect the website's performance or other people's use of the website
- Increasing network traffic on a website to the point that the owner is forced to add infrastructure to meet traffic needs
- Sending excessive quantities of email as to diminish the utility of email or email servers

To better understand trespass to chattels, consider the spider developed by a company called Bidder's Edge, which cataloged auctions on eBay. This centralized spider collected information about auctions in an effort to aggregate the contents of several auction sites, including eBay, into one convenient website. In order to collect information on all eBay auctions, it downloaded as many as 100,000 pages a day.

To put the impact of Bidder's Edge spider into context, assume that a typical eBay web page is about 250KB in size. If the spider requested 100,000 pages a day, the spider would consume 25GB of eBay's bandwidth every day, or 775GB each month. In response to the increased web traffic, eBay was forced to add servers and upgrade its network.

With this amount of requests coming from Bidder's Edge spiders, it was easy for eBay to identify the source of the increased server load. Initially, eBay claimed that Bidder's Edge illegally used its copyrighted auctions. When that argument proved unsuccessful, eBay pursued a trespass-to-chattels case.[10] In this case, eBay successfully argued that the Bidder's Edge spider increased the load on its servers to the point that it interfered with the use of the site. eBay also claimed a loss due to the need to upgrade its servers to facilitate the increased network traffic caused by the Bidder's Edge spider. Bidder's Edge eventually settled with eBay out of court, but only after it was forced offline and agreed to change its business plan.

How do you avoid claims of trespass to chattels? You can start by not placing an undue load on a target server. If the information is available from a number of sources, you might target multiple servers instead of relying on a single source. If the information is only available from a single

---

[10] You can find more information about this case at http://pub.bna.com/lw/21200.htm. Googling *eBay, Inc. v. Bidder's Edge* will also provide links to comments about the succession of rulings on this case.

source, it is best to limit downloads to the absolute minimum number of pages to do the job. If that doesn't work, you should evaluate whether the risk of a lawsuit outweighs the opportunities created by your webbot. You should also ensure that your webbot or spider does not cause damage to a business or individual.

Internet Law

While the laws protecting physical property are long established and reinforced by considerable numbers of court rulings, the laws governing virtual property and virtual behavior are less mature and constantly evolving. While one would think the same laws should protect both online and offline property, the reality is that most laws were written before the Internet and don't directly address those things that are unique to it, like email, frames, hyperlinks, or blogs. Since many existing laws do not specifically address the Internet, the application of the law (as it applies to the Internet) is open to much interpretation.

One example of a law to deal specifically with Internet abuse is Virginia's so-called Anti-Spam Law.[11] This law is a response to the large amount of server resources consumed by servicing unwanted email. The law attacks spammers indirectly by declaring it a felony to falsify or forge email addresses in connection to unsolicited email. It also provides penalties of as much as $10.00 per unsolicited email or $25,000 per day. Laws like this one are required to address specific Internet-related concerns. Well-defined rules, like those imposed by Virginia's Anti-Spam Law, are frequently difficult to derive from existing statutes. And while it may be possible to prosecute a spammer with laws drafted before the popularity of the Internet, less is open to the court's interpretation when the law deals specifically with the offense.

When contemplating the laws that apply to you as a webbot developer, consider the following:

- Webbots and spiders add a wrinkle to the way online information is used, as most web pages are intended to be used with manually operated browsers. For example, disputes may arise when webbots ignore paid advertising and disrupt the intended business model of a website. Webmasters, however, usually want *some* webbots (such as search engine crawlers) to visit their sites.

- The Internet is still relatively young and there are few precedents for online law. Existing intellectual property law doesn't always apply well to the Internet. For example, in the Kelly v. Arriba Soft case, which we discussed earlier, there was serious contention over whether or not a website has the right to link to other web pages. The opportunity to challenge (and regulate) hyper-references to media belonging to someone else didn't exist before the Internet.

---

[11] "SB 881 Computer Crimes Act; electronic mail," Virginia Senate, approved March 29, 1999 (http://leg1.state.va.us/cgi-bin/legp504.exe?991+sum+SB881).

- New laws governing online commerce and intellectual property rights are constantly introduced as the Internet evolves and people conduct themselves in different ways. For example, blogs have recently created a number of legal questions. Are bloggers publishers? Are bloggers responsible for posts made by visitors to their websites? The answer to both questions is no—at least for now.[12]

- It is always wise for webbot developers to stay current with online laws, since old laws are constantly being tested and new laws are being written to address specific issues.

- The strategies people use to violate as well as protect online intellectual property are constantly changing. For example, *pay per click advertising*, a process in which companies only pay for ads that people click, has spawned the arrival of so-called *clickbots*, which simulate people clicking ads to generate revenue for the owner of the website carrying the advertisements. People test the law again by writing webbots that stuff the ballot boxes of online polls and contests. In response to the threat mounted by new webbot designs, web developers counter with technologies like *CAPTCHA devices*,[13] which force people to type text from an image (or complete some other task that would be similarly difficult for webbots) before accessing a website. There may be as many prospects for webbot developers to create methods to block webbots as there are opportunities to write webbots.

- Laws vary from country to country. And since websites can be hosted by servers anywhere the world, it can be difficult to identify—let alone prosecute—the violator of a law when the offender operates from a country that doesn't honor other countries' laws.

Final Thoughts

The knowledge and techniques required to develop a useful webbot are identical to those required to develop a destructive one. Therefore, it is imperative to realize when your enthusiasm for what you're doing obscures your judgment and causes you to cross a line you didn't intend to cross. Be careful. Talk to a qualified attorney before you need one.

If Internet law is appealing to you or if you are interested in protecting your online rights, you should consider joining the Electronic Frontier Foundation (EFF). This group of lawyers, coders, and other volunteers is dedicated to protecting digital rights. You can find more information about the organization at its website, http://www.eff.org.

---

[12] In 2006 a Pennsylvania court ruled that bloggers are not responsible for comments posted to the blog by their readers; to read a PDF of the judge's opinion, visit http://www.paed.uscourts.gov/documents/opinions/06D0657P.pdf

[13] More information about CAPTCHA devices is available in Chapter 27.

A

PHP/CURL REFERENCE

 This appendix highlights the options and features of PHP/CURL that will be of greatest interest to webbot developers. In addition to the features described here, you should know that PHP/CURL is an extremely powerful interface with a dizzying array of options. A full specification of PHP/CURL is available at the PHP website.[1]

Creating a Minimal PHP/CURL Session

In some regards, a PHP/CURL session is similar to a PHP file I/O session. Both create a session (or file handle) to reference an external file. And in both cases, when the file transfer is complete, the session is closed. However, PHP/CURL differs from standard file I/O because it requires a series of

---

[1] See http://us2.php.net/manual/en/ref.curl.php.

options that define the nature of the file transfer set before the exchange takes place. These options are set individually, in any order. When many options are required, the list of settings can be long and confusing. For simplicity, Listing A-1 shows the minimal options required to create a PHP/CURL session that will put a downloaded file into a variable.

```
<?
# Open a PHP/CURL session
$s = curl_init();

# Configure the cURL command
curl_setopt($s, CURLOPT_URL, "http://www.schrenk.com"); // Define target site
curl_setopt($s, CURLOPT_RETURNTRANSFER, TRUE);          // Return in string

# Execute the cURL command (send contents of target web page to string)
$downloaded_page = curl_exec($s);

# Close PHP/CURL session
curl_close($s);
?>
```

Listing A-1: A minimal PHP/CURL session

The rest of this section details how to initiate sessions, set options, execute commands, and close sessions in PHP/CURL. We'll also look at how PHP/CURL provides transfer status and error messages.

Initiating PHP/CURL Sessions

Before you use cURL, you must initiate a session with the curl_init() function. Initialization creates a session variable, which identifies configurations and data belonging to a specific session. Notice how the session variable $s, created in Listing A-1, is used to configure, execute, and close the entire PHP/CURL session. Once you create a session, you may use it as many times as you need to.

Setting PHP/CURL Options

The PHP/CURL session is configured with the curl_setopt() function. Each individual configuration option is set with a separate call to this function. The script in Listing A-1 is unusual in its brevity. In normal use, there are many calls to curl_setopt(). There are over 90 separate configuration options available within PHP/CURL, making the interface very versatile.[2] The average PHP/CURL user, however, uses only a small subset of the available options. The following sections describe the PHP/CURL options you are most apt to use. While these options are listed here in order of relative importance, you may declare them in any order. If the session is left open, the configuration may be reused many times within the same session.

---

[2] You can find a complete set of PHP/CURL options at http://www.php.net/manual/en/function.curl-setopt.php.

CURLOPT_URL

Use the CURLOPT_URL option to define the target URL for your PHP/CURL session, as shown in Listing A-2.

```
curl_setopt($s, CURLOPT_URL, "http://www.schrenk.com/index.php");
```

Listing A-2: Defining the target URL

You should use a fully formed URL describing the protocol, domain, and file in every PHP/CURL file request.

CURLOPT_RETURNTRANSFER

The CURLOPT_RETURNTRANSFER option must be set to TRUE, as in Listing A-3, if you want the result to be returned in a string. If you don't set this option to TRUE, PHP/CURL echoes the result to the terminal.

```
curl_setopt($s, CURLOPT_RETURNTRANSFER, TRUE);          // Return in string
```

Listing A-3: Telling PHP/CURL that you want the result to be returned in a string

CURLOPT_REFERER

The CURLOPT_REFERER option allows your webbot to spoof a hyper-reference that was clicked to initiate the request for the target file. The example in Listing A-4 tells the target server that someone clicked a link on http://www.a_domain.com/index.php to request the target web page.

```
curl_setopt($s, CURLOPT_REFERER, "http://www.a_domain.com/index.php");
```

Listing A-4: Spoofing a hyper-reference

CURLOPT_FOLLOWLOCATION and CURLOPT_MAXREDIRS

The CURLOPT_FOLLOWLOCATION option tells cURL that you want it to follow every page redirection it finds. It's important to understand that PHP/CURL only honors header redirections and not redirections set with a refresh meta tag or with JavaScript, as shown in Listing A-5.

```
# Example of redirection that cURL will follow
header("Location: http://www.schrenk.com");
?>

<!-- Examples of redirections that cURL will not follow-->
<meta http-equiv="Refresh" content="0;url=http://www.schrenk.com">
<script>document.location="http://www.schrenk.com"</script>
```

Listing A-5: Redirects that cURL can and cannot follow

Any time you use `CURLOPT_FOLLOWLOCATION`, set `CURLOPT_MAXREDIRS` to the maximum number of redirections you care to follow. Limiting the number of redirections keeps your webbot out of *infinite loops*, where redirections point repeatedly to the same URL. My introduction to `CURLOPT_MAXREDIRS` came while trying to solve a problem brought to my attention by a network administrator, who initially thought that someone (using a webbot I wrote) launched a DoS attack on his server. In reality, the server misinterpreted the webbot's header request as a hacking exploit and redirected the webbot to an error page. There was a bug on the error page that caused it to repeatedly redirect the webbot to the error page, causing an infinite loop (and near-infinite bandwidth usage). The addition of `CURLOPT_MAXREDIRS` solved the problem, as demonstrated in Listing A-6.

```
curl_setopt($s, CURLOPT_FOLLOWLOCATION, TRUE); // Follow header redirections
curl_setopt($s, CURLOPT_MAXREDIRS, 4);         // Limit redirections to 4
```

Listing A-6: Using the `CURLOPT_FOLLOWLOCATION` and `CURLOPT_MAXREDIRS` options

CURLOPT_USERAGENT

Use this option to define the name of your user agent, as shown in Listing A-7. The user agent name is recorded in server access log files and is available to server-side scripts in the `$_SERVER['HTTP_USER_AGENT']` variable.

```
$agent_name = "test_webbot";
curl_setopt($s, CURLOPT_USERAGENT, $agent_name);
```

Listing A-7: Setting the user agent name

Keep in mind that many websites will not serve pages correctly if your user agent name is something other than a standard web browser.

CURLOPT_NOBODY and CURLOPT_HEADER

These options tell PHP/CURL to return either the web page's header or body. By default, PHP/CURL will always return the body, but not the header. This explains why setting `CURL_NOBODY` to `TRUE` excludes the body, and setting `CURL_HEADER` to `TRUE` includes the header, as shown in Listing A-8.

```
curl_setopt($s, CURLOPT_HEADER, TRUE);    // Include the header
curl_setopt($s, CURLOPT_NOBODY, TURE);    // Exclude the body
```

Listing A-8: Using the `CURLOPT_HEADER` and `CURLOPT_NOBODY` options

CURLOPT_TIMEOUT

If you don't limit how long PHP/CURL waits for a response from a server, it may wait forever—especially if the file you're fetching is on a busy server or you're trying to connect to a nonexistent or inactive IP address. (The latter happens frequently when a spider follows dead links on a website.) Setting a time-out value, as shown in Listing A-9, causes PHP/CURL to end the session if the download takes longer than the time-out value (in seconds).

```
curl_setopt($s, CURLOPT_TIMEOUT, 30);    // Don't wait longer than 30 seconds
```

Listing A-9: Setting a socket time-out value

CURLOPT_COOKIEFILE and CURLOPT_COOKIEJAR

One of the slickest features of PHP/CURL is the ability to manage cookies sent to and received from a website. Use the CURLOPT_COOKIEFILE option to define the file where previously stored cookies exist. At the end of the session, PHP/CURL writes new cookies to the file indicated by CURLOPT_COOKIEJAR. An example is in Listing A-10; I have never seen an application where these two options don't reference the same file.

```
curl_setopt($s, CURLOPT_COOKIEFILE, "c:\bots\cookies.txt"); // Read cookie file
curl_setopt($s, CURLOPT_COOKIEJAR,  "c:\bots\cookies.txt"); // Write cookie file
```

Listing A-10: Telling PHP/CURL where to read and write cookies

When specifying the location of a cookie file, always use the complete location of the file, and do not use relative addresses. More information about managing cookies is available in Chapter 22.

CURLOPT_HTTPHEADER

The CURLOPT_HTTPHEADER configuration allows a cURL session to send an outgoing header message to the server. The script in Listing A-11 uses this option to tell the target server the MIME type it accepts, the content type it expects, and that the user agent is capable of decompressing compressed web responses.

Note that CURLOPT_HTTPHEADER expects to receive data in an array.

```
$header_array[] = "Mime-Version: 1.0";
$header_array[] = "Content-type: text/html; charset=iso-8859-1";
$header_array[] = "Accept-Encoding: compress, gzip";
curl_setopt($curl_session, CURLOPT_HTTPHEADER, $header_array);
```

Listing A-11: Configuring an outgoing header

CURLOPT_SSL_VERIFYPEER

You only need to use this option if the target website uses SSL encryption and the protocol in CURLOPT_URL is https:. An example is shown in Listing A-12.

```
curl_setopt($ch, CURLOPT_SSL_VERIFYPEER, FALSE);    // No certificate
```

Listing A-12: Configuring PHP/CURL not to use a local client certificate

Depending on the version of PHP/CURL you use, this option may be required; if you don't use it, the target server will attempt to download a client certificate, which is unnecessary in all but rare cases.

CURLOPT_USERPWD and CURLOPT_UNRESTRICTED_AUTH

As shown in Listing A-13, you may use the CURLOPT_USERPWD option with a valid username and password to access websites that use basic authentication. In contrast to using a browser, you will have to submit the username and password to every page accessed within the basic authentication realm.

```
curl_setopt($s, CURLOPT_USERPWD, "username:password");
curl_setopt($s, CURLOPT_UNRESTICTED_AUTH, TRUE);
```

Listing A-13: Configuring PHP/CURL for basic authentication schemes

If you use this option in conjunction with CURLOPT_FOLLOWLOCATION, you should also use the CURLOPT_UNRESTRICTED_AUTH option, which will ensure that the username and password are sent to all pages you're redirected to, providing they are part of the same realm.

Exercise caution with using CURLOPT_USERPWD, as it is possible that you can inadvertently send username and password information to the wrong server, where it may appear in access log files.

CURLOPT_POST and CURLOPT_POSTFIELDS

The CURLOPT_POST and CURLOPT_POSTFIELDS options configure PHP/CURL to emulate forms with the POST method. Since the default method is GET, you must first tell PHP/CURL to use the POST method. Then you must specify the POST data that you want to be sent to the target webserver. An example is shown in Listing A-14.

```
curl_setopt($s, CURLOPT_POST, TRUE);          // Use POST method
$post_data = "var1=1&var2=2&var3=3";          // Define POST data values
curl_setopt($s, CURLOPT_POSTFIELDS, $post_data);
```

Listing A-14: Configuring POST method transfers

Notice that the POST data looks like a standard query string sent in a GET method. Incidentally, to send form information with the GET method, simply attach the query string to the target URL.

CURLOPT_VERBOSE

The CURLOPT_VERBOSE option controls the quantity of status messages created during a file transfer. You may find this helpful during debugging, but it is best to turn off this option during the production phase, because it produces many entries in your server log file. A typical succession of log messages for a single file download looks like Listing A-15.

```
* About to connect() to www.schrenk.com port 80
* Connected to www.schrenk.com (66.179.150.101) port 80
* Connection #0 left intact
* Closing connection #0
```

Listing A-15: Typical messages from a verbose PHP/CURL session

If you're in verbose mode on a busy server, you'll create very large log files. Listing A-16 shows how to turn off verbose mode.

```
curl_setopt($s, CURLOPT_VERBOSE, FALSE);        // Minimal logs
```

Listing A-16: Turning off verbose mode reduces the size of server log files.

CURLOPT_PORT

By default, PHP/CURL uses port 80 for all HTTP sessions, unless you are connecting to an SSL encrypted server, in which case port 443 is used.[3] These are the standard port numbers for HTTP and HTTPS protocols, respectively. If you're connecting to a custom protocol or wish to connect to a non-web protocol, use CURLOPT_PORT to set the desired port number, as shown in Listing A-17.

```
curl_setopt($s, CURLOPT_PORT, 234);        // Use port number 234
```

Listing A-17: Using nonstandard communication ports

NOTE *Configuration settings must be capitalized, as shown in the previous examples. This is because the option names are predefined PHP constants. Therefore, your code will fail if you specify and option as* curlopt_port *instead of* CURLOPT_PORT.

Executing the PHP/CURL Command

Executing the PHP/CURL command sets into action all the options defined with the curl_setopt() function. This command executes the previously configured session (referenced by $s in Listing A-18).

```
$downloaded_page = curl_exec($s);
```

Listing A-18: Executing a PHP/CURL command for session $s

You can execute the same command multiple times or use curl_setopt() to change configurations between calls of curl_exec(), as long as the session is defined and hasn't been closed. Typically, I create a new PHP/CURL session for every page I access.

---

[3] Well-known and standard port numbers are defined at http://www.iana.org/assignments/ port-numbers.

Retrieving PHP/CURL Session Information

Additional information about the current PHP/CURL session is available once a curl_exec() command is executed. Listing A-19 shows how to use this command.

```
$info_array = curl_getinfo($s);
```

Listing A-19: Getting additional information about the current PHP/CURL session

The curl_getinfo() command returns an array of information, including connect and transfer times, as shown in Listing A-20.

```
array(20)
  {
  ["url"]=> string(22) "http://www.schrenk.com"
  ["content_type"]=> string(29) "text/html; charset=ISO-8859-1"
  ["http_code"]=> int(200) ["header_size"]=> int(247)
  ["request_size"]=> int(125)
  ["filetime"]=> int(-1)
  ["ssl_verify_result"]=> int(0)
  ["redirect_count"]=> int(0)
  ["total_time"]=> float(0.884)
  ["namelookup_time"]=> float(0)
  ["connect_time"]=> float(0.079)
  ["pretransfer_time"]=> float(0.079)
  ["size_upload"]=> float(0)
  ["size_download"]=> float(19892)
  ["speed_download"]=> float(22502.2624434)
  ["speed_upload"]=> float(0)
  ["download_content_length"]=> float(0)
  ["upload_content_length"]=> float(0)
  ["starttransfer_time"]=> float(0.608)
  ["redirect_time"]=> float(0)
  }
```

Listing A-20: Data made available by the curl_getinfo() command

Viewing PHP/CURL Errors

The curl_error() function returns any errors that may have occurred during a PHP/CURL session. The usage for this function is shown in Listing A-21.

```
$errors = curl_error($s);
```

Listing A-21: Accessing PHP/CURL session errors

A typical error response is shown in Listing A-22.

```
Couldn't resolve host 'www.webbotworld.com'
```

Listing A-22: Typical PHP/CURL session error

Closing PHP/CURL Sessions

You should close a PHP/CURL session immediately after you are done using it, as shown in Listing A-23. Closing the PHP/CURL session frees up server resources, primarily memory.

```
curl_close($s);
```

Listing A-23: Closing a PHP/CURL session

In normal use, PHP performs *garbage collection*, freeing resources like variables, socket connections, and memory when the script completes. This works fine for scripts that control web pages and execute quickly. However, webbots and spiders may require that PHP scripts run for extended periods without garbage collection. (I've written webbot scripts that run for months without stopping.) Closing each PHP/CURL session is imperative if you're writing webbot and spider scripts that make many PHP/CURL connections and run for extended periods of time.

B

STATUS CODES

This appendix contains status codes returned by web (HTTP) and news (NNTP) servers. Your webbots and spiders should use these status codes to determine the success or failure communicating with servers. When debugging your scripts, status codes also provide hints as to what's wrong.

HTTP Codes

The following is a representative sample of HTTP codes. These codes reflect the status of an HTTP (web page) request. You'll see these codes returned in $returned_web_page['STATUS']['http_code'] if you're using the LIB_http library.

```
100 Continue
101 Switching Protocols
200 OK
201 Created
202 Accepted
203 Non-Authoritative Information
204 No Content
205 Reset Content
206 Partial Content
300 Multiple Choices
301 Moved Permanently
302 Found
303 See Other
304 Not Modified
305 Use Proxy
306 (Unused)
307 Temporary Redirect
400 Bad Request
401 Unauthorized
402 Payment Required
403 Forbidden
404 Not Found
405 Method Not Allowed
406 Not Acceptable
407 Proxy Authentication Required
408 Request Timeout
409 Conflict
410 Gone
411 Length Required
412 Precondition Failed
413 Request Entity Too Large
414 Request-URI Too Long
415 Unsupported Media Type
416 Requested Range Not Satisfiable
417 Expectation Failed
500 Internal Server Error
501 Not Implemented
502 Bad Gateway
503 Service Unavailable
504 Gateway Timeout
505 HTTP Version Not Supported
```

NNTP Codes

Listed below are the NNTP status codes. Your webbots should use these codes to verify the reposes returned from news servers.

```
100 help text follows
199 debug output
200 server ready - posting allowed
201 server ready - no posting allowed
202 slave status noted
205 closing connection - goodbye!
211 group selected
215 list of newsgroups follows
220 article retrieved - head and body follow
221 article retrieved - head follows
222 article retrieved - body follows
223 article retrieved - request text separately
230 list of new articles by message-id follows
231 list of new newsgroups follows
235 article transferred ok
240 article posted ok
335 send article to be transferred. End with <CR-LF>.<CR-LF>
340 send article to be posted. End with <CR-LF>.<CR-LF>
400 service discontinued
411 no such news group
412 no newsgroup has been selected
420 no current article has been selected
421 no next article in this group
422 no previous article in this group
423 no such article number in this group
430 no such article found
435 article not wanted - do not send it
436 transfer failed - try again later
437 article rejected - do not try again
440 posting not allowed
441 posting failed
500 command not recognized
501 command syntax error
502 access restriction or permission denied
503 program fault - command not performed
```

C

SMS EMAIL ADDRESSES

Sometimes it is useful for webbots to send Short Message Service (SMS) or text message notifications. In most cases, you can send a text message to a subscriber by simply sending an email to the wireless subscriber's mail server, using the subscriber's phone number or username as the addressee. Below is a collection of email addresses that will send text messages. The email addresses in the table below have not been individually verified, but each entry was found on more than one source.

NOTE *Special charges may apply to the use of these services. Contact the individual service provider for more information regarding charges.*

If you don't see the carrier you need listed below, contact the carrier to check—most wireless services support this service and the carrier's customer service department should be able to help if you have questions.

Wireless Carrier	Text Message Email Address
Alltel	10digitphonenumber@alltelmessage.com
Ameritech Paging	10digitpagernumber@paging.acswireless.com
BeeLine GSM	phonenumber@sms.beemail.ru
Bell Mobility (Canada)	phonenumber@txt.bell.ca
Bell South	phonenumber@bellsouth.cl
Bell South Mobility	phonenumber@blsdcs.net
Blue Sky Frog	phonenumber@blueskyfrog.com
Boost	phonenumber@myboostmobile.com
Cellular One	10digitphonenumber@mobile.celloneusa.com
Cellular One West	phonenumber@mycellone.com
Cingular Wireless	10digitphonenumber@mobile.mycingular.com
Dutchtone/Orange-NL	phonenumber@sms.orange.nl
Edge Wireless	phonenumber@sms.edgewireless.com
Fido	phonenumber@fido.ca
Golden Telecom	phonenumber@sms.goldentele.com
Idea Cellular	phonenumber@ideacellular.net
Manitoba Telecom Systems	phonenumber@text.mtsmobility.com
MetroPCS	10digitphonenumber@mymetropcs.com
MobileOne	phonenumber@m1.com.sg
Mobilfone	phonenumber@page.mobilfone.com
Mobility Bermuda	phonenumber@ml.bm
Netcom	phonenumber@sms.netcom.no
Nextel	10digitphonenumber@messaging.nextel.com
NPI Wireless	phonenumber@npiwireless.com
O2	username@o2.co.uk
Orange	phonenumber@orange.net
Oskar	phonenumber@mujoskar.cz
Personal Communication	sms@pcom.ru (number in subject line)
PlusGSM	phonenumber@text.plusgsm.pl
Qualcomm	name@pager.qualcomm.com
Qwest	10digitphonenumber@qwestmp.com
Southern LINC	10digitphonenumber@page.southernlinc.com
Sprint PCS	10digitphonenumber@messaging.sprintpcs.com
SunCom	number@tms.suncom.com
SureWest Communications	phonenumber@mobile.surewest.com
T-Mobile	10digitphonenumber@tmomail.net
T-Mobile Germany	phonenumber@t-d1-sms.de
T-Mobile UK	phonenumber@t-mobile.uk.net
Tele2 Latvia	phonenumber@sms.tele2.lv

(continued)

Wireless Carrier	Text Message Email Address
Telefonica Movistar	phonenumber@movistar.net
Telenor	phonenumber@mobilpost.no
TIM	10digitphonenumber@timnet.com
UMC	phonenumber@sms.umc.com.ua
Unicel	phonenumber@utext.com
Verizon Pagers	10digitpagernumber@myairmail.com
Verizon PCS	10digitphonenumber@vtext.com
Virgin Mobile	phonenumber@vmobl.com
Wyndtell	number@wyndtell.com

INDEX

computers. *See also* server
distributing tasks across multiple, 186
"constructive hacking," 11
Content-Type line
for email message, 153
in HTTP header, 32
$content_type variable, 163
converting website into function,
167–174
COOKIE_FILE, 244
cookies, 103
about, 211–213
adapting to management
changes, 244
for authentication, 204–207
cURL to read and write, 27
defaults for, 29
deleting, 214–215, 244
for deterring webbots, 261
expiration dates for, 205
and forms, 53
managing multiple users', 215
permanent, 211–212
persistence with, 211
PHP/CURL and, 213–214
purging temporary, 214–215
viewing, 104
and webbot design, 214–215
copyright issues, 69, 267–270
"all rights reserved" notice, 268
and facts, 269
fair use laws, 270
registration, 268
CORBA (Common Object Request
Broker Architecture), 255
crawlers. *See* spiders
cron command, 217
cryptography, 195
CSS. *See* Cascading Style Sheets (CSS)
CSV (comma-separated value)
files, file() function for
downloading, 25
cURL, 6, 21
for executing webbot on remote
server, 218
local certificate and, 197
curl_error() function, 282
curl_exec() function, 281–282
curl_getInfo() function, 282
curl_init() function, 276

curl_setopt() function, 204, 276–281
case sensitivity, 281
CURLOPT_COOKIEFILE option, 207, 279
CURLOPT_COOKIEJAR option, 207, 279
CURLOPT_FOLLOWLOCATION option, 277
CURLOPT_HEADER option, 278
CURLOPT_HTTPHEADER option, 279
CURLOPT_MAXREDIRS option, 277, 278
CURLOPT_NOBODY option, 278
CURLOPT_PORT option, 281
CURLOPT_POST option, 280
CURLOPT_POSTFIELDS option, 280
CURLOPT_REFERER option, 277
CURLOPT_RETURNTRANSFER option, 277
CURLOPT_SSL_VERIFYPEER option, 279–280
CURLOPT_TIMEOUT option, 278–279
CURLOPT_UNRESTRICTED_AUTH option, 280
CURLOPT_URL option, 277
CURLOPT_USERAGENT option, 278
CURLOPT_USERPWD option, 203, 280
CURLOPT_VERBOSE option, 280–281
executing, 281–282
for time-out values, 244
custom logs, and webbot detection, 230

D

daily scheduling of webbots, 219–220
data
fields in forms, 50
networks, access and abuse, 266
set, parsing into array, 39–40
sources, choosing for aggregation
webbot, 124
data management, 61–74
organizing data, 61–69
naming conventions, 62–63
storing images in database, 67–68
storing text in database, 64–67
structured files, 63–64
reducing size, 69–73
data compression, 70–72
removing formatting, 72–73
storing references to image files, 69
thumbnailing images, 73–74
data-only interfaces, 251–256
lightweight data exchange, 253–255
SOAP (Simple Object Access
Protocol), 255–256
XML (eXtensible Markup
Language), 251–252
<data> tags, for insertion parse, 117–118
$data_array, 33, 172

database
    for saving links, 185
    storing images in, 67–68
    storing text in, 64–67
dates, in filenames, 63
DCOM (Distributed Component Object
    Model), 255
`decode_zipcode()` function, 169
deep linking, 241
default file, for web page, 22
delays, inserting between page fetches,
    232, 234
`DELE` command (POP3), 153
deleting
    cookies, 214–215, 244
    HTML formatting, 72–73
    unwanted text, 41–42
    white space, 73
delimiters
    parsing text between, 37–38
    splitting string at, 37
denial of service (DoS) attack,
    preventing, 184
DES (Digital Encryption Standard), 197
`describe_zipcode()` function, 171–173
developers, webbot benefits for, 10–11
digest authentication, 204
digital certificate, 196, 200
    local, 197–198
Digital Encryption Standard (DES), 197
directories, 63
    script for creating, 89, 91
disclaimer, 6
disk swapping, 185
Distributed Component Object Model
    (DCOM), 255
`<div>` tags, parsing data into array, 82
DoubleClick online advertising, 103
`download_binary_file()` function, 86
`download_images_for_page()` function, 86,
    87, 89
downloading
    with FTP, 135
    with `LIB_http`, 28–34
    with link-verification webbot, 93–94
    linked page, 97
    with parsing script, 79–82
    with PHP built-in functions, 23–25
    with PHP/CURL, 26–28
    web pages, 21–34
        vs. files, 22–23
`download_parse_rss()` function, 128, 130

E

eBay, 271
    snipers and, 190
Electronic Frontier Foundation
    (EFF), 273
email
    guidelines, 158
    headers, 160
    keeping legitimate out of spam filter,
        162–163
    for notification
        of FTP transmission failure, 134
        of webbot action, 165
    placing account information in
        script, 154
    reading with webbots, 149–156
    sending, 157–165
        email with webbots, 157–165
        HTML-formatted email, 163–164
        with `mail()` function, 159–161
        with PHP, 158–159
        notifications with webbots, 161–164
    undeliverable as alert to invalid
        address, 164–165
    as webbot trigger, 222–223
email-controlled webbots, 155–156
encryption, 195
    authentication and, 210
    certificate, 197
    for deterring webbots, 261
    overview of web, 197
    webbots using, 196
end-of-message indicator (POP3), 151
error
    handlers, 245–246
    information
        from `http_get()` function, 30
        from `http_get_withheader()`
            function, 31
    logs, and webbot detection, 229–230
`eval()` function, 253–254
event triggers, 53
`exclude_link()` function, 183–184
exclusion list, for spiders, 184
executing webbots
    in browsers, 24–25
    in command shell, 24
`exe_sql()` function, 66–67
expiration dates, for cookies, 205
eXtensible Markup Language (XML).
    See XML

H

hacking
constructive, 11
webbot activity appearing as, 228
handle for file, 23
handshake process, 197
hard drives, compressing files on, 71–72
hardware requirements, 5–6
harvest, separating from payload, 186
harvest_links() function, 181–182
hash, 161
haystack, 42
<head> tag, detecting redirection,
238–239
header tags, and search engine
optimization, 250
headers
in email, 152, 160
redirection, 238
hijacking bandwidth, 88, 241
holidays, scheduling webbots on, 232
Hormel Foods Corporation, 157*n*
hotel room prices, aggregating and filtering data, 14
href attribute
extracting value, 96
of link tag, parsing, 40–41
HTML (Hypertext Markup Language)
formatting, deleting, 72–73
for formatting email, 163–164
parsing
content of reoccurring tags, 39–40
poorly written, 35–36
text between tags, 37–38
removing formatting, 72–73
htmlspecialchars() function, 261
HTMLTidy (Tidy), 36, 44
HTTP codes, 236
from http_get_withheader()
function, 31
HTTP
header, 30–32
exchanging cookies in, 212
and security, 52
protocol, 23
port for, 281
status codes, 97–98, 285–286
http() routine, 29
http_get() function, 29–30, 33, 79, 94,
97, 236
http_get_form() function, 33
http_get_form_withheader() function, 33

http_get_withheader() function, 30–32, 33
http_header() function, 33
http_post_form() function, 33, 172
http_post_withheader() function, 33
HTTPS protocol, 200
port for, 281
human patterns, webbot simulation of,
231–232
Hypertext Markup Language. *See*
HTML (Hypertext Markup
Language)

I

identity, online exposure and, 103–104
image-capturing webbots, 85–92
binary-safe download routine, 88
directory structure, 89
execution, 87
main script, 89–92
overview, 86
image-processing loop, 91
images
borrowing from other sites, 88
single-pixel, 103
storing in database, 67–68
thumbnailing, 73–74
<img> tags
alt attribute, 250
parsing from downloaded web page,
90–91
src attribute from array, parsing, 41
incompatible systems,
communication on, 20
index file, for web page, 22
indexing web pages, by search engine
spider, 248
industry news articles, consolidating, 17
infinite loops, preventing, 278
information, aggregating and filtering
by relevance, 14
initialization
download_images_for page() function,
89–90
link-verification webbot, 93–94
parsing script, 79–82
search-ranking script, 115–116
input tags in forms, 50
insert() function, 65
insertion parse, 112, 117
installing
HTMLTidy, 36
PHP/CURL, 28

S

sale item, verifying availability, 189
saving
    links in database, 185
    source code for form, 170
scheduling, 217–224
    adding variety to, 224
    complex, 221–222
    disabling, 246
    for distributed spider, 186
    and stealth, 231, 232
    webbots to run daily, 219–220
    webbots to run monthly, 222
    Windows Task Scheduler, 218–221
scripts, 4–5
    writing in small steps, 44
Sealand, 109n
search engine
    optimization, 247–250
    spiders
        design techniques hindering,
            250–251
        indexing web pages with, 248
    Terms of Service agreement, 120
search-ranking webbots, 111–121
    fetching search results, 117
    how they work, 114–115
    initializing variables, 115–116
    parsing search results, 117–120
    running, 114
    search results page description,
        112–113
    starting loop, 116
    what they do, 114
search results page, parts of, 113
search term, in URL, 116
Secure Sockets Layer (SSL), 196
    CURLOPT_SSL_VERIFYPEER option for,
        279–280
    sites, downloading images from, 88
seed URL, 178
sending email, 157–165
server
    avoiding undue load on, 271
    error log, form errors in, 58–59
    obtaining clock value, 191–192
    remote, using cURL to execute
        webbot on, 218
session
    authentication, 204–209
    ID, forms with, 54
    value, dynamically assigned, 171–172

set_time_limit() function, 179, 245
Short Message Service (SMS), 165,
    289–291
Simple Object Access Protocol (SOAP),
    255–256
simulating action of person, 117
single-pixel image, uploading, 103
single points of failure, avoiding, 224
size reduction, 69–73
    data compression, 70–72
    removing formatting, 72–73
    storing references to image files, 69
SMS (Short Message Service), 165,
    289–291
snipers, 190–193
    authentication, 191
    clock synchronization, 191–192
    testing, 193
SOAP (Simple Object Access Protocol),
    255–256
socket management, with cURL, 28
software
    for monitoring logs, 230–231
    requirements for, 6
source code
    configuration area of LIB_mysql, 65
    for form
        displaying, 169
        saving, 170
spam, 157–159
    filters, 157
        keeping legitimate mail out of,
            162–163
spam indexing, 248
special characters, 261
SpecificClick online advertising, 103
spiders, 177–185
    adding payload, 179, 185
    distributing tasks across multiple
        computers, 186
    examples, 179–180
    experimenting with, 184
    how they work, 178
    LIB_simple_spider library, 180–184
        archive_links() function, 182
        exclude_link() function, 183–184
        get_domain() function, 182–183
        harvest_links() function, 181–182
    maximum penetration level for, 178
    options for treating unwanted,
        263–264
    potential ideas for, 177–178

U

undeliverable mail, using to prune access lists, 164–165
unformatted text, parsing, 43
unique keywords, 249
US Copyright Office, 267, 268
Unix
    scheduling in, 217
    timestamp, 192
unsubscribe options, for email 158
unwanted text, deleting, 41–42
update() function, of LIB_mysql, 66
updating website, frequency for deterring webbots, 262
uploading files, with FTP, 135
urlencode() function, 116
URLs
    adapting to changes, 236–241
        page redirection, 238–240
        referer values' accuracy, 240–241
        requests for nonexistent pages, 236–238
    defining target for PHP/CURL session, 277
    fully resolved, 96–97
usernames, 200

V

validation point, for downloaded web page, 237–238
variables, passing to webbots, 254–255
verification loop, 95–96
Virginia, Anti-Spam law, 272
virtual
    private networks (VPNs), 200
    property, laws governing, 272

W

weather forecasts, 167
web
    agent, selectively allowing access to specific, 260–261
    pages
        accessibility to webbots, 247
        adapting to content changes, 241–242
        avoiding requests for nonexistent, 236–238
        displaying status of, 97–98
        displaying proxied, 108
        notification of change in, 161–162

        parsing image tags from downloaded, 90–91
        poorly written HTML within, 44
        ranking by search engine spider, 248
        status of request for, 285–286
        validation point for, 237–238
    services, 255
        designing custom lightweight, 174
    spiders. *See* spiders
    technologies, tracking, 19–20
    walkers. *See* spiders
webbot_error_handler() function, 245
WEBBOT_NAME constant, 58
webbots (web robots), 2. *See also* scheduling
    benefits of, 9–10
        for business leaders, 11–12
        for developers, 10–11
    cookies and design of, 214–215
    countermeasures for, 257–264
        with cookies, encryption, JavaScript, and redirection, 261
        embedding text in other media, 262
        obfuscation, 261
        reasons for, 257
        robots meta tag, 260
        robots.txt file, 259–260
        allowing selective access to specific agents, 260–261
        Terms of Service agreements, 258
    creating first script, 23
    daily scheduling of, 219–220
    executing
        in browsers, 24–25
        in command shell, 24
    fault-tolerant, 235–246
    growth in use, 10
    monthly scheduling of, 222
    periodicity of, 219, 224
    preparing to run as scheduled tasks, 218
    preventing negative consequences of, 265–266. *See also* copyright issues
    project ideas, 13–20
    for reading email, 149–156
        and executing POP3 commands, 153–155
        and POP3 protocol, 150–153
    reasons for stealth, 227–231

Electronic Frontier Foundation
Defending Freedom in the Digital World

Free Speech. Privacy. Innovation. Fair Use. Reverse Engineering. If you care about these rights in the digital world, then you should join the Electronic Frontier Foundation (EFF). EFF was founded in 1990 to protect the rights of users and developers of technology. EFF is the first to identify threats to basic rights online and to advocate on behalf of free expression in the digital age.

The Electronic Frontier Foundation Defends Your Rights!
Become a Member Today!
http://www.eff.org/support/

Current EFF projects include:

Protecting your fundamental right to vote. Widely publicized security flaws in computerized voting machines show that, though filled with potential, this technology is far from perfect. EFF is defending the open discussion of e-voting problems and is coordinating a national litigation strategy addressing issues arising from use of poorly developed and tested computerized voting machines.

Ensuring that you are not traceable through your things. Libraries, schools, the government and private sector businesses are adopting radio frequency identification tags, or RFIDs – a technology capable of pinpointing the physical location of whatever item the tags are embedded in. While this may seem like a convenient way to track items, it's also a convenient way to do something less benign: track people and their activities through their belongings. EFF is working to ensure that embrace of this technology does not erode your right to privacy.

Stopping the FBI from creating surveillance backdoors on the Internet. EFF is part of a coalition opposing the FBI's expansion of the Communications Assistance for Law Enforcement Act (CALEA), which would require that the wiretap capabilities built into the phone system be extended to the Internet, forcing ISPs to build backdoors for law enforcement.

Providing you with a means by which you can contact key decision-makers on cyber-liberties issues. EFF maintains an action center that provides alerts on technology, civil liberties issues and pending legislation to more than 50,000 subscribers. EFF also generates a weekly online newsletter, EFFector, and a blog that provides up-to-the minute information and commentary.

Defending your right to listen to and copy digital music and movies. The entertainment industry has been overzealous in trying to protect its copyrights, often decimating fair use rights in the process. EFF is standing up to the movie and music industries on several fronts.

Check out all of the things we're working on at http://www.eff.org and join today or make a donation to support the fight to defend freedom online.

ELECTRONIC FRONTIER FOUNDATION · 454 SHOTWELL STREET · SAN FRANCISCO, CA 94110 · 415.436.9333

THE BOOK OF JAVASCRIPT, 2ND EDITION
A Practical Guide to Interactive Web Pages

by THAU!

This book teaches readers how to add interactivity, animation, and other tricks to their websites with JavaScript. Rather than provide a series of cut-and-paste scripts, thau! takes the reader through real-world JavaScript code examples with an emphasis on understanding. Each chapter focuses on a few important JavaScript features, shows how professional websites incorporate them, and shows readers how they might add those features to their own websites. This thoroughly updated and completely reworked second edition includes coverage of Ajax, revised appendices, and new examples throughout.

DECEMBER 2006, 528 PP., $39.95 ($49.95 CDN)
ISBN 978-1-59327-106-0

WICKED COOL PHP
Real-World Scripts That Make Difficult Things Possible

by WILLIAM STEINMETZ *and* BRIAN WARD

Wicked Cool PHP provides scripts that can be implemented immediately to make programmers' lives easier, including scripts for processing credit cards, getting live shipping quotes, and accepting PayPal payments online. Readers learn how to create robot-blocking security images and on-the-fly graphs to embed in web pages, access email accounts with PHP, design screen scrapers to connect to other sites and download information from them, and much more.

JUNE 2007, 304 PP., $34.95 ($43.95 CDN)
ISBN 978-1-59327-102-2

OBJECT-ORIENTED PHP
Concepts, Techniques, and Code

by PETER LAVIN

Object-Oriented PHP shows developers how to take advantage of the new object-oriented features of PHP. Working from concrete examples, the book begins with code compatible with PHP 4 and 5, and then focuses on object orientation in PHP 5. The author's practical approach uses numerous code examples, which will help developers get up to speed quickly and show them how to apply what they've learned to everyday situations. All code samples are available for download on the book's companion site.

JUNE 2006, 216 PP., $29.95 ($38.95 CDN)
ISBN 978-1-59327-077-3